Henry James and the Visual Arts

HENRY JAMES
AND THE VISUAL ARTS

Viola Hopkins Winner

The University Press of Virginia

Charlottesville

THE UNIVERSITY PRESS OF VIRGINIA
Copyright © 1970 by the Rector and Visitors
of the University of Virginia
First published 1970

FRONTISPIECE: Henry James. (Courtesy of
The Clifton Waller Barrett Library of
the University of Virginia.)

Standard Book Number: 8139-0285-1
Library of Congress Catalog Card Number: 73-109223
Printed in the United States of America

For my mother and father

Preface

THE well-known photograph of Henry James by Alice Boughton, showing him in top hat with cane and gloves in hand, bending slightly forward in the classic Daumier pose, absorbed in a painting, is a portrait perhaps not of the quintessential but certainly of the essential James. His engagement with the visual arts was intense and lifelong, from the house-size canvases of the Düsseldorf school of the 1850's to the Cézannes and Matisses of the London Post-Impressionist Exhibition of 1912. Also spanning his career are his recorded impressions of pictures and places in numerous art reviews, most appearing between 1868 and 1882, some in the 1890's, and travel essays, collections beginning with *Transatlantic Sketches* (1875) and ending with *Italian Hours* (1909). Although the frequency with which art historians quote James attests to his visual perceptiveness and the felicitous phrasing of his writings on art, it is the use he made in fiction of his museum haunting and sight-seeing that primarily concerns us.

Reliving the "agitations, explorations, excitements" of his first trip abroad as an adult, James recalls in *The Middle Years* that he felt the "commonest street-vista" as well as the "great sought-out compositions" such as Hampton Court and Windsor Castle to be "charged somehow with a useability the most immediate, the most urgent. . . . There were truly moments at which they seemed not to answer for it that I should get all the good of them and the finest—what I was so extravagantly, so fantastically after—unless I could somehow at once indite my sonnet and prove my title." It is characteristic of James that the scenic view solicited treatment, that only by converting his experience of it into a work of art did he consider it used and his. So integrally related were his visual responses and creative impulse that an understanding of his mode of vision will certainly deepen an understanding of his theory and practice of fiction. At any rate, that was the assumption with which I began this study; my conclusion, reached by tracing his experience with art and its ramifications in his work, is that the connection is indeed intimate.

In a sense, James never outgrew, but merely developed, his tendency as a child to try to grasp the meaning of the external world through the picture: the controlled point of view and pictorial de-

scription in his fiction similarly give shape and coherence, helping
to create the illusion that relations stop somewhere. The dualism in
his mature response to art—his admiration for both the classical Renaissance and the painterly-picturesque styles—also has parallels in
his fiction: both in the thematic conflict between the ideal and the
real and in the tension, especially in the late work, between his desire
to achieve formal balance and proportion and to represent shifting,
indeterminate, ambient reality. He had much in common with the
contemporary impressionists in technique and in thought but cru-
cially differed from them in his formalism and traditionalism. He
was closer in sensibility and in style to the mannerist Tintoretto, the
Italian painter for whom he felt the deepest affinity. His experience
with art, primarily with pictures, also carried over into his theory of
fiction: the abundance of art terms in his works of criticism is in-
dicative not merely of his feeling a lack of a vocabulary appropriate to
a serious discussion of fiction as an art but also of a visual orientation
leading him to conceive of fiction and painting as analogous in aim
and form and even competitive in the rendering of appearances. His
friendships with artists and familiarity with the contemporary studio
world are reflected in works in which the painter or sculptor and
aesthetic questions are central as well as those in which the artist is a
symbolic figure or an accessory of the social scene. Although the artist
in James's work stands in a special relation to "life," meaning both
the experience he strives to represent as an artist and that which he
seeks as a human being, all of James's favored characters are endowed
with the artistic temperament or perceptive, empathic imagination.
It is the relation of character to "things" as well as to people that
is for James the touchstone of moral sensibility. From his precursors
such as Hawthorne and Ruskin, James inherited the romantic associational aesthetic dominant in the first half of the nineteenth
century in America; while mostly rejecting its idealistic, moralistic,
and religious assumptions, James adhered to this aesthetic, for he, too,
considered "suggestiveness" a supreme value. His chosen associations,
however, are historical, psychological, and social and in the highest
art are not divorced from form. Hence, the ultimate test of sensibility
for James's characters is not whether they are correct in their aesthetic
judgments but whether they also consider things as survivals or as expressions of a common humanity.

As essential background for these general conclusions and for its
own interest, I have devoted chapters 1 through 4 to James's aesthetic
and art criticism: the development of his taste and its underlying
principles from childhood to the end of his career. Chapters 5 and

6 explore his use of the visual arts in technique, first in his conception of fiction and then in his own practice. Chapters 7 and 8 concentrate on theme, the treatment of the artist figure and the connoisseur. There is, of course, a certain amount of overlapping in my discussion of technique and theme: the art devices examined in depth turn out to have meaning, as is characteristic of technique generally in his works.

Whenever feasible, I have followed a chronological order in my analysis of the fiction and therefore have used as texts the earliest available editions for works preceding and including *The Portrait of a Lady*. As the revisions after that work did not seem crucial enough to justify using editions often difficult to obtain, for later fiction I refer to *The Novels and Tales of Henry James* (New York, 1907–9), and for works not included in the New York edition, to *The Novels and Stories of Henry James*, edited by Percy Lubbock (London, 1920–23).

I have preferred discussing one work in detail to several sketchily and have concentrated on the novels rather than on the shorter fiction. The works in which the visual arts play a relatively insignificant part receive little notice or are omitted altogether, although I believe my general arguments could be applied to James's mature work as a whole. The amount of space devoted to any single work is obviously not a sign of intrinsic artistic merit: *Roderick Hudson* requires more attention than *The Wings of the Dove* because it deals specifically with the artist's creative problems; *The Golden Bowl*, more than any of the other late novels because the relation of the self to art, morality, history, and possession is of its essence, and it seems to me to be the culmination, not merely in a chronological sense, of this theme in James's complete works.

I am especially pleased to express here my gratitude to Leon Edel, who presided at the inception of my study, no less for his generous encouragement and many instances of specific kindnesses over the years than for his erudition, insights, and exemplary dedication. For criticism of chapters of an early version, I wish to thank John W. Kinnaird and Carla Gottlieb. From my students in recent seminars, I gained a new awareness of the intricacy of James's figure in the carpet and of the risks and rewards of attempting to discern it. Donald G. Watson painstakingly and intelligently checked references for me but is not responsible for errors. I am also grateful to the American Association of University Women and the University of Virginia for research grants.
V. H. W.

Charlottesville, Virginia
October 1969

Acknowledgments

I WISH to thank those who have granted permission to quote from published and unpublished sources. Quotation from the Charles Eliot Norton papers is by permission of the Harvard College Library; from the James family papers, by permission of Alexander R. James and the Houghton Library, copyright 1970, Alexander R. James; from *The Novels and Tales of Henry James, The Letters of Henry James, The Art of the Novel, A Small Boy and Others, Notes of a Son and Brother,* and *The Middle Years,* by permission of Charles Scribner's Sons; and from *The Painter's Eye,* edited by John L. Sweeney, by permission of Rupert Hart-Davis. I am grateful to the Wayne State University Press for permission to incorporate in this study the article that appeared in *Criticism: A Quarterly for Literature and the Arts,* IX, no. 1 (Winter, 1967), and to the Modern Language Association of America, for the article that appeared in *PMLA,* LXXVI, no. 5 (Dec., 1961). I also wish to thank the institutions cited in the legends for supplying photographs and permitting their reproduction.

Contents

Illustrations

Henry James and the Visual Arts

1 The Apprenticeship of an Amateur

HENRY JAMES'S interest in pictures began early. As a small boy in New York he loved to pore over the volumes of Gavarni's etchings, the set of illustrated Béranger, and the "tall entrancing folios of Nash's lithographed Mansions of England in the Olden Time"[1] that were kept in the piece of furniture that stood between the front parlor windows of the Fourteenth Street house. In fact, his earliest memory was of a living picture—a view of the "admirable aspect of the Place and the Colonne Vendôme" (pp. 32–33), glimpsed through a moving carriage window when he was a baby in long clothes. He saw the view "framed by the clear window of the vehicle as [he] passed," an inkling of a mode of perception that became habitual and of his relation to life as a mature artist. Real as the great square is, with its "splendid perspective" and "tall and glorious column," it was seen and remembered as a picture, the frame circumscribing the scene and creating aesthetic distance between it and the observer. The infant impressed by the view through the window was to become James the observer-artist, passionately involved yet objective and detached, "addicted to seeing 'through' —one thing through another, accordingly, and still other things through *that*."[2]

Cast from the beginning in the role of observer—"foredoomed" to be one "in whom contemplation takes so much the place of action" (p. 17)—young Henry was not, however, exempt from having to cope with the confusing outside world, the otherness. The boy's problem was how to appropriate the real—"the thing of accident, of mere actuality, still unappropriated" (p. 150)—how to reduce the "unreduced impression" of people, places, and situations. It is not surprising given his habitual gazing and gaping and his need to find order and coherence in inchoate impressions that he should have been at an early age attracted to the picture, the art form that most vividly and immediately interprets the visual world. The act of perception requiring preconceptions as well as an object to be perceived, he saw because he had seen, that is, the remembered picture brought into focus for him the otherwise blurred living scene, and, conversely, the

scene reinforced the reality of the picture. Through drawings of her
type, he placed his governess, Mlle. Delavigne: "there she was, to the
life, on the page of Gavarni, attesting its reality, and there again did
that page in return . . . attest her own felicity" (p. 13). Similarly,
London looked familiar to him in 1855 because he had already seen
it in *Punch*. "*Punch* was England; *Punch* was London."[3] The "London view" had for him as a child a "Cruikshank side" that was almost
terrifying. One particular occasion traveling westward from the London Bridge railway station he especially recalled:

It was a soft June evening, with a lingering light and swarming crowds, as
they then seemed to me, of figures reminding me of George Cruikshank's
Artful Dodger and his Bill Sikes and his Nancy, only with the bigger brutality of life, which pressed upon the cab, the early-Victorian fourwheeler,
as we jogged over the Bridge, and cropped up in more and more gas-lit
patches for all our course, culminating, somewhere far to the west, in the
vivid picture, framed by the cab-window, of a woman reeling backward as
a man felled her to the ground with a blow in the face. (p. 175)

But not only in London was there a rich interplay of figures in life
and in art. In America such persons as his dentist and his writing
master called to mind figures in Phiz's or Cruikshank's illustrations
of Dickens's novels. Even within the realm of the fictive, pictures
sometimes seemed to impress him more than the text they illustrated.
In describing a governess as a Becky Sharp type, James recalled specifically Thackeray's drawing, not his text, of Becky neglecting her
charges.[4] To him, *Oliver Twist* seemed "more Cruikshank's than
Dickens's" (p. 69). And on one occasion, illustrated fictional characters had so much reality for the small boy that he expected the
dramatic representation to conform to the pictured one. So great
was the impression of colored plates in volumes "devoted mainly to
heroines of Romance, with one in particular, presenting those of
Shakespeare, in which the plates were so artfully coloured and var-
nished, and complexion and dress thereby so endeared to memory,"
that it was a shock for a long time afterward "not to see just those
bright images, with their peculiar toggeries, come on" (p. 56). James
was confronted at an early age with the problem of the relation of art
to reality, the complexities of which he explored most fully and ex-
asperatingly in *The Sacred Fount*.

Through the illustrated books available to him in childhood Henry
was admitted to a complex and sophisticated society. The raffish
dandy Gavarni introduced him to numerous Parisian types other
than Mlle Delavigne's. Although he could not fathom the racy witty

legends, he must have sensed the subtle social situations in the drawings. The illustrations of Gavarni, who had "a remarkable faculty for indicating character and mood by the position of the body, the twist of the limb, the turn of the head,"[5] piqued the boy's imagination. It is not strange that the novelist who considered it an incident "for a woman to stand up with her hand resting on a table and look out at you in a certain way" should have retained his boyhood admiration for Gavarni, even preferring him to Daumier.

Gavarni was also a frequent contributor to *Les français peints par eux-mêmes,* according to James "one of the fondest of our literary curiosities of that time" (the early Paris period). Its eight volumes consisting of literary and graphic sketches, the titles of a few indicate the range and type of subject: "La mère d'actrice," "L'ami des artiste," "La grisette," "Une femme à la mode," "Le joueur d'échecs," "L'épicier," "Les duchesses," "Le ramoneur." Virtually a visual and literary catalogue of French occupations and classes, it helped introduce the receptive child, whose own country lacked a variety of sharply defined social and occupational types, to the complexities of another social order.

This book, James recalled, was reinforced "in a general and particular way" by the long walks he and his brother William used to take to the Palais du Luxembourg, the same route followed by Lambert Strether on his second morning in Paris. By "in a general way," James must have meant that they met on the streets the types they had seen and read about in the book. The differences they perceived between the "old Paris" of the Luxembourg and the newer one of the Tuileries reinforced "in a particular way" the message of the pictures and essay (mistakenly attributed by James to Balzac) contrasting "L'habituée des Tuileries" with "L'habituée du Luxembourg" (see plate I). James found the text "very *serré*" but "flavoured withal and a trifle lubricated by Gavarni's two drawings, which had somehow so much, in general to say." As sketched by Gavarni, with Lami's collaboration, the contrast between the world of fashion and that of the old royalist aristocracy is presented dramatically and wittily, at least three hundred leagues and three centuries, in effect, separating the gardens. Urbain de Bellegarde in *The American* places no less distance between himself and the court at the Tuileries.

The engravings in the collected poems of Béranger, the popular republican poet, those in Rodolphe Töpffer's *Voyages en zigzag,* an account of the holiday tours through Switzerland and Northern Italy of a Swiss school master and his charges (the source, James surmised, of his family's ideas of the idyllic character of Swiss education), and those in Joseph Nash's *Mansions of England in the Olden Time,* all three books familiar to Henry before 1855, undoubtedly prepared the way for his appreciation of the picturesque, romantic, and historic in Europe. From Nash's views of old English houses peopled with figures in Elizabethan dress, James must have derived in part his sense of the "deep British picturesque," and from Töpffer's book, an object of his "fondest study," his delight in the "romance of travel," which he felt for the first time when the James family traveled by carriage from Lyons to Geneva. The steel engravings in the set of Béranger, "to the strange imagery of which I so wonderingly responded that all other art of illustration, ever since, has been for me comparatively weak and cold" (p. 13), might arouse wonder even in a less imaginative child. Unlike the linear uncluttered astringent Gavarni drawings, these illustrations by Johannot, Daubigny, Pauquet, and others are rich in chiaroscuro, three dimensional in effect, elaborately decorated and detailed, and sentimental rather than satirical in tone.[6] The pictures are a strange mélange of the picturesque and grotesque, the humorous and fantastic, the pathetic and heroic. Louis IX stands next to a smartly dressed bourgeois; smugglers with carbines on their shoulders filing down a mountain ravine appear a few pages after allegorical figures of war and peace; gypsies, beggars, violin players, devils, and peddlers are some of the other characters who play parts in front of varying backdrops of castles, thatched cottages, battlefields, vineyards, inns, and parlors. Memories of the romantic Béranger engravings, replete with castles and peasants in sabots, must have come into play on a biographically crucial occasion. James describes the experience as happening during a pause at a village inn on the same journey from Lyons to Geneva:

The village street . . . opened out, beyond an interval, into a high place on which perched an object also a fresh revelation and that I recognized with deep joy . . . as at once a castle and a ruin. . . . At a point in the interval, at any rate, below the slope on which this memento stood, was a woman in a black bodice, a white shirt and a red petticoat, engaged in some sort of field labour, the effect of whose intervention just then is almost beyond my notation. (p. 161)

Henry had never seen a castle before, except for "the machicolated villa above us the previous summer at New Brighton," much less a real ruin, and this was the first peasant he had ever seen, "or beheld at least to such advantage." "Supremely, in that ecstatic vision, was 'Europe,' sublime synthesis, expressed and guaranteed to me—as if by a mystic gage, which spread all through the summer air, that I should now, only now, never lose it, hold the whole consistency of it: up to that time it might have been but mockingly whisked before me" (p. 161). From his description, the *gestalt* of Europe, a concrete, tangible image, never to be lost, seems to have come to him in the form of a composed living picture. The road leading to the high place and the castle ruin suggest the recessional effects and picturesque subject matter of one of the landscapes in Béranger's books. The image of the real scene touched memories of books read and pictures studied in New York. There would have been no "ecstatic vision" without the shock of recognition.[7]

While the graphic arts, especially caricature, were of the greatest importance in young Henry's appropriation of people and places—he was to write portraits of both—the significance of museums and exhibitions, as well as of his own art efforts and aspirations in the formation of his taste and in the discovery of his métier, should not be underestimated.

Attending art exhibitions was for the young Jameses in New York as much a matter of course as going to the theater, and in England and France the museum overshadowed the theater as an entertainment and cultural resource. If, as James assumed, they were shown "everything there was" in the way of art under the same "genial law" (p. 151) by which they enjoyed the freedom of theater going, Henry must have seen in New York a considerable number of contemporary German, American, and French canvases. Between 1851 and 1855 the New York Gallery of Fine Arts with a permanent collection, the American Art Union with a rotating one, and the National Academy of Design with an annual show exhibited mainly contemporary American paintings, while Goupil's and the Düsseldorf Galleries specialized in contemporary European art and occasionally exhibited the work of an old master. James specifically mentions visits to art exhibitions at the Crystal Palace and at Thomas J. Bryan's Gallery of Christian Art; in both places works of old masters could be seen. As his father's frequent companion, he perhaps accompanied him on visits to the studios or homes of Thomas Hicks, Felix Darley, Christopher Cranch, and Paul Duggan, contemporary illustrators and painter friends of the elder James.

In the period between Sully, Stuart, Copley, West and Hunt, La Farge, Eakins, Inness, Homer, Duveneck, Ryder, the most important American painters belonged to the Hudson River school, but the style of painting taught at Düsseldorf, "European headquarters of spit-and-polish finish at the time,"[8] was in the ascendancy, infecting even those American artists who had not studied there with a passion for minute detail, high finish, and superficial realism, all thinly spread on huge canvases. The monumental *Martyrdom of John Hus* was to Henry "a revelation of representational brightness and charm that pitched once for all in these matters my young sense of what should be" (p. 151), but the picture of this school which seemed to have made the greatest impression on him was Emanuel Leutze's *Washington Crossing the Delaware*, though at least part of the thrill of seeing it may be attributed to the occasion itself—a special excursion at night, as if to the theater, by the Fourteenth Street stage. The picture, in James's words, "showed us Washington crossing the Delaware in a wondrous flare of projected gaslight and with the effect of a revelation to my young sight of the capacity of accessories to 'stand out'" (p. 151). Similarly Henry was struck favorably by "the violently protruded accessories" in Thomas Hicks's portrait of his wife and by "the light of the window playing over the figure and the 'treatment' of its glass and of the flower-pots and the other furniture" which "passed, by my impression, for the sign of the master hand" (pp. 37–38). "Materialism unmastered by intelligence" is how Virgil Barker characterizes works of this type of the mid-nineteenth century.[9]

As James himself treated with tender, nostalgic jocularity his childhood taste for the bigger than life, the garish, the superficially realistic, and the pictorially dramatic or anecdotal, the temptation is to dismiss his early preferences as being entirely the result of the naïve or debased art and taste of the times and of a child's inherent love of imitation. Small wonder that James at the age of ten or eleven admired Leutze when even Proust at thirteen or fourteen, with his opportunities for viewing the masterpieces of the Louvre, named as his favorite the painter Meissonier.[10]

These comments on Leutze and Hicks suggest an early sensitivity to color and light, but his taste otherwise was unprecocious, even, when compared with his brother William's, somewhat slow in developing. One reason the elder James gave for taking his children abroad was that the opportunity for a "sensuous" education was better than at home.[11] Henry's initial response to European art in Europe and his preferences among works in New York indicate that the dramatic, anecdotal, and psychological interest of painting attracted him rather than more formal qualities. Insofar as his aesthetic responses were formed by others, his attention was directed to the literary content or the likeness of a painting to its subject rather than to its technique. His earliest adventure in criticism occurred in a discussion of two pictures of the Tuscany landscape hanging in the

Fourteenth Street house, one by Thomas Cole[12] (see plate II) and the other by a M. Lefèvre.[13] James tells how a visitor questioned the verisimilitude of the Lefèvre:

"Tuscany?—are you sure it's Tuscany?" said the voice of restrictive criticism, that of the friend of the house who in the golden age of the precursors, though we were still pretty much precursors, had lived longest in Italy. And then on my father's challenge of this demur: "Oh in Tuscany, you know, the colours are much softer—there would be a certain haze in the atmosphere." "Why, of course," I can hear myself now blushingly but triumphantly—"the softness and the haze of our Florence there; isn't Florence in Tuscany?" (p. 154)

The boy's perception of the different tonal qualities of the Cole and Lefèvre paintings and of the light in the works by Hicks and Leutze shows a sensitivity to atmosphere, play of light, and intensity of color, but his earliest conscious experience in criticism hinged on the question of representational truth.

Fascinated by monumental art, Henry was charmed by the "great showy sculpture" of Thorvaldsen and Kiss at the New York Crystal Palace Exhibition of 1853. In contrast, the exhibition at the Thomas J. Bryan Gallery of "worm-eaten diptychs and triptychs, of angular saints and seraphs, of black Madonnas and obscure Bambinos," notwithstanding the enchanting label of "Europe" it also bore, disappointed him. Believing that Bryan's collection "was to fall . . . under grave suspicion, was to undergo in fact fatal exposure" (pp. 152–53), James in later life liked to console himself with the thought that if the pictures had been genuine he would have reacted differently to them. Art collections of the works of old masters so often turned out to be fakes in the Barnum age that it is no wonder the cautious author of the 1853 catalogue declined "to express any opinion upon the authenticity of the many pictures here which bear some of the greatest names in art."[14] Actually, however, modern methods of attribution have shown that the paintings in this collection were all originals of the periods to which they were ascribed, even though some have been re-attributed to less famous painters than those listed in the 1853 catalogue. Not perceiving the aesthetic qualities of two-dimensional art, Henry resembled in this respect his cultivated elders who had not yet begun to learn to appreciate quattrocento works.

While this inability of a boy to enjoy what only the sophisticated could may be easily discounted, it is interesting that he seemed impervious to the works of old masters in general. The fact that he did not mention in *A Small Boy and Others* any of the other pictures in Bryan's Gallery, those by Renaissance painters, for example, cannot be used as evidence, but there is his own testimony that when the James family was in London in 1856, the Rubenses and Titians in the National Gallery failed to arouse any enthusiasm. In fact, the kinds of pictures he admired in London and at first in Paris differed little from those that had filled him with wonder in New York. The mammoth works of the historical painter Benjamin Robert Haydon at the Pantheon had "remarkable interest and beauty," in part because of the fascination of his life as recorded in the then-new *Autobiography*, but as James himself added, "I blush to risk the further surmise that the grand manner, the heroic and the classic, in Haydon, came home to us more warmly and humanly than in the masters commended as 'old,' who, at the National Gallery, seemed to meet us so little half-way" (p. 177). Wondering what had become of *The Banishment of Aristides*,[15] James could still see "every attitude and figure . . . especially that of the foreshortened boy picking up stones to shy at the all-too-just" staring out at him, a memory suggesting that it was the illusion of reality, the human interest of the painting which caught and held his fancy.

Even more captivating than Haydon's were the pictures in the collection given in 1847 to the nation by Robert Vernon, a gift of 157 paintings, mainly by nineteenth-century British artists, "more generous at the time than it is now valuable."[16] Though the collection included Turner, Bonington, and Constable landscapes as well as portraits by Reynolds and Gainsborough, Henry seems to have been charmed mainly by the genre and "subject" pictures. He thought Daniel Maclise's picture of the play scene from Hamlet "the finest composition in the world (though Ophelia did look a little as if cut in silhouette out of white paper and pasted on)" (p. 178). Charles Leslie's *Sancho Panza and His Duchess*, an illustration of the chapter which treats of "the relishing conversation which passed between the Duchess, her damsels, and Sancho Panza,"[17] opened the door for Henry "through the great hall of romance to the central or private apartments" (p. 178). Of the other painters James later mentioned, Mulready, Landseer, and Wilkie, only the reputation of Wilkie has shown some sturdiness. The dependency of nineteenth-century academic painting on literary, historical, and sentimental crutches is demonstrated by the works of these painters: Mulready's chefs-d'oeuvre were painted from his wood-block illustrations of *The Vicar of Wakefield*; Landseer's pictures relied on story and humanized animals for their ready appeal; Wilkie, through the depiction of stirring historical events, for example, *John Knox Preaching before the Lords of the Congregation*, and humble character, as in *The Blind*

Fiddler, fulfilled the accepted aims of elevating the mind and warming the heart. It was presumably this pictorialized sentiment and drama to which the thirteen-year-old Henry responded.

Henry's first glimpse of Pre-Raphaelite art was in Paris in 1855 during a brief stopover which included a visit to the exhibition at the Palais de l'Industrie. At the Royal Academy exhibition of 1856 he saw more of the "first fresh fruits of the Pre-Raphaelite efflorescence. . . . The very word Pre-Raphaelite wore for us that intensity of meaning, not less than of mystery, that thrills us in its perfection but for one season, the prime hour of first initiations" (p. 178). Although he retained his high opinion of Millais's *Blind Girl* and *Autumn Leaves*, the initial excitement from the bold colors and sharply defined details characteristic of the earliest Pre-Raphaelite painting was not to deepen into lasting admiration. His reaction, however, to Holman Hunt's *Scapegoat* (see plate VI) is of special interest: he felt that the painting was "so charged with the awful that I was glad I saw it in company—*it* in company and I the same" (p. 178).[18] The picture must have made an intense impression indeed, for it rose to the surface some forty-eight years later in *The Golden Bowl*: Maggie Verver sees herself as carrying the burden of perilously strained family relationships "as the scapegoat of old, of whom she had once seen a terrible picture, had been charged with the sins of the people and had gone forth into the desert to sink under his burden and die."[19] Hunt had intended the picture of the goat to awaken feelings of fear and awe in the spectator, and he had taken the trouble to go to the Holy Land to paint an authentic biblical goat, but it is difficult not to agree with the critic of the contemporary *Art Journal* who saw it as just a goat "meaning nothing."[20] Even Ruskin, who praised Hunt for his sincerity in painting a "real" Semitic goat, implied that the picture had little meaning unless one familiarized oneself with the Hebrew custom of attributing sins to a sacrificial goat.[21] Henry's fear must have been stimulated in part by catalogue notes or comments made by his companions, though it was through the visual symbol that he experienced the emotion. He lived through his eyes, but the visual sense was never isolated from the literary imagination.

Even more thrilling to Henry than the Pre-Raphaelites, however, was Delaroche, painter of historical episodes. Although in his first art essay James spoke disparagingly of Delaroche, he remembered the minutest details of his pictures for half a century. At least part of the attraction of Delaroche's work can be attributed to the "English lore" which one of their tutors, Robert Thomson, had "rubbed" into them, "all from a fine old conservative and monarchical point of view" (p. 195). Before the boy's delighted eyes, the history text was made visible. In *Les enfants d'Edouard* (see plate III) he saw "a reconstitution of far-off history of the subtlest and most 'last word' modern or psychologic kind" (p. 194). Although he had never heard of "psychology in art or anywhere else," he "truly felt the nameless force at play" here; his own practice of psychological analysis "set in, under such encouragements, once for all" (p. 194). His response to this painting is a striking instance of the way in which James grew in awareness through pictures, even if we take into account his tendency toward hyperbole in his memoirs. If Delaroche's picture of the hapless princes did not by itself sire James's numerous innocents in a similar, though less obviously horrendous, plight, it must have helped in the engendering of them and of James's characteristic subordination of overt to inner drama.

More sensitive than Henry to the strictly technical aspects of painting, William not only scorned to reproduce Delaroche but tried instead to copy Delacroix and to create "effects, with charcoal and crayon, in his manner" (p. 195), that is, to imitate his technique. William's admiration for Delacroix was more immediate and intelligent than Henry's. "I could see in a manner, for all the queerness, what W. J. meant by that beauty and, above all, that living interest in La Barque du Dante, where the queerness, according to him, was perhaps what contributed most" (p. 194), James recalled. William was, of course, correct; it is Delacroix's "queerness"—his execution, especially his color technique, figure distortion, and visible brush strokes—which sets him apart from the other contemporary orientalist and historical painters and which led Cézanne to refer to him as the father of modern painting. Henry could see in Delacroix what William meant, but it was *Les enfants d'Edouard* that "thrilled" him "to a different tune." James's taste was to change substantially, but his response to the representational power of painting remained stable. He had, as La Farge said, "the painter's eye," but not in a strict sense. He did not seem to see objects in their integrity as does the painter, who through a combination of talent and training sees patterns of color and masses divorced from intellectual meaning to a high degree. "In La Farge's opinion," according to his biographer, "the literary man did not so much see a thing as think about it."[22] Like his artist character who was "ridden by the twin demons imagination and observation,"[23] James "thought" because he "saw."

The turning point in Henry's aesthetic development came as a result of visits to the Louvre and the Luxembourg where he became aware on his own of the "inscrutable" elements in art—the personal vision of the painter which finds expression through the language of his medium and which penetrates his representation of objects. At the Luxembourg, while Delacroix and to a lesser extent Decamps led to an awareness of "style," other contemporary painters helped to educate his eyes. Here, Henry admired Thomas Couture's *Romains de la décadence*, then thought to be "the last word of the grand manner, but of the grand manner modernised, humanised, philosophised, redeemed from academic death" (now better characterized as the last gasp of the moribund classical school inaugurated by David), and *Le fauconnier*, "a poetic conception" which made James wonder "by what rare chance . . . the heavens had once opened" for Couture (pp. 192–93). James also linked with Couture the Barbizon landscapists—Troyon, Rousseau, Daubigny, and Lambinet—whom he was to consider for a long time the masters of modern painting. But it was the Louvre which James felt in retrospect to have been "educative, formative, fertilising, in a degree which no other 'intellectual experience' our youth was to know could pretend, as a comprehensive, conducive thing, to rival" (p. 197).

The centrality of the Louvre not only in the formation of his taste but in the resolution of his search for a bridge between Self and Others, his inner world and the threatening outer, is evident in the well-known autobiographic passages describing his first visit to the Louvre and the "dream-adventure" in the Galerie d'Apollon in which he unexpectedly put to rout the intruder making for his "place of rest" (p. 197). This "dream-adventure," according to James, "founded in the deepest, quickest, clearest act of cogitation and comparison, act indeed of life-saving energy, as well as in unutterable fear" (p. 196), may symbolize his recognition of where his road to personal power and salvation lay (the life-saving energy) and his awareness of the tolls exacted (the unutterable fear) along this route. Counterpointing these two passages are phrases and words standing for the opposition and reconciliation of the "world," or active experience, and "art." Thus, the Louvre was the "palace of art" and the "house of life"; even the windows of the great gallery "threw off the rest of monumental Paris somehow as a told story, a sort of wrought effect or bold ambiguity for a vista, and yet held it there, at every point, as a vast bright gage, even at moments a felt adventure, of experience" (pp. 195–96). On his first visit to the Louvre, while he gaped "at Géricault's Radeau de la Méduce . . . Guérin's Burial of Atala, Prudhon's Cupid and Psyche,[24] David's helmetted Romanisms, Madame Vigée-Lebrun's 'ravishing' portrait of herself and her little girl," the boy had a prevision "of all the fun, confusedly speaking, that

one was going to have, and the kind of life, always of the queer, so-
called inward sort . . . that one was going to lead. It came of itself, this
almost awful apprehension in all the presences, under our courier's
protection and in my brother's company—it came just there and so;
there was alarm in it somehow as well as bliss" (p. 198).

If the "alarm" may be understood to represent the fear of experiencing only the image of life, not life at first hand, the "bliss" may be
taken for the sense of mastering the world, of appropriating experience, through art. The Galerie d'Apollon with its Delacroix and
Le Brun frescoes and its cases of crown jewels was for him the bridge
to style, but he goes on to identify style here with glory, and "glory
meant ever so many things at once, not only beauty and art and
supreme design, but history and fame and power, the world in fine
raised to the richest and noblest expression" (p. 196).

James's great discoveries about style as "beauty and art and supreme design" carried him beyond Géricault and David and presumably far beyond the glittering gaucheness of Haydon and Leutze
to an appreciation of the subtler art of Veronese, Leonardo, Murillo,
"the treasures of the Salon Carré." However, he associated style not
only with purely aesthetic qualities but also with a reconciliation of
art and the world and with "history and fame and power," as sum-
marized in the following passage.

The beginning in short was with Géricault and David, but it went on and
on and slowly spread; so that one's stretched, one's even strained, perceptions, one's discoveries and extensions piece by piece, come back, on the
great premises, almost as so many explorations of the house of life, so many
circlings and hoverings round the image of the world. I have dim reminiscences of permitted independent visits, uncorrectedly juvenile though I
might still be, during which the house of life and the palace of art became
so mixed and interchangeable—the Louvre being, under a general description, the most peopled of all scenes not less than the most hushed of all
temples—that an excursion to look at pictures would have but half expressed
my afternoon. . . . I had also looked at France and looked at Europe, looked
even at America as Europe itself might be conceived so to look, looked at
history, as a still-felt past and a complacently personal future, at society,
manners, type, characters, possibilities and prodigies and mysteries of fifty
sorts. (pp. 198–99)

Clearly, the Louvre was crucial to James's aesthetic development.
That the "dream-adventure" was experienced by the mature artist
and recounted in his old age merely substantiates the intensity with
which his youthful imagination fixed upon it. If the autobiographical
passages from which I have quoted extensively did not exist, we would

still have the evidence of his fiction, the classic opening scene of *The American,* for example. The Louvre began his initiation into the mysteries of international society as well as of art, of picture-viewers as well as of pictures.

James's own picture making apparently began when he was a child in New York. In *A Small Boy* he describes his practice of filling three pages of lined paper with "scenes" and then illustrating them on the fourth unlined page, thus casting his dramatis personae.

The odd part of all of which was that whereas my cultivation of the picture was maintained my practice of the play, my addiction to scenes, presently quite dropped. I was capable of learning, though with inordinate slowness, to express ideas in scenes, and was not capable, with whatever patience, of making proper pictures; yet I aspired to this form of design to the prejudice of any other, and long after those primitive hours was still wasting time in attempts at it. (p. 149)

His persistence in following this "false scent," according to his own analysis, was largely due to his brother William's example. But there were probably other reasons why he continued to nurture his early ambitions: the romantic legend of his cousin Bob, Gus Barker's brother, who had shown promise as a sculptor and died young; his father's acquaintance with New York artists, who, in turn, gave the Jameses "a sense of others" (p. 36), of the Hudson River school— Cole, Kinsett, and Cropsey—and the American sculptors in Rome— Mozier and Ives. Eyre Crowe, Thackeray's secretary, painted his father's portrait in a New York hotel, an operation that held Henry spellbound. In New York and Europe, as already mentioned, the James children visited special exhibitions and museums. In short, the cultural atmosphere of the James family and Henry's fascination with painting provide, apart from fraternal emulation, sufficient explanation for his aspirations.

The only teachers James remembered having as a child "directly desired or invoked" were Mr. Coe, the art instructor, and Mr. Dolmidge, the writing master, at Richard Pulling Jenks's school in New York. But apparently Henry's parents failed to take his art aspirations seriously; probably he took them more seriously retrospectively than he had at the time.[25] It was William, not he, who took private lessons from Coe and later from Léon Coigniet in Paris, and his desire to embark on an art career provided the James family with what Henry thought an odd reason for abandoning Europe in favor of Newport—to give William the opportunity to study with William Morris Hunt, who had settled there. Henry also studied informally with Hunt. Not officially a pupil, he copied antique casts in a room apart from the others—his brother, John La Farge, and Theodora Sedgwick, Charles Eliot Norton's sister-in-law. Still he felt himself in the studio "at the threshold of a world." "Frankly, intensely—that was the great thing—these were hours of Art, art definitely named, looking me full in the face and accepting my stare in return—no longer a tacit implication or a shy subterfuge, but a flagrant unattenuated aim" (p. 285). Hunt apparently made occasional comments on his work, and Henry probably joined the regular pupils and the master for the daily tea when Hunt's talk was at its best.[26] Whether any of Hunt's ideas were assimilated by James, it is not easy to say because of the aphoristic mode of Hunt's speech which often led him to be contradictory and inconsistent. His originality lay not in what he said but in his manner of speaking. While some of Hunt's ideas seem to be echoed in James's fictional art discussions, traces of his brilliant paradoxical talk and mimetic talents are more clearly evident in artist characters like Roderick Hudson. James also must have acquired from Hunt some knowledge of the technical aspects of painting and the painter's terminology.[27] But the impress of Hunt on James's imagination was not so much what he said but what he was— "the living and communicating Artist." He felt that "'the man the great mystery could mark with its stamp, when wishing the mark unmistakable," taught him "just in himself the most and best about any art that I should come to find benignantly concerned with me" (p. 286). "Since the time of his association with Millet," according to Virgil Barker, "Hunt had known and taught that art is found inside the artist himself rather than outside him in the subject."[28] Though James held the conventional view that some subjects are intrinsically better than others, his stress on the value of the artist's power to penetrate through surfaces to the inner reality was surely reinforced by Hunt's example. His resemblance to Don Quixote was not merely physical, as James knew. "William Hunt, all muscular spareness and brownness and absence of waste, all flagrant physiognomy, brave bony arch of handsome nose, upwardness of strong eye-brow and glare, almost, of eyes that both recognized and wondered, strained eyes that played over questions as if they were objects and objects as if they were questions, might have stood, to the life, for Don Quixote" (p. 286). In spite of his madness, or rather because of it, Don Quixote perceives truths about objects which the grosser senses of ordinary people prevent them from detecting. It takes an artist's eye to see that the barber's basin is Mambrino's golden helmet.

More exotically the archetypal artist was John La Farge; for James in the Newport days he was a man of the world, "of the type—the 'European.' " A romantic figure, wearing a black velvet jacket, riding an Arabian horse, a mount from a Fromentin painting, La Farge stood out as "an embodiment of the gospel of esthetics" (pp. 289–90) in a utilitarian America before the days foundations and universities made the artistic career respectable. La Farge, moreover, acted on his vision of artistic truth regardless of negative criticism and indifference to his experiments. Even Hunt reportedly told him that he carried his refinements of tone and color too far as not even "one in a hundred or five hundred artists [were] capable of appreciating such differences of accuracy." "So much the better," La Farge answered, "if only one man in a thousand could see it; I should then have exactly what I wanted in the appeal to the man who knew and to the mind like mine."[29] James's refinements of psychological tone and color seemed oversubtle, even to his "confrères." No less uncompromising than La Farge, James tried, however, in his Prefaces, as Richard P. Blackmur notes, "to prove how much the reader would see if only he paid attention."[30]

While it may not be said that from him alone James learned the importance of conscious concern for composition in literary art, La Farge was a highly intellectual artist with clearly articulated aims, and at the least he helped James justify his bent. Equally at home in literature and art, La Farge introduced James to Balzac, stimulated his interest in Browning, and encouraged him to translate Mérimée's *La Venus d'Ille*. He not only held out to James the much-needed hand of friendship and support, but he led him to see, as James put it, that "even with canvas and brush whisked out of my grasp I still needn't feel disinherited" and that "the arts were after all essentially one" (p. 294). To La Farge must be given much credit for helping James grasp the fact that literature was no less art than painting—not an entirely common view at the time—and that his aesthetic impulses would find successful issue in the practice of the art of fiction.

The realization that he lacked the ability to be a painter came to him dramatically. Paying a visit to the studio where he found his cousin posing in the nude on a pedestal, he saw that here was the "living truth" which he could not hope to capture on canvas, especially not with the dazzling skill William displayed in his rendering of "the happy figure." Nor could he hope to equal William's achievement in his portrait of their Albany cousin, Katherine Temple, "a really mature, an almost masterly, piece of painting" (p. 293). The awareness that he could not compete successfully with William may have been instrumental in his abandoning hopes of a painting career.

At least as decisive, however, may have been the sense of his own inadequacy in portraying the "living truth" and an urgent desire to do so. Copying casts, imitations of imitations of life, could not have satisfied him for long.

Exemplifying the family gift of converting waste into use, James found that his excursion into the studio had not been fruitless; he discovered that in fiction "the picture was still after all in essence one's aim" (p. 150). The implications of the complex conception of the novel underlying this simple statement will be explored later. Most obviously, however, his early art efforts disciplined his eye: he not only copied antique casts but drew rock formations in the Ruskin manner and tried to paint landscapes *en plein air* with La Farge. The degree of his knowledge of painting technique may only be surmised from his art criticism and fictional treatment of the visual arts and artists. Informal as his training was, he learned enough of the craft and its vocabulary to borrow from it extensively for literary purposes. Perhaps most influential was the studio ambience: initially, for the support he derived in pursuing an artistic career and, eventually, as a literary resource. Although the studio settings and artist types changed with the times and with James's personal history and professional preoccupations, their presence in his fiction is a constant throughout his career.

THE third quarter of the nineteenth century, when James's mature aesthetic was formed, was marked by transitions in attitudes toward art, both of the past and of the present, and more importantly by a transformation of art itself. Not only had the furor raised by Delacroix's romantic baroque style subsided by the 1850's, but sentimental, historical, patriotic, exotic, and allegorical subjects, treated in a debased Ingres manner, were the stock in trade of the official artist. The great French controversy in art and literature of the 1850's and 1860's was between the exponents of a new realism and the defenders of tradition, or idealism. The latter, who vehemently attacked what they called the "cult of the ugly," fought in theory to conserve the old humanistic concept of ideal beauty and in practice to defend the sterile academic tradition typified by slick Bouguereau nudes posing as Mary Magdalenes or Judiths. The realists, on the other hand, believed that the artist should reproduce man and nature faithfully without recourse to traditional idealized views of man or abstract conceptions of beauty. Eventually, still a third attitude, an outgrowth of the second, conceived the painter as a disinterested spectator who should paint what he sees, namely, the variations of light received by the eye. According to the now familiar impressionist theory, not only should the painter make no effort to interpret man or nature intellectually or spiritually, but he should carry realism to its logical conclusion by recording literally what he sees before him, not what he knows is there. In practice, of course, this means that the artist paints not the object itself but his way of seeing the object. As André Malraux points out, there is more of Manet in his portrait of Clemenceau than of Clemenceau.

The English counterparts of the French realists, the Pre-Raphaelites, had by 1860 become assimilated into the mainstream of academic art. Rossetti was still poeticizing in paint, and his disciples Burne-Jones and Morris, having given up the priesthood at Oxford, were through their work spreading the gospel of beauty; however, as Ruskin only eight years after the founding of the Brotherhood noted with satisfaction, Pre-Raphaelite paintings at the Royal

Academy exhibitions no longer stood out as a separate class, "but . . . between them and the comparatively few pictures remaining quite of the old school, there is a perfectly unbroken gradation."[1] Although not without influence in stimulating a wider taste for early Italian paintings, "in spite of its name," as J. R. Hale observes, "the movement, which originated in Rossetti's enthusiastic perusal in 1848 of Lasinio's engravings of the frescoes in the Campo Santo, did nothing in the way of history or criticism to rehabilitate the loved centuries."[2] The significance of this rehabilitation of painters before Raphael can be fully understood only in the light of the fact that the dominant influence on English taste for Italian paintings for virtually two hundred and fifty years had been Vasari, who held that the criterion of good art was the "naturalism, philosophic energy and classical discipline of Raphael and Michelangelo"[3] and who considered the so-called primitives of the fourteenth and early fifteenth centuries merely signposts pointing to the summit–the art of the sixteenth-century masters. But by 1868, the year of James's first art review, Ruskin, Palgrave, Pugin, and popularizers such as Anna B. Jameson had awakened considerable enthusiasm among cultivated persons in England and America for the long-neglected masters—Fra Angelico, Giotto, Gozzoli, Ghiberti, Masaccio, Ghirlandajo. Corollary to the new appreciation of the primitives was the downgrading of *seicento* painting and of late Renaissance architecture, the test of religious "sincerity" to some extent replacing the idea of progress.

Not only was James exposed in a general way to these widely diffused ideas and attitudes and to poetic and fictional treatment of artists and art ideas, but also he was familiar with the art criticism of leading French and English writers of the mid-century. The main French critics whose works he either reviewed or specifically referred to were Stendhal, Planche, Vitet, Taine, Fromentin, Sainte-Beuve, Gautier, Champfleury, Montégut, and Cherbuliez, belletrists whose domain included the visual arts as well as the literary. He was equally familiar with current English art criticism and felt that Ruskin exerted such a powerful influence that independent thought in others was stultified. Considering the French—in art as well as in literature and drama—masters of the science of criticism, he noted in 1868 a lack of books in the English language "belonging in form to literature, in which the principles of painting, or certain specific pictures, are intelligently discussed." The "small library" available consisted of "a small number of collections of lectures by presidents of the Royal Academy, the best of which are Reynolds's; there is Leslie's *Handbook*; there are the various compilations of Mrs. Jameson; and there is the translation of Vasari, and the recent valuable *History of Italian Art* by Crowe and Cavalcaselle."[4] He might have added to this list Charles R. Leslie's biography of Constable, which Thomas Sergeant Perry remembered him as reading the first time they met. He did add, in the same article, the names of W. M. Rossetti, F. T. Palgrave, and P. G. Hamerton as the "three principal art-critics now writing in England" whose criticism was not merely ephemeral. Later, he also referred to Pater and Burckhardt in translation. The absence of any reference to English aestheticians, such as Edmund Burke, Archibald Alison, Richard Payne Knight, and Lord Kames, suggests that James's reading, with the exception of Reynolds, was mainly of works having an empirical rather than an abstract emphasis.

How does James's criticism reflect the often conflicting theories and attitudes of the time? That he himself felt the impress of Ruskin is clear from his observation that Ruskin had "achieved a very manifest and a very extended influence over the mind and feelings of his own generation and that succeeding it,"[5] the latter "generation" surely being James's. The precise extent to which Ruskin shaped James's preferences and views on art cannot be ascertained: Ruskin's theory of art is notoriously tortuous and contradictory, and wide dissemination of his ideas makes attribution specifically to him risky. Still, there are places in James's thought where it seems quite clear that, in his own phrase, "Ruskin has *passé par là*," in some instances making an indelible impression.

Ruskin served as James's cicerone to north Italy through Murray's guidebook—passages from Ruskin appeared from the second edition in 1846 on and finally became absorbed in the text—and to Venice through *The Stones of Venice*. Charles Eliot Norton, Ruskin's friend and James's mentor on his first trip abroad as an adult, advised him to use it, especially the "Venetian Index," as a guide to buildings and pictures worth seeing,[6] or, in Ruskin's words, those "it is a duty to enjoy and a disgrace to forget." Ruskin's championship of Tintoretto undoubtedly led to James's initial interest, though he felt in 1871 that "not even Ruskin" had done justice to him, a phrase he tactfully amended to "save Ruskin"[7] after hearing from Norton of Ruskin's warm praise of his article on Tintoretto that appeared in the *Nation*.

Ruskin also introduced him to the early Florentine painters, whose abstract decorative qualities did not evoke in him, however, an enthusiasm comparable to Ruskin's, and taught him to question the taste of the preceding generation for late sixteenth-century and seventeenth-century paintings, especially the Bolognese school, and to regard classical Palladian and baroque architecture as decadent. James's early essays are redolent of Ruskin in other respects. To support his reaction to the Cathedral of Milan he argued that "beauty in great architecture is almost a secondary merit and that the main point is mass—such as may make it a supreme embodiment of sustained effort." A "great building is the greatest conceivable work of art" because it "represents difficulties annulled, resources combined, labor, courage, and patience." His conclusion was even more characteristically Ruskinian: "And there are people who tell us that art has nothing to do with morality! Little enough, doubtless, when it is concerned, ever so little, in painting the roof of Milan Cathedral within to represent carved stone-work."[8] Similarly, his opinion in 1873 that "the great source of his [Tintoretto's] impressiveness is that his indefatigable hand never drew a line that was not, as one may say, a moral line,"[9] was derived from Ruskin, who believed that the artist's moral qualities are reflected in technique itself. Evaluations of specific paintings were almost certainly colored by Ruskin's prior judgment: James's disappointment in Titian's *Assumption* in the Academy in Venice is an almost word-for-word echo of Ruskin's remarks in *Stones of Venice*. But "Ruskin-haunted" as he was, James was not a servile disciple. In his very first art essay his call for a criticism independent of Ruskin's indicates his determination to see by his own light. In spite of Ruskin's spirited public patronage of Turner and his personal amiability in showing the young American his Turner collection, James was not persuaded that Turner was of old master caliber. "I think I prefer Claude. He had better taste, at any rate," he declared in a letter to John La Farge.[10] Nor did he hesitate to criticize Ruskin in print, calling him to task for attributing "various incongruous and arbitrary intentions to the artist." In his 1877 essay "Italy Revisited," he chided Ruskin for being hysterical about the "desecration" of old Italy by the new government; James found the "familiar asperity of the author's style" and his "pedagogic fashion" comic and his legislative tone inharmonious: "For many persons he will never bear the test of being read in this rich old Italy, where art, so long as it really lived at all, was spontaneous, joyous, irresponsible. If the reader is in daily contact with those beautiful Florentine works which do still, in a way, force themselves into notice through the vulgarity and cruelty of modern profanation, it will seem to him that Mr. Ruskin's little books are pitched in the strangest falsetto key."[11] James's apology in 1884 for imputing morality to the church of Saint-Sernin in Toulouse—"As a general thing I favor little the fashion of attributing moral qualities to buildings; I shrink from talking about tender cornices and sincere campanili"[12]—contrasts sharply with his earlier statements on the relation of morality to architecture. In 1906 James gave what seemed to be his final opinion of Ruskin in a letter to Edwin A. Abbey, the American illustrator, who had enlisted his help in a search for a motto on art for a mural: "Look into Ruskin and he's all about Nature—splendidly often, but *loathing* Art."[13] A far cry from the young critic's assertion in 1868 that Ruskin, in spite of his sorties into economics and social theory, "has been unable to abandon the aesthetic standpoint. Let him treat of what subjects he pleases, therefore, he will always remain before all things an art-critic."[14]

Even in his early criticism, at the height of Ruskin's influence on him, James was at the most only stiff and unduly solemn rather than "pedagogic." Closer in tone to Gautier than to Ruskin, he held a relaxed view of his critical duties: "a person whose sole relation to pictures is a disposition to enjoy them," he wrote in an essay on Delacroix (1880), "can rest upon his personal impressions; and in the case of the writer of these lines such an impression has been conscious of no chilling responsibilities."[15] He was the obverse of Christopher Newman in taste and cultivation, but he cast himself most frequently in the role of the man who takes his pleasure in art with a large easiness wherever he can, apparently having found the part of the "sincere," moralistic young minister from Dorchester, Newman's foil on the grand tour, uncongenial. James's tone is self-deprecatory, ironic, playful; his pace, leisurely; his fund of tolerance, large enough to meet drafts on it with good-humored generosity. Even the severity of his criticism of "bad" art was tempered with mercy. After describing Domenichino's *Communion of St. Jerome* as a picture which ought to hang in every art school as an example to students of what they should avoid, James added that he hated to leave as final an unkind verdict "upon any great bequest of human effort."[16] Ever conscious of the fraternity of artists, their debts to one another, and the human uses of art, he found it difficult to ridicule any artistic effort.

Despite these essential differences in tone and approach, basic affinities between James and Ruskin did exist. Though James, unlike Ruskin, did not try to construct a theory of art, lacking not only the metaphysical tools but, more importantly, the intellectual temperament and desire to do so, he did apply in his criticism of specific works a theory of representation similar to the one Ruskin evolved in *his* attempt to justify beauty, reconcile art and morality, truth and the imagination.

"Art is the one corner of human life in which we may take our

ease," James said, criticizing Ruskin's view of the world of art as "a
sort of assize-court, in perpetual session . . . a region governed by a
kind of Draconic legislation." Through art we enter an ideal world in
which we find ourselves free from the confusions, conventions, and
limitations of real life, but James made clear that he was not espousing art for art's sake or art for escape or entertainment by adding
that our freedom in the sphere of art is qualified by a necessary "passion for representation."[17] That crucial qualification, a "passion for
representation," in addition, of course, to the evidence of his art
criticism as a whole, suggests that he owed more of his basic assumptions and even terms to Ruskin than he perhaps realized. But the influence of Ruskin's ideas—his conception of the imagination and of
the relation of art to nature—can be gauged only after consideration
of what James meant by "representation" in his criticism.

James often praised artists for literally reproducing a scene or
object. Of the trees in a Troyon painting he approvingly said: "They
stand there solid and mighty, without the smallest loss of their
hugeness and dignity,"[18] *loss*, that is, in the transfer from nature to
canvas. Of a painting by Theodore Rousseau, another realist, he
wrote, "It is all admirably true; you seem, as you look, to be plodding
heavy-footed across the field and stumbling here and there in the
false light which is neither night nor day. The struggle and mixture
of the dusk and glow in all the little ruts and furrows of the field
is perfectly rendered. If we are asked for an example in painting of
that much-discussed virtue 'sincerity,' we should indicate this work
as a capital instance."[19] Opposed to Rousseau's and Troyon's sincerity was the artificiality of the orientalist Decamps (see plate IV),
one of the class of artists "whose mission is the pursuit of effect, without direct reference to truth." Representing "the opposite pole of art
from even the most skeptical of the great pietistic masters," Decamps
in his painting *The Centurion* made the scriptural subject "the mere
pretext for a bit of picturesqueness;" his picture had "about the same
relation to probable fact as some first-rate descriptive tidbit of Edgar
Poe or Charles Baudelaire." Decamps did not have the "generous
imagination" of Delacroix; still, "only a supremely vivid fancy . . .
could have conceived those dizzy and mellow-toned walls and towers
and distilled that narrow strip of morbidly tender sky."[20] In his
analysis of *The Gallery of the H.M.S. Calcutta* (see plate V), the work
of another contemporary, James Joseph Jacques Tissot, James applied similar standards: he found the painting brilliantly realistic but
the "sentiment . . . sterile and disagreeable . . . . What is it that makes
such realism as M. Tissot's appear vulgar and *banal*, when an equal

degree of realism, practised three hundred years ago, has an inexhaustible charm and entertainment?" The only answer he could offer was that "the realism of the Dutch painters seems soft and that of such men as M. Tissot seems hard. His humour is trivial, his sentiment stale. Is there then to be no more *delightful* realism?" Without referring in any detail to technique, he judged George Frederick Watts's portrait of Mrs. Percy Wyndham as having "a style which is distinctly removed from the 'stylishness' of M. Tissot's yellow-ribboned heroine." Watts had what presumably Tissot lacked: "the art of combining the imagination and ideal element in portraiture with an extreme solidity, and separating great elegance from small elegance."[21]

James's "palace of art" had "many mansions"; however, only works which combined the real and the ideal were worthy of the highest, most unqualified reception. Neither truth to an empirical reality nor technical skill in itself sufficed. More receptive than Ruskin to a painting that reproduced nature or one whose subject was used for technical display, he nevertheless believed as Ruskin did that what made a painting truly valuable was evidence the painter had "lingering relish for something in objects over and above their literal facts."[22] Thus, in his review of the Metropolitan Museum's purchase of 1871 he described the Ruisdaels, Teniers, and Brueghels in sympathetic detail, but he did not rank them among the world's greatest pictures. The Dutch, on the whole, he felt, "please by giving one the sense of rest that results when aim [to copy nature] and end [picture] coincide," but to him the finest works were those which had "intellectual charm," "allusiveness," "style," "tone," "invention," "sentimental redundancy," "reflection," "emotional byplay," or "imagination." All these words do not stand for the same degree of excellence in James's scale—he usually reserved *imagination* or *reflection* for the best—but when he used one of these words to describe a work of art, he was invariably referring to a quality that to him raised it above the realistic or skillful. All paintings with "imaginative qualities" were not great, but in order to be great a painting had to have them. "The principal charm . . . ," he said of the minor American painter Mrs. Spartali Stillman, "is the intellectual charm—that thing which, when it exists, always seems more precious than other merits, and indeed makes us say that it is the only thing in a work of art which is deeply valuable. Imagination, intellectual elevation, cannot be studied, purchased, acquired; whereas everything else can; even, in a degree, the colourist's faculty."[23]

On the surface, the implication of James's criticism is that what makes a picture superior to nature is the artist's intensification of the scene, his creation of values over and above those of the object in nature, and the more intensification, that is, the more stylized the presentation, the better the picture. However, not only did James consider certain realists to be without imagination, but also he included in this category painters like Decamps, a romantic orientalist, and others like Ingres who belonged to the nonrealistic, neoclassical tradition. Accordingly, the best way to approach James's conception of imagination in painting is through Ruskin, for, though James's theory of representation is relatively free from moral overtones and abstract categorizing, it rests largely on Ruskin's. James could have derived the idea that the highest value in art depends on the imagination from any theorist espousing a romantic view of art. The idea of the imagination as an innate faculty, a sign of genius, and the "highest intellectual power of man" which "works not by algebra, nor by integral calculus"[24] was a romantic commonplace. Also, in placing greater emphasis on the technical than on the inspirational or intuitional aspect of the creative process, James had much in common with Constable, who declared "there has never been a boy painter, nor can there be. The art requires a long apprenticeship, being *mechanical*, as well as intellectual."[25] However, for his conception of the perceptive imagination—that power which enables the artist through contemplation to perceive the essence of a thing—James was mainly indebted to Ruskin.

To Ruskin, the imagination, which he identified with perception and contemplation, was "a piercing, Pholas-like mind's tongue that works and tastes into the very rock heart" of things. Originality to him, was "not newness . . . it is only genuineness; it all depends on this single glorious faculty of getting to the spring of things and working out from that."[26] Likewise, for James, though he placed more emphasis on the contemplative aspects of the process, "the highest result" in painting was obtained when to the perception of appearances "a certain faculty of brooding reflection is added. I use this name for want of a better, and I mean the quality in the light of which the artist sees deep into his subject, undergoes it, absorbs it, discovers in it new things that were not on the surface, becomes patient with it, and almost reverent, and, in short, enlarges and humanizes the technical problem."[27]

Ruskin, unfortunately, did not describe exactly how the presence of imagination in painting was to be detected, though he gave some clues: "The fancy sees the outside, and is able to give a portrait of the outside, clear, brilliant, and full of detail. The imagination sees the heart and inner nature, and makes them felt, but is often obscure, mysterious, and interrupted, in its giving of outer detail."[28] The one sign by which it could be known was suggestiveness. Ruskin believed the painter's object to be the transfer to the viewer's mind of the emotional atmosphere of the real scene. James, following in Ruskin's footsteps, praised Delacroix for his sensitivity to the "mystery" of a scene which he made the viewer feel through the canvas. This imaginative quality, as described by James in an 1880 essay, was a "metaphysical emanation" one felt in looking at a painting. Actually, as I shall show, imagination in painting to James depended on the number and quality of literary, historical, and psychological associations it aroused in the beholder as well as such pictorial qualities as color and movement. James did not insist that a painting convey, in Ruskin's terms, "the greatest ideas," but his appreciation of a painting was deeply influenced by extrapictorial considerations.

James thus continued the associational aesthetic of the first half of the nineteenth century in America; however, for spiritual truth, which, for example, Allston, Hawthorne, and Cole sought as the primary value in pictorial representation, James substituted historical and cultural complexity and continuity. The touchstone of greatness for a work of art lay in its power to evoke a sense of human relationships, especially of the past to the present. Like Irving, he needed the humanizing touch of the past to see beauty in a natural scene. At times, he almost equated history and art. An intuitive historical consciousness was a sign of the artistic temperament; beauty resided largely in the past that the art object preserved. History humanized landscape: "Everything in the landscape," he said of some English scenery, "is something in particular—has a history, has played a part, has a value to the imagination."[29] The lack of historical continuity could be a positive detraction from beauty: the "multitudinous sky-scrapers" of New York "standing up to the view, from the water, like extravagant pins in a cushion already overplanted, and stuck in as in the dark, anywhere and anyhow," to his eye neverthless had "the felicity of carrying out the fairness of tone, of taking the sun and shade in the manner of towers of marble, . . . Crowned not only with no history, but with no credible possibility of time for history, and consecrated by no uses save the commercial at any cost, they are simply the most piercing notes in that concert of the expensively provisional into which your supreme sense of New York" resolved itself. It was not the upward thrust of the skyscraper that was appalling, but its "*invented* state,"[30] the New York practice of tearing down a building whenever it "pays" to do so, the deliberate denial of the beauty and identity that come from the accretions of "slow time."

James underrated the bourgeois Protestant paintings of the North because he could not find in them the complex manners, elaborate ceremony, colorful pageants, and the storied past of an aristocratic society and the Roman Catholic church. A Titian painting, in itself only of "average Titianesque merit," in Belgium attracted his attention because of its title—"John, Bastard of Sforza, Lord of Pesaro, husband, by her first marriage, of Lucretia Borgia, and then Bishop of Paphos and Admiral of the Pontificial Galleys, is presented to St. Peter by the Pope Alexander VI"—and because of its further reach into a complex past through its depiction of St. Peter as "seated upon a fragment of antique sculpture, surrounded by a frieze representing a pagan sacrifice!" It was the historical and social suggestiveness of this kind of picture that struck in him a responsive chord and that he missed in the paintings of the Lowlands. "Even that harshly sincere genius, Quentin Matsys, who shines hard by in a brilliantly pure piece of coloring, can hardly persuade us that we are in simple Flanders, and not in complex Italy,"[31] he concluded. Only in "complex Italy" could one hear the concert of past and present, sacred and profane, the "historical whisperings" of ecclesiastical and social manners that the keenest ears in a new, provincial, and democratic culture hopelessly strained to catch.

But James did not simple-mindedly advocate a return to the past. As would be expected in view of his Ruskinian attitude toward art and nature, he felt that the artist should depict the living present, not imitate the old masters. Not sentimental about necessary reconstruction, he preferred, however, "in every case the ruined, however ruined, to the reconstructed, however splendid," because history was more romantic than the reconstructed fiction. "One is positive, so far as it goes; the other fills up the void with things more dead than the void itself, inasmuch as they have never had life."[32] It was the past as a living part of the present that he responded to, as indicated by his words on the Roman theater in Arles, "one of the most charming and touching ruins I had ever beheld." He did not think there was "profanation in the fact that by day it is open to the good people of Arles, who use it to pass, by no means in great numbers, from one part of the town to the other; treading the old marble floor and brushing, if need be, the empty benches. This familiarity does not kill the place again; it makes it, on the contrary, live a little—makes the present and the past touch each other."[33] Delighting in the dynamic and organic relationship of the present to the past, he had an "unspeakably tender passion" for Italy, a "jumble of the sternest antiquity and the most frivolous modernness, of pagan and Christian pontiffs, of soldiers and priests, of the extreme of profanity and the greatest pomp of ecclesiasticism, of the brutality of destruction and the ecstasy of creation, the superimposition of the later clerical arts and manners upon [all] the rugged heritage of the previous time, and of the fine fresh Italian rule of today upon the whole promiscuous deposit." For him "this huge historic compound" had "a potent and inexhaustible savor."[34]

Corollary to his ideal of an organic living relation of the past to the present was his belief that a work of art was seen to its best advantage in its native setting. Stendhal's wish that the Maison Carrée in Nîmes might be exactly duplicated in Paris led James to remark that "Stendhal found it amusing to write in the character of a *commis-voyageur* and sometimes it occurs to his reader that he really was one."[35] The paintings in the long gallery in the Uffizi might be inferior and the curtains shabby, but the setting and general atmosphere charmed away harsh criticism.[36] The Van Dycks in an English country house acquired a luster from their historic setting; the pictures at Warwick reminded him of his "old conclusion . . . that the best fortune for good pictures is not to be crowded into public collections,—not even into the relative privacy of Salons Carrés and Tribunes,—but to hang in largely spaced half-dozens on the walls of fine houses. Here the historical atmosphere, as one may call it, is almost a compensation for the often imperfect light."[37] (It was the draining of English treasures from the country, which had become a national scandal in the early 1900's, that occasioned *The Outcry*, which centers on the efforts of two young persons to keep intact the collection of a great English house.) Sensitive to "gathered detail and clustered associations," he believed that the removal of a painting from a private house to a museum did essentially modify its character and value.

For James, then, the pleasures of picture viewing were not narrowly aesthetic, and therefore the imaginative qualities of a painting could not be analyzed in strictly pictorial terms. Inheriting Ruskin's prejudice in favor of thought-evoking art, James also derived from him the belief that the source of great style was nobility of character. In *Roderick Hudson* James explored in fictional terms the relation of the artist's conduct to creativity. In his criticism James contended that the painter's capacities for, and qualities of, thought and feeling in a mysterious, undefinable way do matter. Ruskin believed that there was "reciprocal action between the intensity of moral feeling and the power of imagination; for, on the one hand, those who have keenest sympathy are those who look closest and pierce deepest, and hold securest; and, on the other, those who have so pierced and seen the melancholy deeps of things, are filled with the most intense passion and gentleness of sympathy.[38] This dictum is echoed in James's criticism of Delacroix:

His vision of earthly harmonies leaves nothing to be desired; only his feeling about it, as he goes, is that of a man who not only sees, but reflects as well as sees. It is this reflective element in Delacroix which has always been one of the sources of his interest, and I am not ashamed to say that I like him in part for his moral tone. . . . A painter is none the worse for being of a reflective temperament, or for having a good deal of feeling about the things he represents. In such questions as this, it is easy to say more than one intends, or than one is sure of. So it is enough to express the belief that a large part of the legitimate value of the pictorial power of such painters as Tintoretto and Delacroix lies in their having felt a good deal about the things they represented. In the arts, feeling is always meaning.[39]

Though Ruskin was the greatest single source of James's aesthetic, other contemporary critics added to his stock of general notions and taught him some of the secrets of eye-catching display. To Taine's philosophy of art, he had a mixed reaction. He preferred Sainte-Beuve's "frank provisional empiricism" to what he called Taine's "premature philosophy." Taine was a "singular and methodical observer" who commented cogently on English art and presented his impressions vividly, but James felt that his theory of milieu led him to ignore subtle distinctions and even trapped him into inconsistencies. For instance, James pointed out that if English painting, as Taine claimed, reflected the atmospheric light of England just as Flemish and Dutch paintings did of their countries, then English paintings should have "their lowness of tone, their patient science and finish."[40] Still, he found Taine's *Notes on England* a suggestive book. "I never go into an exhibition of English pictures," James wrote later, "without being strongly reminded of M. Taine; I put on his spectacles; I seem to see so well what he meant."[41] And, indeed, in several of his reviews of English exhibitions, James drew heavily on Taine in taking a social approach to art and speculating on the relation of English painting and art acquisitions to the English temperament and country house life.

While James was largely attracted to Taine's descriptive and stylistic powers, he was even more struck by Gautier's visual perceptiveness, his "descriptive brio and grace." "He sees pictures where most people find mere dead surfaces, and where common eyes find the hint of a picture he constructs a complete work of art."[42] "Not the least of

his charms, . . ." to James's mind, "has always been a certain sensuous
serenity, the imperturbable levity of a mind utterly unhaunted by
the metaphysics of things,"[43] but he also felt that Gautier paid the
price for this levity in feebleness of thought: "his powers of reflection
were about equivalent to those of an intelligent poodle."[44] Well
aware of Gautier's shallowness, James probably did not desire to be
his literary analogue in English. But his remark that "no English
writer has as yet taken stock of the capacity of our language for light
descriptive prose"[45] (like Gautier's) suggests that the French writer's
achievements in this limited respect were a challenge which James
tried to meet in his own travel and art essays.

While Taine represented the realist point of view, and Gautier, the
art for art's sake, Gustave Planche[46] most authoritatively and force-
fully made a last ditch stand in the *Revue des deux mondes* for the
conservative, or idealist, cause. James seemed to value Planche, not for
his views or taste, but for what he felt was Planche's beneficial effect
in forcing the realists to an awareness of the implications of their
position. James was aligned, however, with the conservatives in virtue of his belief that the artist should strive to create beauty and that
some subjects because of their intrinsic handsomeness were more
suitable for artistic treatment than others.[47] James never really grap-
pled with slippery abstractions such as beauty and ugliness; his assumption seemed to be that the artist with imagination was sensitive
to beauty in external reality. Thus, in 1883, he admitted that "what
is called ideal beauty . . . is usually a matter of not very successful
guesswork."[48] Maneuvering past the metaphysical issues, he slipped
beauty into the work of art through the artist's perceptions. Du
Maurier, according to James, had a passion "for loveliness observed
in life and manners around him, and reproduced with a generous desire to represent it as usual."[49] One of the points in favor of the
Hungarian painter Munkácsy was his not using literary or mythological subjects. He belonged "to the school of painters for whom a 'subject' is simply any handsome object whatsoever—anything materially
paintable."[50] The import of the qualifying "handsome" is grasped
when juxtaposed to this statement about Winslow Homer: "He has
chosen the least pictorial features of the least pictorial range of
scenery and civilization; he has resolutely treated them as if they
were pictorial, as if they were every inch as good as Capri or Tan-
gier."[51] But even when James found a subject, such as the gruesome,
prize Salon painting of 1876 entitled *Locusta Trying the Effects of
Poisons before Nero*, "detestable, inasmuch as it allows no chance
for beauty," he was not prejudiced as to its possible merits; he praised

this picture for being "an accomplished and picturesque piece of painting of the younger, larger, and richer academic sort, combining a good deal of reality with a good deal of arrangement."[52] In short, James valued most highly the painting which he thought reflected the beauty to be found by the painter with imagination in an observable reality, but he could appreciate good painting as painting regardless of the offensiveness or inanity of the subject.

On the whole, however, he preferred the quiet, humble, undramatic subject treated sincerely to a notably pictorial subject which displayed "mere artifice and manner." Thus, in contrast to Guardi's "torpid and silent" pictures of Venice, he characterized Jan van der Heyden's *Quay in Leyden* as "a compact pictorial sonnet . . . to the homely charms of brick-work,"[53] an apt description of van der Heyden but an injustice to Guardi whose pictures sing with vibrant light.[54]

What James had most in common with the conservatives was the conception of the grand style—which did not mean the individual painter's mode of expression or characteristic vision but grandeur in theme, size, conception, and treatment. The grand style was moreover specifically associated with the art of the Italian Renaissance and of classical antiquity. For James, Italy and, to a lesser extent, France meant style in this sense. Although he praised Millet, for example, as equal in his own terms to Veronese,[55] Italian Renaissance painting, sculpture, and architecture surpassed for him the art of all other countries and periods.

HENRY JAMES'S appreciation of Italian art should not be considered apart from his attitude toward the Renaissance. As Bernard Berenson points out, interest in Italian painting is as much in the period as in aesthetic qualities. "A serious student of art will scarcely think of putting many of even the highest achievements of the Italians, considered purely as technique, beside the works of the great Dutchmen, the great Spaniard, or even the masters of today."[1] Even before embarking on his passionate pilgrimage James considered Italy a land consecrated by two great periods of artistic creativity, the Renaissance and the Roman "prime." It was the place to go to "gaze upon certain of the highest achievements of human power" which represent "the *maximum* of man's creative force." In fact, he went on to say, "So wide is the interval between the great Italian monuments of art and the works of the colder genius of the neighboring nations, that we find ourself willing to look upon the former as the ideal and perfection of human effort, and to invest the country of their birth with a sort of half-sacred character."[2]

James's love affair with Italy was lifelong, and his interest in the Renaissance was deep enough for him to tackle Burckhardt's and Symonds's studies on the Renaissance as well as Crowe and Cavalcaselle's history of Italian painting and works by the German historian Gregorovius. It was the period as an "aesthetic explosion" that fascinated him, not its political and social aspects, nor its lurid, violent, and sensational side; for him, it was a golden age, possessing a love of beauty for its own sake and producing an art expressive of a new delight in man's life in this world.

Indeed, implicit in all of James's art criticism is the assumption that High Renaissance art is in the first rank in architecture, in painting, and in sculpture. But in his comments on each of these art forms there is a curious dualism in his responses. On the one hand, he valued monumentality, symmetry, proportion, and clearly defined contours and lines—the qualities of High Renaissance art as embodied in Leonardo's *Last Supper*, Michelangelo's *David*, and the Farnese Palace (see plate VII)—and explicitly denigrated or ignored the fully developed baroque. On the other hand, he keenly enjoyed the picturesque in art and in scenery: shifting color, light, and tone; the crooked and irregular; the moss covered and angle softened; spectacle and movement; views and perspectives—all visual qualities detached from objects themselves. In short, utilizing the polar concepts introduced by Heinrich Wölfflin in *Principles of Art History*, we see that James seemed to combine a painterly vision with a linear feeling for form.[3]

In architecture he admired works in the grand style, which he found embodied in structures of the Renaissance, but disliked the full-blown baroque and Palladian classicism.[4] "Great lines, great spaces, great emphasis, great reserve—if the grand style abides in them all they yet scarce suffice to make it,"[5] he declared, moved by the great interior doors of the Barberini Palace to apply his response to architecture in general. Style did not, in his view, reside in sheer monumentality. "It was all really, with the very swagger of simplicity, a wrought refinement, a matter of the mixture of the elements, a question, like everything else indeed in the whole place, of the mutual relation of parts."[6] Emphasizing the importance of the monumental and of a surface broken only at large intervals—better a house with three stories than six or seven given the same height, he thought—he preferred dignified and well-proportioned buildings, those of the early Renaissance, which predominate in Florence,[7] or those reflecting the more chaste, classical side of the Roman High Renaissance as opposed to those presaging the exuberant, spectacular, often florid aspects of the baroque. The only building worth speaking of in Rome was the massive but restrained Farnese Palace; though "highly impressive," St. Peter's, its giant orders typical of the more grandiose side of the High Renaissance, was on the outside "literally hideous" to James, as were all the other Roman churches.[8] In a less critical mood, James did have a good word for the basilica of Santa Maria Maggiore as a place which proved "so endlessly suggestive."[9] Gesù, which has been characterized as combining the formality of the High Renaissance style with mannerist tendencies, James aptly described as having "great picturesqueness" and as piquing the curiosity but not impressing the imagination.[10] In Venice architecture, according to him, reached its prime in the Byzantine and Gothic periods, though he expressed an uneasy pleasure in buildings of the "decadence." He was surer, however, that the Gothic Ca' Foscari had "more formal greatness" than the "seventeenth century pile" Rezzonico Palace, the former being "one of the noblest creations of the fifteenth century, a masterpiece of symmetry and majesty."[11]

Similarly, the buildings which appealed to James the most during his *Little Tour in France*, apart from the Gothic, were examples of the early French Renaissance, a style combining a medieval structure with Italianate decoration. Unlike Stendhal, he was no "votary of the new classic . . . of tall, square, regular buildings,"[12] and dipping his pen into Ruskin's inkpot, he expressed a dislike for Mansart's wing of the Chateau at Blois, a seventeenth-century embodiment of the Italian High Renaissance, an antipathy not entirely explained by the fact that this wing is inconsistent in style with the older parts of the chateau. He considered it as an example of the "stupidity of a taste which had ended by becoming an aggregation of negatives." It had the *bel air* of the later Louis Quatorze architecture, but "taken in contrast to its flowering, laughing, living neighbor," he thought it marked "the difference between inspiration and calculation."[13] Of course, the absence of the golden Italian light had something to do with this reaction; he certainly did not justify his views in terms of principles of structure and design or of historical development of a style. Although James considered architecture in the grand style a superior type, he found other edifices almost as pleasing if they satisfied his sense of the picturesque. But before pursuing further this aspect of his taste, a glance at the various meanings of this ubiquitous word in James's art and travel essays is necessary.

Picturesque is used by James least frequently in the Ruskinian sense to describe the strictly technical aspects of a painting, for example, to describe Rembrandt's chiaroscuro which forms an aesthetically pleasing pattern but does not contribute to verisimilitude. *Picturesque* in this sense comes close to meaning painterly, the style of painting which, having emancipated itself from things as they are, represents not the continuous outline of objects but only the visual semblance of things. An extreme example of the painterly is Monet's treatment of the Rouen cathedral, while Raphael's *School of Athens* epitomizes the classical linear style.

Much more frequently James used *picturesque* to designate the aesthetic aspects of any object or natural scene, the elements of which please the eye as a picture does through color, light, and movement. James defined the "pure picturesque" in one of his early travel pieces as "simply the presentation of a picture, self-informed and complete."[14] The following analysis by the art historian Heinrich Wölfflin of the picturesque in nature is worth quoting at length for it reveals the aesthetic basis of this type of beauty, to which James was especially sensitive. After pointing out that any object may be perceived in a picturesque manner, Wölfflin goes on to say:

But now it cannot be denied that there are in nature certain things and situations which we denote as "picturesque." The character of the picturesque seems to be inherent in them apart from perception by a painterly eye. Naturally, there is no absolute "picturesque," and even the so-called "picturesque" object only becomes so for a perceiving eye, but for all that, we can still isolate as something special those themes [of paintings] whose picturesque character consists in actual conditions which can be demonstrated. These are themes in which the single form is so entwined in a great context that any impression of all-pervading movement arises. If real movement is present, so much the better, but it is not necessary. It may be intricacies of the form which of their very nature produce a picturesque effect, or peculiar aspects and illuminations; over the solid, static body of things there will always play the stimulus of a movement which does not reside in the object and that also means that the whole only exists as a *picture* for the eye, and that it can never, even in the imaginary sense, be grasped with the hands.[15]

Thus, the beggar's rags are picturesque because the surface is broken up, the very tears creating a movement which the perfect garment hanging on a store rack does not have. The play of light on form creates especially picturesque effects, as James noted: "The white light in the lower part of Rheims really contributes to the picturesqueness of the interior. It makes the gloom above look richer still, and throws that part of the roof which rests upon the gigantic piers of the transepts into mysterious remoteness."[16] He was also responsive to the object dissolved in atmosphere, as indicated by his preference for viewing buildings at twilight, the time when, according to Wölfflin, "instead of a number of separate objects, we see indeterminate lighter or darker masses which flow together in common tonal movement."[17]

Picturesque was used in a slightly different sense when applied to scenes with eye appeal because they resembled pictures with which James was familiar, usually paintings having picturesque themes, namely, genre or landscapes of the type originated by Hobbema, Ruisdael, van Ostade, and the early Rembrandt—crooked streets, thatched cottages, dusky interiors, and brown-faced peasant women wearing white caps or, to take Christopher Hussey's list, "old gnarled trees, sandy banks, water and windmills, rough heaths, rustic bridges, stumps, logs, ruts, hovels, unkempt persons, and shaggy animals."[18] James also called a landscape or view picturesque if it reminded him of the informal landscapes of the Barbizon school or of landscapes in the Claude Lorrain manner, depicting pipe-playing shepherds seated by jagged columns in the foreground with castle ruins in the distance.[19]

A final usage should be distinguished. Something is picturesque because of its historical or poetic associations or because of its quaintness. Often the word vaguely signifies the deeply felt but inexpressible, as James's revisions changing "picturesque" to "impressiveness," "intensity," and "vague and immensely deep" suggest.

Picturesqueness often proved to be an adequate substitute for style. Thus the coloring, tone, and atmospheric effects in London made up for its architectural poverty,[20] and the absence of proportion, perspective, balance, and height in St. Mark's in Venice was compensated for by its pictorial beauty.[21] Similarly, though Florence lacked the "ragged picturesqueness—the picturesqueness of poverty" of Naples and Rome, it did have some "romantic shabbiness," the rows of houses on the Arno, for example, proving that "often what is literally hideous may be constructively delightful."[22] A monument which architecturally failed to be of "absorbing interest" pleased when viewed picturesquely. The picture James painted of the Arch of Triumph at Orange, in Provence, shows how much of its beauty was due to light, color, position, and historical sentiment. The charm of the arch came,

partly from its soft, bright yellow color, partly from a certain elegance of shape, of expression; and on that well-washed Sunday morning, with its brilliant tone, surrounded by its circle of thin poplars, with the green country lying beyond it and a low blue horizon showing through its empty portals, it made, very sufficiently, a picture that hangs itself to one of the lateral hooks of the memory. I can take down the modest composition and place it before me as I write. I see the shallow, shining puddles in the hard, fair French road; the pale blue sky, diluted by days of rain; the disgarnished autumnal fields; the mild sparkle of the low horizon; the solitary figure in sabots, with a bundle under its arm, advancing along the *chausée*; and in the middle I see the little ochre-colored trio of apertures, which, in spite of its antiquity, looks bright and gay, as everything must look in France of a fresh Sunday morning.[23]

Just as the grand style in architecture was conceived of in terms of well-proportioned monumentality, in city vistas it was dependent on a "certain degree of height" of buildings and on "great expansive symmetries and perspectives," or at least, as in London, an atmosphere which "magnifies distances and minimizes detail."[24] Having also an eye for the picturesque, he delighted in crooked streets, unexpected corners, and projecting second stories and at times expressed irritation with the "tiresome monotony of the 'fine' and the symmetrical, above all, the deathly passion for making things 'to match' " of Parisian taste.[25] Haussmann's regularization of Paris, especially the creation of the Avenue de l'Opera, did not please him because it deprived the city streets of their "ancient individuality" and introduced instead a "huge, blank, pompous, featureless sameness," but admittedly "there is something fine in the vista that is closed at one end by the great sculptured and gilded mass of the former building."[26] In a cityscape, as in a single building, beauty of line, perspective, massiveness, proportion—all associated with the High Renaissance style—and movement, color, light detached from the object, irregularity, crookedness—all qualities of the picturesque—were the two poles of his aesthetic judgment.

Although sculptors, however outnumbered, rub shoulders with painters in James's novels and short stories, and although a sculptor, William Wetmore Story, was the subject of a biography by James, he wrote much less frequently on sculpture than on any other visual art. In part, this emphasis reflects the proportion of exhibitions of sculpture to those of painting and the relative public interest in the two arts. But it is also evident that James, generally, found sculpture, primarily a presentational, not a representational, art, less suggestive than painting, in spite of what may be taken as a protest to the contrary: "With this to point to," referring to the Antinous in the Villa Albani, "it is not for sculpture to confess to an inability to produce any emotion that painting can." Of "imagination" in this work, he found "five hundred times as much as in the 'Transfiguration.' "[27] His own writing, however, bears witness to the fact that he responded more readily to the visual than to tactile qualities. Even the Albani Antinous is a relief, the statue verging on picture; some art critics consider the relief as a type of painting rather than of sculpture. James commented, to be sure, on tombs and on the sculpture on church façades, but in the main it was the building, not the sculpture, that he focused on.

As relatively infrequent as his comments on sculpture were, there is a perceptible pattern which suggests that classical and Renaissance sculpture, especially the latter, were the sources of his conception of excellence. The purportedly Greek statues, actually Roman copies of works of the great period four and five centuries before Christ, over which James's contemporaries swooned, did not move him deeply. The Antinous is an exception, and that, as Sir Kenneth Clark points out, is not typical of the bankrupt Hellenistic art as it is "taken from real life, and not from a copy book."[28] The Vatican, the main repository of classical sculpture in Rome, James thought padded with "third and fourth rate statues," the "great thing" there being the "impression of the whole place . . . the feeling that through these solemn vistas flows the source of an incalculable part of our present conception of Beauty."[29]

While the classical evoked a generalized piety but rarely a specific enthusiasm, the Renaissance in sculpture—no less than in painting and in architecture—provided a concrete standard. Thus, James came away from Rome in late 1869 so inspired by Michelangelo's statue of Moses in San Pietro in Vincoli as to declare him the greatest of all Italian artists. The sculptural ideal embodied in Michelangelo's work—classical restraint combined with Renaissance expressiveness —was the criterion by which he judged all later statues with pretentions to high seriousness, even though his subsequent allusions to Michelangelo were relatively few. Typical of a later comment was his statement that all the sculpture in St. Peter's, except Michelangelo's "ineffable" *Pietà*, which was "the rarest artistic *combination* of the greatest things the hand of man has produced," was "either bad or indifferent."[30] The Florentine realists—Donatello, Luca della Robbia, Matteo Civitali, Mino da Fiesole—on the other hand, became for him a standard for less sublime sculpture, for portraiture.

One of James's most explicit statements on the art of sculpture is in a criticism of the sculptor Paul Dubois, whose clay models of *Charity* and *Military Courage* for General Larmoricière's tomb in the Cathedral in Nantes were exhibited in the Paris Salon of 1876.[31] "M. Dubois is certainly a sculptor, and sees things as a sculptor—sees lines and forms and contours, and not intentions, motives, and dramatic effects. But his two figures seem to me to lack just that supreme element of ease and independence which makes the work that is rarest in quality. Still, in its intelligence, purity, and high plastic tendency, the quality of his work is rare."[32] Later, after seeing the figures in bronze, James referred to Dubois as "one of the most interesting of that new generation of sculptors who have revived in France an art of which our over-dressed century had begun to despair. . . . The whole monument is proof of exquisitely careful study [mainly of Michelangelo]; but I am not sure that this impression on the part of the spectator is the happiest possible. It explains much of the great beauty, and it also explains perhaps a little of the slight pedantry."[33] In short, James praised Dubois for creating sculptural forms having volume, contours, and lines, but he was fully aware of his academicism—his ability to imitate Michelangelo's forms but not the effect of suppressed power and energy. Dubois's statues, however, had the monumentality as well as the generalized features which for James represented ideal beauty in sculpture.

His taste formed by works in the classical and Renaissance tradition, James thought William Wetmore Story's romantic and anecdotal statues clever but much overrated;[34] was appreciative of the power of Barye (see plate VIII), a "diligent and profound observer," to trap in sculpture the animal in action but considered him "a man of genius"[35] only within the limits of his speciality; and was faintly embarrassed by Carpeaux's "undressed lady and gentleman," so "pitifully real" were their "poor, lean, individualized bodies."[36] While not unsympathetic to the realists, James in the 1870's failed to perceive that the means of rescuing sculpture from the sterility of pseudoclassicism lay in the direction of the work of Barye, his pupil Rodin, and Carpeaux, that is, in the reintroduction of movement and life based upon accurate observation, rather than in the imitation of Renaissance masterpieces, the practice of the academicians, even the good ones, like Dubois, Chapu, and Mercié, whom James admired. Hence, uniting a keen sense of actuality with a strain of idealism inherited from Michelangelo and Donatello, his masters of the Renaissance, the American sculptor Augustus Saint-Gaudens was the most radical of contemporary sculptors whom James could without qualification praise.

The list of Italian paintings James mentioned favorably is too extensive to be enumerated, even though his taste was mostly limited to works from the early fifteenth through the sixteenth century. What should be noted is that, as with architecture and sculpture, he looked for a combination of classical, or linear, and picturesque qualities. Thus, in 1869 he "admired" Raphael, a master of composition and of tranquil harmonies of form and restrained color, but he "passionately" loved Titian,[37] who epitomized the Venetian love of splendid color and dramatic movement. Similarly, while paying his respects to Raphael's genius, he considered him more expendable than the artists of the early Florentine school—Fra Angelico, Filippo Lippi, Ghirlandajo, and Botticelli, the last being the equal, in his opinion, of Leonardo and Michelangelo. Leonardo he thought a supreme master of line and form and more vigorous than the "sweet optimist" Raphael. His association of Leonardo's *Last Supper*, the "saddest" and "greatest" work of art, with the ruins of the Abbey of Glastonbury,[38] which he thought revealed to the spectator sheer architectural beauty in their very ruin, illustrates the extent to which Leonardo's genius for coordinated and monumental design impressed him.

With the best works of the early Florentine school, James ranked the "ripest performances of the Venetians" as "the most valuable things in the history of art."[39] He was, however, aware of basic differences in style between the Venetians and other Italian painters. He thought the Venetians felt the "indissoluble unity" of the "great spectacle"; "form and color and earth and air were equal members of every possible subject." Other painters, particularly the early Florentines, Leonardo, Raphael, and Michelangelo, saw "in beautiful, sharp-edged elements and parts."[40] But though it is true that the Venetians were more painterly, the similarities, as Wölfflin points out, were greater and more basic than the differences among the various schools of the sixteenth century. Like the Umbrians and the Florentines, the Venetians, with the exception of Tintoretto and Titian in his late period, invariably created the "multiple" unity of classic art, the parts existing independently as free members and the line being sovereign. If a comparison is made between Titian's recumbent *Bella* and Velásquez's *Venus*, the classical quality of Titian's design becomes apparent. If the figure in Titian's painting were cut out, it would suffer from its loss of setting, but it would not disintegrate. Velásquez's figure, however, is inextricably woven into the movement of the background and the texture of light and dark. "While Titian's beautiful figure possesses a rhythm in itself alone, in Velásquez the figure is only completed by what is added to it in the picture."[41] James did not formulate this distinction between "multiple" and "fused" unity in precisely these terms, but clearly he recognized in Tintoretto the fused unity, uncharacteristic of the High Renaissance style, that distinguished this painter from his peers.

The deep and lasting appeal of Tintoretto to James's imagination is indicated by both his essays and his letters. After seeing Tintoretto in Venice for the first time, he declared him to be the equal of Shakespeare in feeling "the great, beautiful, terrible spectacle of human life. . . ." His seemingly infinite energy and inventiveness stirred in James the desire for emulation: "I'd give a great deal to be able to fling down a dozen of his pictures into prose of corresponding force and colour."[42] To show this was not hyperbole, a momentary rapture, here is a passage from a letter to Charles Eliot Norton two years later: "My own memory of him [Tintoretto] remains singularly distinct and vivid and I feel as if the emotions wrought by his pictures had worked themselves into the permanent substance of my mind, more than I can feel it of any other painter—or of any works of art perhaps, save those good people at San Lorenzo.—May you know this good fact in later years!"[43] Even without this letter, his first essay on Venice would have given a hint of his sense of Tintoretto's supremacy and influence on him. Recording the impressions of his second visit to Italy in "From Venice to Strasburg," James said that his earlier estimates of painters had not changed. "I still found Carpaccio delightful, Veronese magnificent, Titian supremely beautiful, and Tintoret altogether unqualifiable."[44] In a later essay on Venice, reprinted in *Portraits of Places*, he devoted less space to Tintoretto and more to Carpaccio, Veronese, and Bellini, even momentarily ranking Carpaccio with Tintoretto by calling them the "two great realists." However, in an essay first printed in 1892, there is this evaluation of Tintoretto, indicating that James still responded to him as deeply as he had in his youth:

The plastic arts may have less to say to us than in the hungry years of youth, and the celebrated picture in general be more of a blank; but more than the others any fine Tintoret still carries us back, calling up not only the rich particular vision but the freshness of the old wonder. Many things come and go, but this great artist remains for us in Venice a part of the company of the mind. The others are there in their obvious glory, but he is the only one for whom the imagination, in our expressive modern phrase, sits up.[45]

Further measure of his feeling for Tintoretto may be taken by the order he gave in 1901 to the Venice-bound Edmund Gosse: *"Go to see the Tintoretto Crucifixion at San Cossiano [sic] or never more be officer of mine."*[46] This is the Crucifixion that had once made him feel that he "had advanced to the uttermost limit of painting; that beyond this another art—inspired poetry—begins, and that Bellini, Veronese, Giorgione, and Titian, all joining hands and straining every muscle of their genius, reach forward not so far but that they leave a visible space in which Tintoret alone is master."[47]

What did James see in Tintoretto that he did not see in the other Venetians? First of all, there was the fused unity he did not find in Veronese or Titian. Tintoretto's great merit was

his unequalled distinctness of vision. When once he had conceived the germ of a scene, it defined itself to his imagination with an intensity, an amplitude, an individuality of expression, which makes one's observation of his pictures seem less an operation of mind than a kind of supplementary experience of life. Veronese and Titian are content with a much looser specification, as their treatment of any subject which Tintoret has also treated abundantly proves. There are few more suggestive contrasts than that between the absence of a total character at all commensurate with its scattered variety and brilliancy, in Veronese's "Marriage of [sic] Cana," in the Louvre, and the poignant, almost startling, completeness of Tintoret's illustration of the theme at the Salute Church.[48]

To compare Tintoretto's *Presentation of the Virgin in the Temple* at the Madonna dell'Orto or his *Annunciation* with Titian's paintings on the same themes, according to James, "is to measure the essential difference between observation and imagination," meaning by the artist of "observation" one who paints effectively the single figure or easily balanced group but who cannot paint successfully the "great dramatic combinations—or, rather, leaves them ungauged." Tintoretto saw the whole scene "in a flash of inspiration intense enough to stamp it ineffaceably on his perception; and it was the whole scene, complete, peculiar, individual, unprecedented, which he committed to canvas with all the vehemence of his talent."[49]

A comparison of Tintoretto's *Last Supper* in San Giorgio Maggiore (see plate IX) with another famous treatment of the same subject reveals explicitly how he violated the practice of High Renaissance painting. In Leonardo's painting, the model of the highly developed classical Renaissance style, unity comes from coordination of elements, for example, from the careful balancing of figures in units of three with Christ occupying the center of the table, which is on a horizontal plane. The room in which Leonardo sets his scene is carefully defined; chiaroscuro creates volume and defines patterns of horizontals and verticals. Psychological values are achieved through gesture and facial expression and through the grouping of the figures in the design: all figures, except that of Judas, are related in horizontal movement to Christ, and all lines converge at his head, which is silhouetted against the background.

In contrast, Tintoretto created unity through fusion rather than through coordination of elements. The figures are not placed in front of a background, but figures and background are so fused that neither single figures nor objects are detachable. The entire surface of the canvas is filled with movement created by objects bathed in light; that is, Tintoretto does not depend on facial expression, gesture, and arrangement for dramatic effect; the servants, the dog, the burning censer, the angels, the cloudy atmosphere, the diagonally placed tables—all are handled so as to be as dramatic as the human figures in the scene. This painting differs from the classical Renaissance type in still other significant ways. Instead of figures or objects placed parallel to the lower horizontal picture edge, an arrangement which creates the effect of a stage, diagonal lines lead the viewer into the picture and create an illusion of great depth and movement. Similarly, Tintoretto's vertical staircases in *The Presentation* at the Madonna dell' Orto and the receding pavements of *The Finders of St. Mark's Body* lead the eye deeper and deeper into space to provide an especially satisfying aesthetic experience for the lover of perspectives. Moreover, in contrast with the closed composition of the classical picture in which the rectangle of the frame or edge is em-

phasized in the design, Tintoretto's receding diagonals suggest that
the scene on the canvas continues beyond or behind the surface while
creating a feeling of aesthetic completeness. "You seem not only to
look *at* his pictures, but *into* them," James observes.[50] It is perhaps
this effect of the fullness of represented life contained within a form
and unified tonally which James had in mind when he said that
Tintoretto's *Last Supper* at San Giorgio should be compared with
"the usual formal, almost mathematical, rendering of the subject, in
which impressiveness seems to have been sought in elimination rather
than comprehension."[51] In contrast to the classical Renaissance ideal,
in which light and shade are used to clarify figures and motives, none
of the faces can be seen clearly; the shadows and bursting light ignore
the individual forms in favor of creating an over-all flickering movement and emotional highlighting.

As might be expected, the nineteenth-century artist who meant
the most to James was also "dedicated to colorist, dynamic movement" and attempted to achieve a similar synthesis of content, form,
and color.[52] Delacroix was linked with Tintoretto by James himself.
He thought Delacroix "a great colourist and a great composer: in this
latter respect he always reminded me of Tintoretto. He saw his subject as a whole; not as the portrait of a group of selected and isolated
objects, but as an incident in the continuity of things and the passage of human life."[53] The affinity James felt for both Delacroix
and Tintoretto arose from this common characteristic: their discovery of psychological equivalents in the movement of color and
light, in the dilation of space so that shapes seem to appear and
dissolve, without, however, abandoning stable composition and the
traditional subjects of the grand style.

Michelangelo's "good people" at San Lorenzo, it will be recalled,
were mentioned by James as having had an effect on him similar to
that of Tintoretto. Both Tintoretto and Michelangelo in the period
in which he created the figures in the Medici Chapel waver between
the classical Renaissance and the baroque and exhibit traits of the in-
termediate mannerist style: Tintoretto's elongated figures owe much
to Michelangelo's, and he is traditionally said to have aimed at combining Michelangelo's line with Titian's color. I discuss more fully
the specific traits of the mannerist style in another context. (Some of
the characteristics just mentioned, such as open form, diagonal recession, fused unity are, of course, elements of some examples of
mannerist style.) My point here is that James was attracted to
Michelangelo and Tintoretto because in the works of these transi-
tional artists he could find both the monumental effects of the clas-

sical Renaissance tradition and the light, the movement, and the fused unity that appealed to his picturesque vision.

James was probably unable fully to appreciate Rubens, in whom the baroque style is most completely expressed, because he was far removed from the serene harmonies of classical Renaissance art. In a facetious mood, James wondered if the Flemish painter

was lawfully married to Nature, or did he merely keep up the most unregulated of flirtations? Three or four of his carnal cataracts ornament the walls of the Pitti. If the union was really solemnized it must be said that the ménage was at best a stormy one. He is a strangely irresponsible jumble of the true and the false. He paints a full flesh surface that radiates and palpitates with illusion, and into the midst of it he thrusts a mouth, nose, an eye, which you would call your latest-born a blockhead for perpetrating.[54]

Unlike Michelangelo, who deferred to nature even in his most contorted figures, and Tintoretto, who knew, as Malraux notes, that "Much reality goes to the making of a fairytale,"[55] Rubens carried the baroque passion for appearances far beyond the boundaries of the real world. Moreover, it was probably his total rejection of the relative stability of Renaissance design that led James naïvely to think he painted purely by impulse: "He never waits to choose; he never pauses to deliberate; and one may say, vulgarly, he throws away his oranges when he has given them but a single squeeze."[56]

Satisfying James's love of the picturesque and opening his eyes to the pictorial unity which may be achieved by light and shadow and atmosphere as well as by formal arrangement, Tintoretto spoke to him with more authority than perhaps any other painter. Dutch painters with baroque painterly characteristics—van Ostade, Dou, Ruisdael—were pleasing to James, I surmise, not merely for their realism, which was his professed reason for admiring them, but for the very picturesque technical qualities they had in common with Tintoretto. Of course, their humble subjects, not to mention their lack of scope as compared with that of Tintoretto, precluded their being considered on the same plane as a painter in the grand manner.[57] There are, however, two other reasons why Tintoretto made a lasting impression on James. His breaking the plane line by favoring diagonals has already been mentioned, but not its dramatic effectiveness. The works of a "magnificent stage manager," as Malraux points out, Tintoretto's great epic scenes must have been especially appealing to a writer committed to picture and scene and even to melodramatic effects in his own medium. But even more suggestive is the quality in Tintoretto's painting which Berenson calls "the feeling that whatever existed was for mankind and with reference to man." His treatment of classic fables and biblical stories has "a feeling for the human life at the heart of the story."[58] Conversely, as Malraux notes:

His dogs, palm-trees and jewelry meant much to him, but he needed no less those flights of steps which give the impression of leading up to some Acropolis. Forever listening-in to a celestial threnody heard by him alone, he achieved its orchestration in the San Rocco *Crucifixion*, in which all the aspects of his many-sided genius are harmonized in an infinite variety of earthly forms. Indeed this is the only presentation of the sublime in terms of lavish decoration that Christianity has known.[59]

It is Tintoretto's expression of the sublime, the spiritual in the material, which led James to call him "not a poet but a prophet." Tintoretto on canvas and Michelangelo in stone fixed in material the reality of the inner life. This high achievement becomes especially significant in the light of James's conception of the artistic aims of fiction, as reflected in his criticism of the French realist novelists—Flaubert, the Goncourts, Zola, Daudet, Loti, and Maupassant. He granted them great success in painting "aspects and appearances" but deplored their failure to make "the life of the soul equally real and visible."[60] The great Renaissance artists he most admired—Tintoretto and Michelangelo—succeeded in rendering visible the inner through the outer life.

ANTICIPATORY though it was of the art-for-art's-sake movement of the 1880's, the aestheticism of Rossetti, Morris, and Burne-Jones was more a reaction against the materialism and ugliness of mid-nineteenth-century England than a positive assertion of the self-sufficiency of art. In intention at least, not even Pater or Swinburne encouraged concentration on form in art at the expense of meaning.[1] In considering James's relation to aestheticism, therefore, a distinction must be made between his responses to its early and late manifestations.

The young James, fresh in 1869 from "aesthetic Boston," relished the queerness of the Pre-Raphaelite personalities and Bohemian atmosphere to which Charles Eliot Norton introduced him. He admired Morris's "superb and beautiful" handiwork, "but more curious than anything is himself," he wrote his sister Alice, and even "curiouser," he seemed to think, was Morris's "medieval" wife, "a figure cut out of a missal—out of one of Rossetti's or Hunt's pictures."[2] Rossetti, who lived in a "most delicious melancholy old house at Chelsea on the river" and did not "shame his advantages," was considered by the young critic a great painter and poet, though narrow in range. Burne-Jones's paintings were "literary" but had "great merit."[3] Pater's *Studies in the History of the Renaissance*, a seminal book to which both Bernard Berenson and Oscar Wilde acknowledged a debt, he read shortly after publication in 1873: his description of Botticelli in "Florentine Notes" (1874) is a virtual paraphrase of it. One would expect Pater to have struck a deep responsive chord in James because of basic similarities—a sensitivity to the visible and concrete, a concomitant distaste for the abstract and theoretical, an emphasis on the personal impression,[4] a belief in the relativity of beauty, and a concentration on style. That he did not may be at least partially attributed to the lack of energy, robustness, "manliness" in Pater and to the strength of Ruskin's moral influence on James. "Faint, pale, embarrassed, exquisite Pater," James wrote in 1894 to Edmund Gosse after reading Gosse's study of Pater. "He reminds me, in the disturbed midnight of our actual literature, of one of those lucent matchboxes which you place, on going to bed, near the candle, to show you, in the darkness, where you can strike a light: he shines in the uneasy gloom—vaguely, and has a phosphorescence, not a flame. But I quite agree with you that he is not of the little day —but of the longer time."[5] The unwitting and misconstrued prophet eliciting this qualified praise, no wonder the disciple who preached concentration "upon the moments of life that is itself but a moment" and the "Botticelli women, with wan cheeks and weary eyes, enveloped in mystical crumpled robes," speaking "in strange accents, with melancholy murmurs and cadences"[6] seemed to James fair game for satirical attack.

James expressed his attitude toward the new aesthetic movement explicitly in a little-known essay on George Du Maurier (1883), observing that the English are constitutionally unaesthetic: "there is always a strange element either of undue apology or of exaggerated defiance in their attempts at the cultivation of beauty. . . . their revivals of taste are even stranger than the abuses they are meant to correct. They are violent, voluntary, mechanical; wanting in grace, in tact, in the sense of humour and of proportion."[7] But more important than the fact that the fastidious James recoiled from the self-advertisements, affectations, and improprieties of the aesthetes was that he did not accept Oscar Wilde's principle that "Art never expresses anything but itself."[8] James had no quarrel with their anti-Philistinism, their emphasis on the importance of craftsmanship to the point of considering imperfection in art immoral, or their insistence on the artist's right to treat freely and honestly all of life. His "The Art of Fiction" may be viewed as a manifesto of the aesthetic movement. But it is the aestheticism of the Pre-Raphaelite variety that James associated himself with, not that of the second generation.[9] Ambient, "The Author of Beltraffio,"[10] reads Browning and Balzac—not Huysmans; he much more closely resembles Rossetti or Morris than Oscar Wilde, who, according to James, was "never in the smallest of degree"[11] interesting to him. The image that Ambient uses in this story of the golden vessel of form filled with the liquor of life is close to the one Rossetti used in cautioning against separating style from content: "Work your metal as much as you like, but first take care that it is gold."[12] In *The Tragic Muse*, James satirizes most completely and explicitly the Wildean aesthete in the character of the brilliant but futile Gabriel Nash, who gives up the "doing" necessary to creation because he thinks communication through an art form vulgarizes his personal style.[13]

But what were James's reactions to specific art works of this movement? Just as he apparently liked Henry Harland, the editor of

Plate I Gavarni: *L'Habituée du Luxembourg*; E. Lami: *L'Habituée des Tuileries*. (Prints Division, The New York Public Library; Astor, Lenox, and Tilden Foundations.)

Plate II Thomas Cole: *View of Florence from San Miniato.* (The Cleveland Museum of Art, Mr. and Mrs. William H. Marlatt Fund.)

Plate III   Paul Delaroche: *Edward V and the Duke of York in the Tower.* (Courtesy of the Wallace Collection, London.)

Plate IV Alexandre-Gabriel Decamps: *Arabs Fording a Stream*. (Courtesy of the Wallace Collection, London.)

Yellow Book, but disliked, at least initially, his magazine, he found Aubrey Beardsley "touching and extremely individual" but "hated his productions and thought them extraordinarily base." He "couldn't find (perhaps didn't try enough to find!)," he admitted in 1913, "the formula that reconciled this baseness aesthetically, with his being so perfect a case of the artistic spirit."[14] The vehemence of James's "hated" and "base" suggests that it was the eroticism of this "Fra Angelico of satanism," as Roger Fry called him, that prevented James from appreciating his exceptional powers of design and decoration.

But of more importance than his distaste for Beardsley was his criticism of Whistler for indulging in pure painting. "To be interesting it seems to me that a picture should have some relation to life as well as to painting,"[15] was the reason he gave in 1877 for dismissing Whistler's color symphonies. His eventual modification of his unfavorable opinion of Whistler's paintings, though not of this basic belief in the relation of art to life, paralleled an increasing disenchantment with Burne-Jones's pictured dream world peopled by languid epicene figures after Botticelli and Mantegna.

In the same review in which he "will not speak of Mr. Whistler's 'Nocturnes in Black and Gold' and in 'Blue and Silver,' of his 'Arrangements,' 'Harmonies,' and 'Impressions,' because I frankly confess they do not amuse me," he places Burne-Jones at the "head of the English painters of our day, and very high among all the painters of this degenerate time." At the same time he did express some boredom with "that square-jawed, large-mouthed female visage" of the Pre-Raphaelite school of twenty-five years ago which in Burne-Jones's paintings looked "very weary of its adventures,"[16] and he had reservations about his excessively literary qualities with which his "plastic powers" were not wholly commensurate. The following year, in 1878, though he criticized the lack of modeling in Burne-Jones's figures, he found that "the compositions of which they form part have the great and rare merit that they are *pictures.* They are conceptions, representations; they have a great *ensemble.*" Whistler's paintings in the same review were judged to be "pleasant things to have about, so long as one regards them as simple objects—as incidents of furniture or decoration. The spectator's quarrel with them begins when he feels it to be expected of him to regard them as pictures."[17]

James's tendency to use more disguised wording in his reviews than he did in his letters, so that even in his early reviews he may have had stronger reservations about Burne-Jones than he overtly expressed, should be taken into account; there is evident, nevertheless, a deepening dissatisfaction by 1889 with Burne-Jones's work, as this comment in a letter to their mutual friend Norton suggests: Burne-Jones was painting in a direction "more and more away from the open air of the world and the lovely study of the aspects and appearances of things and the real—or at any rate to me fascinating—problems of the painter's art. He might paint exactly as he does if there were *no* open air, no light, nor atmosphere, nor aspects, nor appearances, nor moving, flashing, changing, larking, ambient life."[18] By 1899 James felt that "even the poetry—the kind of it—that he tried for appeared to me to have wandered away from the real thing."[19]

He found the real thing in Whistler's "exquisite image of Henry Irving as the Philip of Tennyson's *Queen Mary*" (see plate X). Betraying a short memory—*he* certainly had not shown unusual intelligence in his comments on Whistler in the past—James presented himself on viewing this portrait in 1897 as lost

in wonder reintensified at the attitude of a stupid generation toward an art and a taste so rare. Wonder is perhaps, after all, not the word to use, for how *should* a stupid generation, liking so much that [*sic* what?] it does like, and with a faculty trained to coarser motions, recognize in Mr. Whistler's work one of the finest of all distillations of the artistic intelligence? To turn from his picture to the rest of the show—which, of course, I admit, is not a collection of masterpieces—is to drop from the world of distinction, of perception, of beauty and mystery and perpetuity, into—well, a very ordinary place. And yet the effect of Whistler at his best is exactly to give to the place he hangs in—or perhaps I should say to the person he hangs for—something of the sense, of the illusion, of a great museum.[20]

Significantly, James did not discuss this painting as a composition in tones of gray and black, as its alternate title *Arrangement in Black No. 3* might have predisposed him to do. Instead, it was its "charm of a certain degree of melancholy meditation" that he commented on. Similarly, he was struck with Whistler's portrait of his mother because of the evidence it gave of the painter's "power to render life," not because of the somewhat finicky balancing of rectangular forms and tones that Whistler called attention to in his title *Harmony in Gray and Black, No. 1*. In short, James came to terms with Whistler on his own ground; by 1897 Whistler's idiosyncratic technique was not seen by James as an end in itself.

Eventually, in any discussion of a nineteenth-century art critic, his response to the new French art must be considered. One of the tests of a critic is his ability to recognize excellence in works which violate the conventions of the art currently most respected. Of course, it must be remembered that the last word on art is never said. The "see-saw of fortune," to use James's phrase, is always in motion, and not only are there bad Monets and good Courbets, but the transition from one to the other is not so abrupt as it may seem. The current revival of nineteenth-century academic art as manifested in exhibitions and criticism has called into question blanket condemnation of painters such as Couture and Decamps. Moreover, the impressionist method had its limitations. Seurat and Cézanne absorbed its discoveries but in their work returned to the traditional painter's problems of composition and of the rendering of objects in space. Rodin, because of his too exclusive reliance on the pictorial effects of light and shadow, at times failed to respect sufficiently the resources and limitations of his own medium.

Still, vicissitudes of reputation and even the most negative reevaluation of impressionist art do not alter the fact that James initially scorned not only Whistler's flat tonal arrangements and nocturnes for being mere decoration but also the impressionists' seemingly spontaneous color-spotted canvases, alive with the light that makes Whistler's art by comparison seem static and dead. At the same time, he praised Salon and Academy pictures which by any disinterested aesthetic standard must be judged as inferior. Of course, as I have pointed out, James did not judge only by an aesthetic standard. He looked for literary and psychological suggestiveness and more or less traditional subjects. Velásquez's and Delacroix's rough brush strokes and broken color technique he could appreciate, as well as Tintoretto's rendering of objects bathed in light and atmosphere, but these painters were traditional enough in subject matter and in composition not to alienate him. His taste having been formed on traditional art, he could not immediately adjust to an art which did away with values—gradations of darkness and light in color—replacing them with variations in hue, eschewed traditional composition to the point of seeming entirely unpremeditated, and offered as a completed picture a sketch in which brush strokes were not only visible but exaggerated.

In his review of the impressionist exhibition at Durand-Ruel's, James criticized them for being "partisans of unadorned reality and absolute foes to arrangement, embellishment, selection." Their attitude called to mind the Pre-Raphaelites, according to James, in a Ruskinian identification of morality with technique, but the

English realists "went in," as the phrase is, for hard truth and stern fact, an irresistible instinct of righteousness caused them to try and purchase forgiveness for their infidelity to the old more or less moral proprieties and conventionalities, by an exquisite, patient, virtuous manipulation—by being above all things laborious. But the Impressionists, who, I think, are more consistent, abjure virtue altogether, and declare that a subject which has been crudely chosen shall be loosely treated.[21]

Seventeen years later, by which time histories of impressionism had already been written, a sign of the extent to which the movement had won general acceptance, James wrote about Sargent's Manet-like painting *El Jaleo*: "This singular work . . . has the stamp of an extraordinary energy and facility—of an actual scene, with its accidents and peculiarities caught, as distinguished from a composition where arrangement and invention have played their part. It looks like life, but it looks also, to my view, rather like a perversion of life."[22] In other words, the weakness of the impressionists, he still felt, was that they did not "represent" reality by distilling its essence from a welter of sense impressions. *El Jaleo* seemed to James like an enormous leaf from a sketchbook which contained the raw material for pictures. The impressionist practice of cutting off part of a figure, as in this painting, must have been especially disturbing. Obviously, like a photographer who inadvertently cuts off heads, the painter who does not bother to work in a figure lays himself open to James's complaint that he seeks "the solution of [his] problem exclusively in simplification."

To render the impression of an object may be a very fruitful effort, but it is not necessarily so; that will depend upon what, I won't say the object, but the impression, may have been. . . . If a painter works for other eyes as well as his own he courts a certain danger in this direction–that of being arrested by the cry of the spectator: "Ah! but excuse me; I myself take more impressions that that." We feel a synthesis not to be an injustice only when it is rich.[23]

James recognized, but could not entirely approve, that the "method of judging value only by the eye meant a break with traditional art, in which a painted landscape was subordinated to what is known and thought about it; in Impressionist landscapes distance is not representative but allusive, and very different from Leonardo's distance."[24] To James's way of thinking, the painter who records a quick visual impression of a scene runs the risk of being shallow if his perceptions are limited. To achieve the highest result, the painter must take time to see deeply into his subject.

But even though in this essay on Sargent the "latent dangers of the Impressionist practice"[25] are stressed, James also points out "the victories it may achieve," as exemplified by Sargent's portrait of the Boit children (see plate XI). Moreover, through scattered references an acceptance of impressionist art, not just a growing familiarity with it, may be detected. In an essay first published in 1877, the French landscape at Gâtinais reminded him of the works of the Barbizon school.[26] In 1884 he apparently still had in his mind's eye as the norm of French art the Barbizon painters, for he characterized the "tone of French landscape art" as "bright grayness,"[27] a phrase hardly descriptive of the impressionist palette. Moreover, the picturesque sketchable "bits" referred to repeatedly in *A Little Tour in France*—the crooked streets, ruined fortresses, old peasant women cleaning pots—were not the subjects to which the impressionists, preferring city dwellers, often in outdoor settings on pleasure excursions, were especially attracted. But by 1888, in *The Reverberator*, James was making casual allusions to the impressionists' palette: Gaston Probert "defended certain of Waterlow's [a fictional American-impressionist painter] purples and greens as he would have defended his own honour."[28] Eleven years later his designation of Frederick Walker, the English illustrator, "in the full, present welter of the opposite wave" as "the most distinguished product of which the age of expressionism was capable"[29] shows not only that he was cognizant of the impressionist revolution in taste, as anyone intellectually alive at the time would have been, but that he himself had experienced a change in aesthetic values. Further evidence that he had assimilated the impressionist method is found in an 1894 notebook entry: the "formula" that would enable him to contain the idea of "The Coxon Fund" in a story of only 20,000 words "is to make it an *Impression*—as one of Sargent's pictures is an impression."[30] Though a consideration of the extent to which the methods of the pictorial arts were actually transposed into fictional technique is reserved for later analysis, it should also be noted that *The Ambassadors* was informed by the impressionist mode of vision. Moreover, as John L. Sweeney has shown, there is specific evidence that James modified his earlier attitude toward the impressionists in his essay "New England: An Autumn Impression" (1905), reprinted in *The American Scene*. Here James refers to a house in which

an array of modern "impressionistic" pictures, mainly French, wondrous examples of Manet, of Degas, of Claude Monet, of Whistler, of other rare recent hands, treated us to the momentary effect of a large slippery sweet inserted, without a warning, between the compressed lips of half-conscious inanition.[31]

As would be expected in view of James's changed opinion of Whistler and eventual acceptance of the impressionists, his idols of the sixties suffered with time. In the 1870's he expressed some doubt about the direction La Farge and Hunt were taking, but not until his valedictory *Notes of a Son and Brother* did he publicly, though regretfully, admit that they had not fulfilled the promise of the Newport days. Hunt was a victim of "the merciless manner in which a living and hurrying public educates itself";[32] La Farge was "never to surpass" two or three of his early illustrations of Browning's *Men and Women*.[33] Similarly, when in 1914 James spoke of the "so finely interesting landscapists . . . Troyon, Rousseau, Daubigny, even Lambinet and others" as summing up "for the American collector and in the New York and Boston markets the idea of the modern in the masterly,"[34] his tone had the slight condescension of one who has witnessed a truly radical revolution in taste.

Considering that James's aesthetic had its roots in the Victorian morality, his modification of former views reveals an unexpected flexibility. Unfortunately, as most of his art essays appeared between 1868 and 1882, a continuous record of his expressed views is unavailable, and there are only a few works—he briefly resumed art reviewing in the 1890's—informed by his latest aesthetic. By the last years of the century, he came to stress the importance of design over content and even came close to conceiving of art as an annexation rather than a representation of life, as shown by the following passage from a letter (1906) to Edwin A. Abbey, in reply to his request for a motto on art for a mural:

Here is, after all, a small thing out of Emerson's *Essays*–but I am omitting half a sentence that spoils it. "Art is the need to create; but in its essence immense and universal, it is impatient of working with lame or tied hands. Nothing less than the creation of men and nature is its end. . . ." Should you think of it you must make the image in her hand, [that is, the figure of Art in the mural] not the model of the Parthenon, but of a small and exquisite human (male) figure, and as a form she ought to be "tramping" on something that symbolizes the Void and the Vague–or *standing* on *all* plastic material! (a ball of putty!) But give me a little more time, as I say.[35]

As has frequently been pointed out, James became increasingly aware that the artist created by drawing on nature, but not by reproducing it. "Art makes life" may be taken as his motto in his nowfamous quarrel with Wells about the relationship of art to life. As his idea for the mural indicates, the artist with godlike powers creates man and nature, that is, palpable, visible life, whereas before there was only the enemy, nothingness, the "Void and the Vague." His suggestion, however, that the male figure be substituted for the Parthenon model shows the strength of his belief in art not as divorced from, but as vitally related to, human life. Difficult as it is to imagine this idea translated into pictorial terms—Abbey apparently (probably fortunately) could not as he used a quotation from Plotinus and retained the model of the Parthenon—it is notable as an expression of his view of art in general as additive, not imitative.

The modernity of his taste in painting will not be exaggerated if it is kept in mind that two revolutions in art took place in James's lifetime. Gauguin, Cézanne, Seurat, and van Gogh about 1885 and Picasso, Matisse, and Braque at the turn of the century began to stir up a public which had just become comfortably settled with impressionism. One wonders what James, who said that "there is no greater work of art than a great portrait," thought about the portrait treated as still life, the dehumanizing of art, as Ortega y Gasset called it. He praised Sargent's portrait of Mrs. Meyer for its "truth of characterization, a wonderful rendering of life, of manners, of aspects, of types, of textures, of everything."[36] To consider Picasso's portrait of Gertrude Stein (1906) from the point of view of its "truth of characterization" still has relevance, but confronted with *Les desmoiselles d'Avignon* (1907) what could James have done with his belief that "the artist, in any field, essentially and logically" must love the nude?

Evidence of James's reactions to postimpressionism is slight. According to Virginia Woolf, he saw the 1912 Post-Impressionist Exhibition in London, the second large-scale showing of Gauguin, Seurat, Cézanne, Matisse, Picasso, and Rouault in England. Roger Fry, who had arranged these exhibitions, took "old friends"

down to the basement where, among the packing cases and the brown paper, tea would be provided. Seated on a little hard chair, Henry James would express "in convoluted sentences the disturbed hesitations which Matisse and Picasso aroused in him, and Roger Fry, exquisitely, with something of the old-world courtesy which James carried about with him," would do his best to convey to the great novelist what he meant by saying that Cézanne and Flaubert were, in a manner of speaking, after the same thing.[37]

How convincing Fry was can only be surmised. It is doubtful that, even if James had overcome his "disturbed hesitations," he would have been able by that time in his life to respond with enthusiasm to the new art or so to absorb it that it would have influenced his own work. Even by 1892 he felt he had ceased to react to paintings as he had in his youth, though he continued to go to exhibitions and remained interested in new art developments. Probably even in viewing impressionist paintings he never felt the intense pleasure that he had when standing on his first trip abroad as an adult "in the immediate presence of Titian and Rembrandt, of Rubens and Paul Veronese" at the National Gallery and "the cup of sensation was thereby filled to overflowing."[38] The old paintings—crystallized history, manners, psychology—spoke to him with a voice that reached chambers of his consciousness closed to the appeals of modern art.

An evaluation of his art criticism on its own merits, apart from its relation to his literary theory and practice, would conclude that the emphasis on literary, psychological, and historical associations extraneous to art *qua* art is one of its greatest weaknesses. For this shortcoming the Ruskin influence alone cannot be blamed. Much of Victorian criticism suffers from the same abstractness: a tendency to use criteria of spirituality and truth to life, to focus on subject rather than on the total work, in short, to avoid the more purely technical by approaching the visual arts through avenues other than the one leading to its center. Of course, when James's contemporaries came to such equations in his writing as "beauty is sincerity" and such terminology as "noble," "good faith," "the scale of the ideal," and "masculine completeness," they probably understood him well enough for his and their purposes. Phrases of approval and disapproval of this type must have had a degree of content for them they do not have for the present-day reader. Judged ahistorically, James's art criticism suffers from being based on an inadequate theory of art with a ready-made critical vocabulary. His literary criticism is enriched by technical terms drawn from the visual arts, but despite an awareness of essential differences in art forms, his approach to the visual arts is not specifically in terms of, to quote Walter Pater, "its own special mode of reaching the imagination, its own special responsibilities to its material,"[39] that is, in terms of craft. The debit side of his art criticism is traceable to his incorrigibly literary approach. As a result it goes without saying that a student today who wishes to learn about Delacroix, for example, will first turn to interpretations by professional art critics and historians, who analyze his work in terms of structure, iconography, and historical development of form, rather than to the often perceptive but fragmentary notes of an amateur. And as James was an amateur in the original sense of the word, a lover of art, he cannot and should not be compared with a Berenson or Burckhardt for erudition, a Ruskin or Pater for effecting a widespread change in taste, and a Fry or Malraux for approaching art with a viable theory that strengthens rather than attenuates perception. However, in spite of weaknesses due to false and confused assumptions, outmoded terminology, and an old-fashioned ignorance of the obeisance owed to significant form, James's criticism (apart from the interest any of his writing has in throwing light on his mind and fictive art) justifies rescue from the death-in-life of periodicals. This judgment leads to the problem of the purpose and value of art criticism.

James himself conceived of the critic as an "honest and intelligent mediator" between painters and the public, someone who deals "with painters and paintings as literary critics deal with authors and books."[40] (Presumably, these remarks would also apply to the criticism of sculpture and architecture.) He admitted that "even an indifferent picture is generally worth more than a good criticism," but criticism had a purpose: "It keeps the question of art before the world, insists upon its importance, and makes it always in order."[41] He admired French critics who "give a sense of the great breadth of the province of art, and of its intimate relations with the rest of men's intellectual life" and who in criticizing a picture "neither talk pure sentiment (or rather, impure sentiment), like foolish amateurs, nor . . . confine their observations to what the French call the *technique* of art."[42] In other words, the critic should neither use the painting as a pretext for self-expression and a purely emotional response nor limit himself to the problems of execution, which are of interest only to other painters. The main fault he found with Fromentin's *Les maîtres d'autrefois*, a classic on Rembrandt and Rubens, was its abstruse, oversubtle technical analysis: Fromentin did not realize that "a man may be extremely fond of good concerts and yet have no relish for the tuning of fiddles."[43] On the other hand, he also agreed with painters that critics tended to write about art too exclusively from a literary standpoint, but he also thought that artists were no better as self-critics, because in general they were incapable of expressing themselves coherently. In short, James's ideal critic had a grasp of the medium through which the painter expresses himself, but since his main purpose was to interpret paintings and awaken interest in them, he concentrated on those aspects of the picture which could be readily and gracefully described for the benefit of the layman. (This view of the critic's function partially explains his admiration for the amiable but undistinguished Hamerton and his petulance toward the difficult but more original Fromentin.)

The problems of expressing in language judgments about a nonverbal art and the value of the attempt itself are perennially debated. Some aestheticians doubt whether any valid judgment of a nonverbal art can be communicated. "Since aesthetic experience takes place in a universe other than that of language, how can it communicate itself by means of words?" asks Étienne Gilson, who concludes that the best the critic can do is to make known his experience by "contagion."[44] Other writers on the problem of the relation of the visual arts to language take a less defeatist attitude. As Rudolph Arnheim points out, the relation of a critical analysis of any art, be it literary, musical, or visual, to the art work itself is the same: all language by its nature can only approximately, never actually, communicate the qualities of a concrete thing or experience. Bernard Berenson, skeptical of the value of interpretations of art that reduce it to a concept, suspecting even some of his own "more abstract statements" of being "merely the rattle of the dangling tin can," believes that the function of the critic is to put the reader "into a state of eager and zestful anticipation," to help him "to 'live' the work of art."[45] The problem of communication is mitigated, however, when the modernist theory of "pure" art is challenged; as Lionel Trilling has suggested in a discussion of Sir Kenneth Clark's study of the nude, the past half century may have gone too far in viewing aesthetic experience as divorced from literary, psychological responses.[46]

In the light of the foregoing criteria as well as James's own, his art criticism, in spite of its technical weaknesses, its lack of scholarly ballast, and the limitations of the taste it reflects, is well worth reading as an independent text, not merely as marginal to his fiction. Whether he tried to capture in prose the flicker of light and illusory movement of the little kings on the Chartres façade, the stillness of Carpaccio's *St. Ursula at Rest*, or the "rich brown bloom" of a minor painter like Crome, James usually succeeded in conveying a unified impression of the appearance and meaning of what he saw. These re-creations of the art work, at their best integrating subject and technique, the human and aesthetic responses, so admirably serve the critical function of communicating contagiously an aesthetic experience that only the reader determined to be unmoved remains unenriched and unenlightened. James had the faculty he admired in Matthew Arnold of "reproducing in their integrity the impressions made by works of art and literature," of conveying "the manner, the meaning, the quality, of an artistic effort."[47]

In a sentence or phrase he captures the quality of a painting, as for example, the grotesqueness of Frank Duveneck's portrait of a German professor, who looks "as to complexion and eyeballs, as if he had just been cut down after an unpractical attempt to hang himself"[48] or the slick superficiality of Lord Leighton's nudes whose "texture is too often that of the glaze on the lid of a prune-box; his drawings too often that of the figures that smile at us from the covers of these receptacles."[49]

In his best and more extended descriptions of pictures, insofar as it is possible to translate from one medium to another, he reproduces the feeling of the created world of the picture at the same time that aspects of composition are not neglected, as in the following passage on Sargent's portrait of the Boit children (see plate XI):

The artist has done nothing more felicitous and interesting than this view of a rich, dim, rather generalized French interior (the perspective of a hall with a shining floor, where screens and tall Japanese vases shimmer and loom), which encloses the life and seems to form the happy play-world of a family of charming children. The treatment is eminently unconventional, and there is none of the usual symmetrical balancing of the figures in the foreground. The place is regarded as a whole; it is a scene, a comprehensive impression; yet none the less do the little figures in their white pinafores (when was the pinafore ever painted with that power and made so poetic?) detach themselves and live with a personal life. Two of the sisters stand hand in hand at the back, in the delightful, the almost equal, company of a pair of immensely tall emblazoned jars, which overtop them and seem also to partake of the life of the picture; the splendid porcelain and the aprons of the children shine together, while a mirror in the brown depth behind them catches the light. Another little girl presents herself, with abundant tresses and slim legs, her hands behind her, quite to the left; and the young-est, nearest to the spectator, sits on the floor and plays with her doll. The naturalness of the composition, the loveliness of the complete effect, the light, free security of the execution, the sense it gives us as of assimilated secrets and of instinct and knowledge playing together—all this makes the picture as astonishing a work on the part of a young man of twenty-six as the portrait of 1881 was astonishing on the part of a young man of twenty-four.[50]

In a totally different vein is his devastating tongue-in-cheek description of Alma-Tadema's painting entitled *Summer*—"in its way a marvel."

M. Alma Tadema's people are always ancient Romans, and in this case he has depicted a Roman bath in a private house. The bath is of yellow brass, sunk into a floor of yellow brass, and in the water, up to her shoulders, sits an ugly woman with a large nose, crowned with roses, scattering rose-leaves over the water, and fanning herself with a large, limp, yellow ostrich-plume . . . . The whole thing is ugly, and there is a disagreeable want of purity of drawing, sweetness of outline. But the rendering of the yellow stuffs and the yellow brass is masterly, and in the artist's manipulation there is a sort of ability which seems the last word of consummate modern painting.[51]

His detailed descriptions of individual art works and his apt characterizations of the general style of a painter are doubly rewarding: they please stylistically, and they heighten one's enjoyment of the visual arts. Of the quickly sketched synopses at which James excelled, this description of Watteau's "scheme of life," "delicious" but "extremely impracticable," is typical:

a scheme of lounging through endless summer days in grassy glades in a company always select, between ladies who should never lift their fans to

hide a yawn, and gentlemen who should never give them a pretext for doing so (even with their guitars), and in a condition of temper personally, in
which satisfaction should never be satiety. Watteau was a genuine poet; he
has an irresistible air of believing in these visionary picnics. His clear good
faith marks the infinite distance, in art, between the light and the trivial; for
the light is but a branch of the serious. Watteau's hand is serious in spite
of its lightness, and firm with all its grace. His landscape is thin and sketchy,
but his figures delightfully true and expressive; gentle folks all, but moving
in a sphere unshaken by revolutions. Some of the attitudes of the women are
inimitably natural and elegant. Watteau, indeed, marks the high-water point
of natural elegance. With the turn of the tide, with Lancret, Nattier,
Boucher, and Fragonard—masters all of them of prettiness, and all here in
force—affectation, mannerism, and levity begin. Time has dealt hardly with
Watteau's colouring, which has thickened and faded to a painfully sallow
hue. But oddly enough, the dusky tone of his pictures deepens their dramatic
charm and gives a certain poignancy to their unreality. His piping chevaliers
and whispering countesses loom out of the clouded canvas like fancied
twilight ghosts in the garden of a haunted palace.[52]

But James is perhaps at his best in his full-length essays on Sargent,
du Maurier, Daumier, and Delacroix and on his London and Italian
"hours" and the American scene, because in these there is sufficient
room to make comparisons, to trace developments of an artist's work,
to relate the art to the milieu, to suggest the individual tone of
artists and places through descriptions of specific works and scenes.

Although his proposal to the publisher James Osgood in 1883 to
collect a number of art and travel essays under the title "Impressions
of Art and Life" was not acted on,[53] the title indicates the qualities
of his art criticism which make it still highly readable even for the
non-Jamesian. Just as James chiefly valued the sense of "felt life" in
fiction, feelings about events and actions rather than these external-
ities in themselves, his evocation in prose of the life he felt in paintings, sculpture, and architecture constitutes the highest value of his
criticism. Through this evocation of the "felt life," at his best, he
fused art and life, the aesthetic and human experiences, and gen-
erated the excitement an art critic should generate in order, as
Berenson put it, to help the reader "to 'live' the work of art." E. M.
Forster said of James, perhaps overmodestly, that "he had in his early
thirties a background of culture and a foreground of information that
have been denied me in my late seventies."[54] Granting that "printed
talk"—cultivated, well informed, articulating a keen and loving response to art with precision and wit—is a pleasure to read, then
James's criticism of the visual arts should be judged, apart from his
fiction, as a minor but nevertheless true achievement.

W ILLIAM MORRIS HUNT'S Newport studio, it will be remembered, represented for James an opening into the world of free creativity, a world from which he was not debarred even after he realized the futility of his ambition to be a painter. As a writer he too could be an artist, for he discovered that "the arts were after all essentially one."[1] In itself this dictum cannot be taken as a considered view on the aesthetics of art interrelations; in its historical context of an essentially puritanical and utilitarian America of the 1860's, it justified a disinterested dedication to fiction as an art form. From the painter-designer John La Farge he derived this early faith in the aesthetic dignity and possibilities of fiction, and in La Farge's uncompromising devotion to the refinements of his craft, he had a model of artistic integrity. Even if James exaggerated Hunt's and La Farge's influence on him and his youthful determination to become a painter for dramatic purposes in his autobiography, in his maturity his vindication of the novel as a work of art was primarily on the grounds of its kinship with the visual arts. In the now-classic essay "The Art of Fiction," containing his "core of conviction" on the subject, he consistently uses examples from the visual arts to make his case. Rightfully read for its main intention—a declaration of freedom for the novel from critical and moral prohibitions and an apologia for his own kind of novel, that of consciousness—it may also be read as an exposition of James's conception of the relation of painting to fiction.

While James stresses the unity of the arts in this essay, underlying his view of their relation is the assumption that they are parallel, not merging, forms. "The *analogy* between the art of the painter and the art of the novelist, is so far as I am able to see, complete" [italics mine]. It is "complete," he continues, with respect to "inspiration," "process (allowing for the different quality of the vehicle)," and "success." "They may learn from each other, they may explain and sustain each other."[2] James then proceeds in the essay to explain and sustain fiction by this analogy, which derives from his assumption that painting is essentially representational. Contrary to modern formalist or expressionist aesthetic theory, James assumes that the painter, aiming at creating the illusion of reality, begins with "nature" and then organizes and shapes his perceptions into an aesthetically appropriate form.

Able to rely implicitly on his reader's acceptance of this view of painting—that its aim is to "represent real life"—James could insist that likewise "the only reason for the existence of a novel is that it does attempt to represent life."[3] The general public tolerates fiction if it does not pretend to deal with life seriously, an attitude symptomatic of a lingering Puritan hostility toward fiction and the stage. The way to combat this attitude is "to insist on the fact that as the picture is reality, so the novel is history."[4] Likewise, "conscious moral purpose" is problematic: "What is the meaning of your morality and your conscious moral purpose? Will you not define your terms and explain how (a novel being a picture) a picture can be either moral or immoral? You wish to paint a moral picture or carve a moral statue: will you not tell us how you set about it?"[5] Furthermore, as fiction is one of the fine arts, the novelist should have the right to treat any subject he pleases, and the "search for form" is as legitimate in writing as it is in painting. It follows, then, that the novelist must not be judged by his choice of subject but rather by his execution, the rules or laws of which, however, must not be prescribed. "The form . . . is to be appreciated after the fact." There is "no limit to what he [the novelist] may attempt as an executant—no limit to his possible experiments, efforts, discoveries, successes. Here it is especially that he works, step by step, like his brother of the brush, of whom we may always say that he has painted his pictures in a manner best known to himself."[6]

While James employs the analogy between painting and the novel for rhetorical purposes, and hence emphasizes similarities, his qualification of the *rapprochement* has bearing on his adaptations of the terminology of painting. "The painter *is* able to teach the rudiments of his practice" in contrast to the literary artist who "would be obliged to say to his pupil much more than the other, 'Ah, well, you must do it as you can!' It is a question of degree, a matter of delicacy. If there are exact sciences, there are also exact arts, and the grammar of painting is so much more definite that it makes the difference."[7] James was endowed with the visual sensibility which made pictorial metaphor natural to him, but he was also aware of the absence in English letters of a serious consideration of fiction and a critical terminology. To fill this gap, he helped himself generously to one that was available, the painter's, without, however, feeling obliged to maintain a strict correspondence. As literature is not an "exact art," its critical language cannot be so fixed or so definite as that of painting.

Differing most from the painter in his ability to teach or transmit technique, the novelist comes closest in descriptive writing to sharing the painter's aim. It is in the attempt to render "the look of things, the look that conveys their meaning, to catch the colour, the relief, the expression, the surface, the substance of the human spectacle" that the novelist "competes with his brother the painter." The creation of the "air of reality (solidity of specification)" is, James maintains, "the supreme virtue of the novel—the merit on which all its other merits . . . helplessly and submissively depend."[8] He is frequently critical of works for their "lack of the note of visibility": Stevenson's *Catriona* subjects his visual sense, his "*seeing* imagination, to an almost painful underfeeding."[9] He wonders what Thackeray intended by his "extraordinary avoidance of picture" in *Denis Duval*: "The impression of to-day's reader is that the chapters we possess might really have been written without the author's having stood on the spot."[10] One of Howells's deficiencies is that he "forgets sometimes to paint, to evoke the conditions and appearances, to build in the subject."[11] A running refrain in James's comments on the French realists is his praise for their "visual curiosity," validating his belief that "in any description of life the description of places and things is half the battle."[12]

But only half the battle. James expresses skepticism of efforts in literature to create purely pictorial effects ungoverned by a larger literary purpose. Description in literature is necessary to create the "illusion of reality" on which acceptance of everything else depends —all psychological, moral, social meanings. But it cannot and should not be an end in itself or even the sole means of expression as it is in the visual arts. The attempt of the Goncourt brothers to vie with painting in prose is given as an instance of failure to make sufficient distinction between the ends and means of the two arts. Having the visual artist's sensibility, they try to do with words what the painter does with paint and the sculptor with stone. "The most general stricture to be made on their work is probably that they have not allowed enough for the difference of instrument, have persisted in the effort to render impressions that the plastic artist renders better, neglecting too much those he is unable to render."[13] As an example of the deficiency of their method James cites their treatment of the religious conversion of the heroine of *Madame Gervaisais*: "When the great spiritual change takes place for their heroine, the way in which it seems to the authors most to the purpose to represent it is by a wonderful description of the confessional, at the Gesù, to which she goes for the first time to kneel."[14] Though James concedes that the Goncourts perform "an almost impossible feat of translation" giving "this manner unmistakable life,"[15] he contends that the effort to render purely painterly effects in prose is bound to be self-defeating. By attempting to appeal purely to the eye, not only does the writer fail to convey the essence of literature—the workings of the mind and the emotions verbally comprehended—but he is also by the very nature of his medium doomed to indirection in depicting the physical world: the difference between the novelist's rendering of the visible world and the visual artist's is "the difference between the roundabout, faint descriptive tokens of respectable prose and the immediate projection of the figure by the pencil."[16] James himself while taking notes on the spot in preparation for a book on London (never written) occasionally made sketches, an indication that at times he resorted to drawing as a more direct and economical way of fixing immediate impressions than hastily describing the scene in words.

Given James's views on translation from one medium to another, his attitude toward the amalgamation of literature and painting follows logically. Pictures inspired by fiction or literary themes he considered legitimate as long as they existed independently of the text as interpretations and aesthetic objects in their own right. Pictures "grafted" to fiction and thus in competition with the writer's creation of "more or less visible appearances" were another matter altogether. Although he was friends with several painter-illustrators and even produced on their behalf mainly appreciative evaluations of their works collected in a slender volume called *Picture and Text*, he often complained to publishers and editors in letters about the illustrations of his own work and also stated his general objections in print. It was not the poor quality of most contemporary illustration that he objected to, but rather the fact that illustrations invaded the writer's domain: "Anything that relieves responsible prose of the duty of being, while placed before us, good enough, interesting enough and, if the question be of picture, pictorial enough, above all *in itself*, does it the worst of services." Illustration to be acceptable should be self-contained, "on its own feet and thus, as a separate and independent subject of publication, carrying its text in its spirit, just as that text correspondingly carries the plastic possibility."[17] Thus he praised Alvin Langdon Coburn's frontispiece photographs to the New York edition, for they did not compete with the text. They made no attempt "to keep, or to pretend to keep, anything like dramatic step with their suggestive matter" but were instead "mere optical symbols or echoes, expressions of no particular thing in the text, but only of the type or idea of this or that thing."[18] Illustration, in short, should be complementary, symbolic, or evocative of the spirit of the work. Although unusually sensitive to the pictorial in art and nature, James nevertheless was too much the literary craftsman to view the relationship between the visual arts and fiction, even in combination, as other than inspirational, analogous, or enhancing.

In his more or less explicit statements on the interrelations of the arts James retains a clear sense of the distinctions among them. It is more difficult to separate the means of expression from the meaning in analyzing the pictorial elements in his theory of fiction and critical practice, for in a unified sensibility such as his, the metaphor *is* the thought. Nevertheless, it may be attempted with the knowledge of the genesis of his taste and of his mature art appreciation to help elucidate his concepts and vocabulary. The tension in his taste between romantic painterly suggestiveness and classical High Renaissance clarity of form has its counterpart in his definition of the novelist's most fundamental dilemma:

To give the image and the sense of certain things while still keeping them subordinate to his plan, keeping them in relation to matters more immediate and apparent, to give all the sense, in a word, without all the substance or all the surface, and so to summarize and foreshorten, so to make values both rich and sharp, that the mere procession of items and profiles is not only, for the occasion, superseded, but is, for essential quality, almost "compromised" –such a case of delicacy proposes itself at every turn to the painter of life who wishes both to treat his chosen subject and to confine his necessary picture.[19]

Approaching the problem from the creator's point of view rather than from the appreciator's, James is concerned here with the difficulty of producing in art a sense of completion and of closure without sacrificing the richness of its reference to the "continuity of things and the passage of human life." In other words, the novelist's "chosen subject" does not provide its own limitations, for subject consists "obviously of the related state, to each other, of certain figures and things"; the crux of the matter is that "relations stop nowhere, and the exquisite problem of the artist is eternally but to draw, by a geometry of his own, the circle within which they shall happily *appear* to do so."[20]

Every artist, no matter how indifferent to formal considerations, faces the problem of selection. What is peculiar to James is that he

believed both that art should be true to the complexities of reality—
the "multitudinous references" and cross-references to developments
that every experience calls forth—and that it should be in form balanced, proportioned, unified. His ideal was to realize in fiction Tintoretto's achievements in painting—works encyclopedic in scope, rich
in variety, and evocative of meanings over and beyond what could
be specifically pointed to in the picture itself, yet self-contained, all
of the diverse elements synthesized to make an organic whole.

The key word in James's discussions of the relation of form to reality is *foreshortening*. What did he mean by it? Joseph Warren
Beach limits the term to the device used to maintain "the desired
balance between the first and second halves of a novel,"[21] but clearly
it has a more inclusive application. Better defined, it is the "economic
device"[22] by which the illusion of complexity is created without loss
of compactness, the compromise the novelist has to make between the
demands of form and the expansiveness of meaning. Obviously, the
relation between pictorial and fictional foreshortening is only a loose
one: in painting it refers to the representation of some lines of an
object as shorter than they are in actuality in order to give the illusion
of relative size, according to the laws of perspective. It is a commonplace that a painting may display miracles of foreshortening and yet
be a bad painting; conversely, no illusional effect may have been attempted and yet the work may be masterful. Some aestheticians
argue that what is left when representational values are omitted is
the essence of the picture. In painting, then, foreshortening refers to
representational or illusional values which may have aesthetic implications. As applied by James to fiction, it refers to the technique
of reconciling representational truth with aesthetic aims. Moreover,
pictorial foreshortening is achieved by the application of optical
laws; there is no comparable scientific basis for fictional foreshortening. In this respect, James was quite correct in believing the "grammar of painting" to be more exact than that of fiction.

But if not done scientifically, how is foreshortening achieved in
fiction? Of James's comments on the principle the most seminal are
those on the composition of *Roderick Hudson* and on Balzac, praised
by James for practicing the "art of the brush" rather than that of the
"slate-pencil." By the "art of the brush" Balzac created the "solidity
of specification" without literally itemizing or reproducing the
imagined setting. He "minutely described" the "scenes and persons of
his drama" (in *Eugénie Grandet*) yet "these things are all described
only in so far as they bear upon the action, and not in the least for

themselves."[23] While he penetrated his subject by a mastery of detail, it was not submerged by detail; he foreshortened by selecting only those details that were relevant to the over-all composition, making them do double duty as strategy for visualization and as accessories to action. Crucial to his meaningful selection was that, like Tintoretto, who perceived his subject "as the whole scene, complete, peculiar, individual, unprecedented," Balzac began with the totality of the work in mind: "his story exists before it is told; it stands complete before his mind's eye."[24]

James applied the "lesson of Balzac" when he came to write *Roderick Hudson*, but he also discovered a second foreshortening device which proved to be of even greater value. In the course of composition, James came to realize that if Roderick's downfall were to be plausible, he would have to have more experiences than could be presented in the novel. The challenge was to create "the *effect* of the great lapse and passage, of the 'dark backward and abysm of time,' by the terms of truth, and . . . the effect of compression, of composition and form, by the terms of literary arrangement."[25] Though he clung to the Balzacian principle that he was dealing with an Action, what really saved him, James recalled, was the discovery of his "center" in the consciousness of Rowland, Roderick's friend and patron; that is, by straining the action through the mind of this character he was able to reconcile form with truth. The novel "hangs together" to the degree that it does because the subject is presented, not as Roderick's experiences, but as Rowland's consciousness of them.

The center of consciousness character (also called *central intelligence*, *reflector*, and *register*) resembles the painter in relation to his subject and the painting's viewers: like the painter, he provides a "frame" which organizes and brings into focus the otherwise inchoate external world. By transforming it with the imagination, or to use Susanne Langer's phrase, by "subjectifying nature," he makes it available to the reader. In effect (even taking into account all of the variations and permutations of this method of narration in James's later fiction), it is as if James placed the painter in the novel so that the reader has a view of the action or the life depicted in the novel both clarified through the formal unity provided by the individual perspective and enriched, for the center of consciousness is almost inevitably endowed with the "penetrative imagination," as Ruskin called it, of the artist. As one on whom "nothing is lost," he sees or comes to see beyond the surface to the meaning at the heart of things.

James did not, however, consciously or directly learn this foreshortening technique from painting. Because of the differences in kind, it is doubtful if technique in any but a theoretical sense is ever transferable from one art to another. But is it not farfetched to assume that his tendency from childhood to view the world outside of himself through the interposing medium of picture as well as his mature affinity for painterly art on a grand scale, such as Tintoretto's, should have predisposed him to this method. Much of his pleasure in landscapes was in the shock of recognition, in seeing a Claude Lorrain in the Roman campagna or a Constable in the English countryside. Viewing nature through pictures and seeing pictures as verified by nature were characteristics of his sensibility which necessarily made themselves felt in his conception and practice of fiction.

Though James considered the novelist in closest competition with the painter in the rendering of the "look of things," the narrative passages he designated in his fiction as "picture" are not strikingly visual. His analysis of his fully elaborated fictional method, primarily a development of the two basic foreshortening devices (Action, or Scene, and Center of Consciousness), explains this seeming contradiction and once again shows how James's experience with painting, at the least, provided him with a critical vocabulary and at the most influenced his theory and practice of fiction. According to his preface to *The Ambassadors*, his compositions are divided "into the parts that prepare . . . for scenes [the Action], and the parts, or otherwise into the scenes, that justify and crown the preparation." Everything that is *not* scene is the "fusion and synthesis of picture,"[26] that is, the narrative passages presented through the central consciousness. James's emphasis on "fusion and synthesis" is well placed, for the picture—the narrative passages, as noted—is not vividly pictorial. The least visual are the introspective passages in which a character is "motionlessly *seeing*":[27] in *The Portrait of a Lady* Isabel's vigil before the fire when she reviews her past and sees its meaning; in *The Golden Bowl* Maggie's meditations while waiting at Portland Place for the Prince to return from Matcham. Consisting mostly of a weaving together of meditations and memories, these contemplative pictures sometimes contain startling visual metaphors, as, for example, the famous pagoda figure in *The Golden Bowl*, but present little or nothing of the setting or of the character's appearance. Much more visual than the contemplative passages are those dealing not only with the character's feelings and thoughts but also with his immediate visual impressions or the interplay between the two: in *The Ambassadors* Strether's glimpse of Mamie Pocock on the balcony; in *The*

Wings of the Dove Milly Theale's hour of solitude in taking possession of her Venetian palace. As may be seen, by referring to these narrative passages as pictures, James did not have in mind an abundance of visual detail or of description used conventionally to set the place and time. Instead, he was expressing his adherence to the ideal of integration that he found supremely realized in Tintoretto and Delacroix: thoughts, gestures, speech, and décor in the novel should be fused just as color and line, detail and mass, and figures and background are made inseparable in the greatest paintings. Moreover the central consciousness subjectifies the action in the picture or narrative passages as does the painter in his treatment of the external scene he is representing on canvas.

In contrast to the picture passages the dramatic ones call for more objective treatment. Dialogue, James felt, should be "organic and dramatic, speaking for itself, representing and embodying substance and form."[28] Because Balzac's dialogue was *not* self-contained, James considered him a "great painter" but not a "great dramatist"; his dialogue was simply "illustrational."[29] The law of the picture is clearly different from that of the drama: the former subjectifies the outer world, the latter objectifies the inner.

In the glossary, I have listed art terms recurring in James's nonfictional writing, apart from those discussed previously. The list, though not presented as exhaustive, suggests the pervasiveness of pictorialism in James's view of the novel and is intended to be of use, of course, only with reference to James's work. He did not develop a terminology sufficiently fixed and technical to furnish subsequent literary critics with a viable critical vocabulary. His adoption of art terms was precise enough, however, for his own purposes. It enabled him to develop and express a theory of the novel which has had an undisputed influence on modern criticism and fiction. Lionel Trilling sees him as having had a dual significance: "From him many of us learned how high, even sacred, is the mission of the artist, and from him we derived many of the tenets by which we judge success in art."[30] That these tenets have been absorbed into the lifeblood of the novel, working unalterable change, seems likely; as Graham Hough remarks, referring to the effects of the literary revolution of which James was a forerunner, "The novel has often got on pretty comfortably without much self-consciousness in formal matters; but I doubt if it can do so again."[31] But it is doubtful that the Jamesian approach in and by itself may be used as a guide for the writing and judging of fiction of the present, nor, for that matter, may its criteria be applied without reservation to the fiction of the past. The charge that the limitations, exclusions, sacrifices to "life" that James's method entails is not worth its aesthetic rewards was in part refuted by the Jamesian revival of the 1940's. A new literary spirit, in turn, has rejected the extravagant claims of the Jacobins and ignored the Alexandrian criticism of the 1950's. But polemics and literary fashion aside, it falls within my province here to suggest briefly the relation of these exclusions, limitations, and sacrifices to James's pictorial approach.

The foundation of James's defense of the novel as an autonomous art form rests on the resemblances he notes between it and painting: representational art does not require a moral or social excuse for being. Moreover, the center of consciousness, which, in conjunction with the scene, is at the heart of James's method, is essentially visual in conception. What has not been pointed out is that the center of consciousness in performing the function of the painter confronting his subject places James's subject at another remove from the raw material, the reality the author finally wants to represent; that is, the center of consciousness is interpreting a fictional world, a world which is, to begin with, the author's distillation of "real" life. Of course, to James subject is what is perceived. "Felt life" is the primary concern of art. Addicted as he was to seeing things through other things, the *process* of seeing in effect is his subject. Not only is life in the raw—active and sensual—excluded, but also more aesthetic distance is placed between the author and his work than there would be were he himself the painter, the omniscient author, as Tolstoi or George Eliot is. This detachment of the author from his creation James considered a necessity for the maintenance of illusion and creation of form: hence his impatience with the "loose and baggy monsters" which attempt to include *all* of life regardless of form and with the unwarranted (in his eyes) authorly intrusions of a Thackeray or a Trollope. By taking the reader backstage, they admitted that the show was only make-believe rather than, as James believed, more real than the world outside the theater.

Likewise, the classical element in James's aesthetic precluded his appreciation of the autobiographical, organic, fluid literary mode, the romantic fiction of self-discovery and growth which *Moby-Dick* and *Sons and Lovers* represent. The painter-writer grasps his subject whole in a flash of insight, as did Balzac and Tintoretto. James himself, as his Notebooks and Prefaces demonstrate, generally conceived of the outlines of his work prior to composition, though in the process of composition the "germ," or seminal idea, was transformed. His conception of the form of a work was even on occasion diagrammatic: an extreme example was his preconception of *The Awkward Age* as "a circle consisting of a number of small rounds disposed at equal distance about a central object."[32] This visualization of psychological situations in formal patterns led Roger Fry to derive from even such a minor work as *Confidence* a pleasure similar to that gained from the "counterpoint of Poussin's designs"[33] and, negatively, E. M. Forster to doubt that the sacrifices made to form are worth the price since "most of human life has to disappear before he can do us a novel."[34] One may think Forster willfully ingenuous, but the drawbacks of approaching "organic" art with James's rather specialized conception of form as a critical criterion are indisputable.

Finally, the question of "general ideas" or the philosophical quest. Although James's mind could be violated by an idea on occasion, social or metaphysical or even moral ideas as such are largely absent from his fiction and from his theory of the novel. This absence is not due to his preoccupation with form. Rather, it is a matter of vision. The "painter of life," one of James's favorite metaphors for the novelist, confronts what he sees, that is, begins with an empirical reality rather than with an abstract idea. The "ideas" of the novel, like those of a painting, are necessarily arrived at through imaginative penetration of surfaces, not by a priori or abstract reasoning. Inclining to the classical in form, he placed his faith, nevertheless, in the romantic imagination, the power of empathy and penetration.

As may be seen, James's visual approach to the novel did entail losses as well as gains, though the appropriateness of viewing an aesthetic in debit and credit terms is questionable. More to the point is that James's love and knowledge of painting helped him to develop a method and articulate a theory of fiction that, though it may be judged limited and incomplete, nevertheless created a new awareness of the aesthetic possibilities of fiction. His case illustrates the way in which the painter and the novelist "may learn from each other . . . explain and sustain each other. Their cause is the same, and the honour of one is the honour of another."[35]

J AMES'S view of the novel as picture—a composition in which all elements are fused—and of the compositional center as the chief means of achieving unity is profoundly related to his experience of the visual arts. But it is obvious that the most carefully composed of James's novels is still a novel, not a picture, and that the experience of reading fiction is different in kind from that of looking at paintings. What then does *pictorial* mean when applied to fiction? I use the term to designate the practice of describing people, places, scenes, or parts of scenes as if they were paintings or subjects for a painting and the use of art objects for thematic projection and overtone. Aside from pictorial devices in fiction, there is the question of resemblance in style and structure of the novel to the work of a particular school of painting, assuming that all the arts reflect in certain ways the pervasive time-spirit. Applied to James, what did he have in common with the impressionists? Assuming, moreover, that there exist certain families of style transcending periods, what is James's relation to mannerism, the art of the past that impressed him perhaps most deeply? Just as metaphors communicate with immediacy the feel of experience as abstract or discursive language cannot, comparisons between the arts sensitize the reader or viewer to qualities in the works otherwise difficult to define; but each art having its own techniques and traditions, this critical approach necessarily becomes less and less valuable the more one tries to penetrate to the formal structural elements of the works being compared.[1] Therefore, my emphasis is on James's pictorialism; only secondarily am I concerned with the question of style and period affinities.

An outgrowth of James's habit of seeing a landscape or figures composed so that the scene appears to the spectator as a living picture perhaps recalling a real one or as a subject for a picture is his use of the framing device.[2] Any scene or part of a scene may be considered framed if through visual imagery or description it is circumscribed and set apart from the rest of the narrative. Framing serves various purposes: to integrate description with action or with characterization, especially if the scene is presented through the consciousness of a character with a painter's eye; to convey with great precision the particular tone of the setting or appearance of a character; and, most importantly, to symbolize relationships and underline themes.

Thus, the opening of *Confidence* consists of a series of scenes viewed pictorially, that is, as they are or might be seen by the hero, Bernard Longueville, who, having a "fancy for sketching," likes to take "pictorial notes."[3] For example:

Longueville, every morning after breakfast, took a turn in the great square of Siena—the vast *piazza*, shaped like a horse-shoe, where the market is held beneath the windows of that crenellated palace from whose overhanging cornice a tall, straight tower springs up with a movement as light as that of a single plume in the bonnet of a captain. Here he strolled about, watching a brown *cantadino* disembarrass his donkey, noting the progress of half an hour's chaffer over a bundle of carrots, wishing a young girl with eyes like animated agates would let him sketch her, and gazing up at intervals at the beautiful, slim tower, as it played at contrasts with the large blue air.[4]

Note that though Longueville is said to be strolling about, the scene is described from the point of view of a spectator who remains at a sufficient distance from the market to be able to glance up to see the tower that dominates the scene. In the suggestion of movement—Longueville's walking about, the upspringing effect of the tower, the animation and sparkle of the girl's eyes—the scene is presented as a typical picturesque subject. As Heinrich Wölfflin points out, "restless architectural forms" and "real movement" create essentially picturesque effects, and "there is nothing more picturesque than the busy crowd of the market."[5] While Longueville is sketching another picturesque scene, the heroine walks into his picture, into his foreground. Description becomes part of the action; the girl he sketches turns out later to be the same one his friend has fallen in love with in Baden-Baden. However, the hero's sketching propensities are not essentially a part of the story. Angela Vivian walks in and out of his life in the same way as she has walked in and out of his subject, and finally stays in his life just as she has become a part of his sketch, but his having an eye for the picturesque is chiefly a device to introduce the local color of Siena into the novel and to show that Longueville is clever and accomplished.

An art object itself sometimes provides the center of James's living pictures: "Travelling Companions" opens with the heroine, Charlotte Evans, and her father looking at Leonardo's *Last Supper* while they are being looked at by the hero. Similarly, in the first paragraph of *The American* Christopher Newman is seen "reclining at his ease on the great circular divan which . . . occupied the centre of the Salon Carré, in the Museum of the Louvre" staring "at Murillo's beautiful moon-borne Madonna."[6] In one sharp visual image the theme of American confronting Europe is presented with immediacy and economy. Sometimes the *tableau vivant* comes as a climax to a scene, gathering together in one image its meaning. A striking instance of this kind of framing occurs in *Roderick Hudson* at the conclusion of the dinner party given in honor of Roderick's successful completion of his first works. Coming back to the drawing room after seeing the ladies to their carriage, Rowland

paused outside the open door; he was struck by the group formed by the three men. They were standing before Roderick's statue of Eve, and the young sculptor had lifted up the lamp and was showing different parts of it to his companions. He was talking ardently, and the lamplight covered his head and face. Rowland stood looking on, for the group struck him with its picturesque symbolism. Roderick, bearing the lamp and glowing in its radiant circle, seemed the beautiful image of a genius which combined sincerity with power. Gloriani, with his head on one side, pulling his long moustache and looking keenly from half-closed eyes at the lighted marble, represented art with a worldly motive, skill unleavened by faith, the mere base maximum of cleverness. Poor little Singleton, on the other side, with his hands behind him, his head thrown back, and his eyes following devoutly the course of Roderick's elucidation, might pass for an embodiment of aspiring candor, with feeble wings to rise on. In all this, Roderick's was certainly the *beau* rôle.[7]

In the dramatic lighting and expressive posture, this picture suggests a Caravaggio, though James's dislike of *seicento* art probably precludes this effect as intentional. More to the point is that through the picture the major art themes of the novel presented as table talk in the preceding scene are recapitulated succinctly and vividly. Furthermore, as it is Rowland who sees the group as a picture and then proceeds to read it in conformity with his own taste and romantic idealism, the picture viewed by the spectator in turn symbolizes Rowland's relation to the active life and adumbrates his lost illusions and ultimate exclusion from the "radiant circle" of fulfillment.

In the later fiction, framing devices are used less stagily, more suggestively. Thinly motivated picture passages like those in *Confidence* all but disappear. What a character feels about a scene or person mingles with his visual impressions. While "the look of things" is not neglected, it is more conditioned by the point of view. Description is presented more indirectly and made to serve multiple purposes. Thus,

Isabel Archer is first presented after her marriage as she appears to Ned Rosier: "dressed in black velvet ... brilliant and noble ... framed in the gilded doorway she struck our young man as the picture of a gracious lady."[8] Between the first visual details, however, and the image of her in her gilt frame is the impression she makes on Rosier, who has known her before her marriage. It is as if James were interpreting a great portrait, touching on visual detail and decorative qualities but emphasizing the character it reveals.

In contrast, the portrait of the Man with the Mask in *The Sacred Fount* is described in a straightforward objective fashion:

The figure represented is a young man in black–a quaint, tight black dress, fashioned in years long past; with a pale, lean, livid face and a stare, from eyes without eyebrows, like that of some whitened old-world clown. In his hand he holds an object that strikes the spectator at first simply as some obscure, some ambiguous work of art, but that on second view becomes a representation of a human face, modelled and coloured, in wax, in enamelled metal, in some substance not human. The object thus appears a complete mask, such as might have been fantastically fitted and worn. (NS, XXIX, 44–45)

But the meaning of the portrait is debated by the characters grouped before it. Is the man's own face Death and the mask Life, or is it the other way around? Is he taking it off or putting it on? Is the mask beautiful, or is it hideous with an awful grimace? Does the mask really resemble Mrs. Server and the face, "poor Briss"? The conflicting interpretations which the ambiguous portrait elicits symbolize the central problem of reality and appearance. As Leon Edel observes about this episode, "What has been underlined here for us if not the very theme of the book?"[9]

At moments of recognition in which sight merges with insight, the framing device is used to its greatest effect. Faced with the obligation of carrying out his terrible assignment for a cause in which he no longer believes and superseded by Paul Muniment in his relationship with the Princess, Hyacinth Robinson seeks out Millicent Henning in her shop "as by the force of the one, the last, sore personal need left him." The futility of his hope of gaining solace from her becomes apparent to him when he comes upon Captain Sholto in the middle of the room, one of two figures in a tableau:

It next became plain to him that the person standing upright before the Captain, as still as a lay-figure and with her back turned to himself, was the object of his own quest. In spite of her averted face, he instantly "spotted" Millicent; he knew her shop-attitude, the dressing of her hair behind and the long grand lines of her figure draped in the last new thing. She was showing off this treasure to the Captain, who was lost in contemplation. He had been beforehand with Hyacinth as a false purchaser, but he imitated a real one better than our young man, as, with his eyes travelling up and down the front of their beautiful friend's person, he frowned consideringly and rubbed his lower lip slowly with his walking-stick. Millicent stood admirably still–the back view of the garment she displayed was magnificent. (NY, VI, 423)

Likewise in *The Wings of the Dove*, Milly seeing Kate Croy standing in the French window opening on the balcony "very handsome and upright, the outer dark framing in a highly favourable way her summery simplicities and lightnesses of dress" sees that Merton Densher has returned from America. "Kate had positively but to be there just as she was to tell her he had come back" (NY, XIX, 272). The earlier scene centering on the Bronzino is of this same type but more complex. The climactic recognition scene of "The Jolly Corner" when Spencer Brydon is confronted by his alter ego, the person he would have been had he stayed in America, is similarly rendered: "No portrait by a great modern master could have presented him with more intensity, thrust him out of his frame with more art, as if there had been 'treatment,' of the consummate sort, in his every shade and salience." And indeed the figure as presented could easily pass as a description of one of Sargent's brilliant, slightly dehumanized and sinister portraits, such as that of John D. Rockefeller or Asher Wertheimer. Brydon "took him in . . . his planted stillness, his vivid truth, his grizzled bent head and white masking hands, his queer actuality of evening-dress, of dangling double eye-glass, of gleaming silk lappet and white linen, of pearl button and gold watch-guard and polished shoe" (NY, XVII, 475). What is suggested is a pure optical image without depth or outline, all surface texture and the gleam of light. The framing device is used here to great effect: Brydon's other self, who represented to him "the triumph of life" and who is outwardly as elegant as one Sargent's American financiers, when unmasked fills him with horror, so "evil, odious, blatant, vulgar" (NY, XVII, 477) is his face.

The richest and most fully developed of framed scenes in James's fiction is the thirtieth chapter of *The Ambassadors*, the account of Strether's excursion to the French countryside "into which he had hitherto looked only through the little oblong window of the picture frame." He has hopes when he sets out that he may see "something somewhere that would remind him of a certain small Lambinet that had charmed him, long years before, at a Boston dealer and that he had quite absurdly never forgotten." Unable to afford it, he always remembers it as "the picture he *would* have bought—the particular production that had made him for a moment overstep the modesty of nature" (NY, XXII, 245–46). The picture itself, he realizes, might now disappoint him:

It would be a different thing, however, to see the remembered mixture re-solved back into its elements—to assist at the restoration to nature of the whole far-away hour: the dusty day in Boston, the background of the Fitch-burg Depot, of the maroon-coloured sanctum, the special-green vision, the ridiculous price, the poplars, the willows, the rushes, the river, the sunny silvery sky, the shady woody horizon. (NY, XXII, 246)

When he gets off the train he imagines himself walking into the pic-ture: "The oblong gilt frame disposed its enclosing lines; the poplars and willows, the reeds and river—a river of which he didn't know, and didn't want to know, the name—fell into a composition, full of fe-licity, within them; . . . it was all there, in short—it was what he wanted: it was Tremont Street, it was France, it was Lambinet" (see plate XII). His past and his present join hands as he wanders about "boring so deep into his impression and idleness that he might fairly have got through them again and reached the maroon-coloured wall" (NY, XXII, 247). Through the work of art which distills the essence of experience freeing it from irrelevant, distracting detail, he is en-abled to grasp the essence of the scene before him, and in turn through the living scene he recovers the picture. Still staying within the frame of the picture, he finally stops at an inn toward evening, and while resting, waiting for his dinner to be prepared, he perceives that "at bottom, the spell of the picture—that it was essentially more than anything else a scene and a stage, that the very air of the play was in the rustle of the willows and the tone of the sky" (NY, XXII, 253); that is, the play in which he has been engaged—the drama of which the main characters are Chad and Madame de Vionnet, he and the other "ambassadors" from Woollett—has occupied the center of his consciousness here no less than it has in Paris. For on this ramble in the country even more than in Paris he has felt the quintessence of what distinguishes the conditions of life in France from those in Woollett.

The conditions had nowhere so asserted their difference from those of Woollett as they appeared to him to assert it in the little court of the Cheval Blanc while he arranged with his hostess for a comfortable climax. They were few and simple, scant and humble, but they were *the thing*, as he would have called it, even to a greater degree than Madame de Vionnet's old high salon where the ghost of the Empire walked. "The" thing was the thing that implied the greatest number of other things of the sort he had to tackle; and it was queer of course, but so it was—the implication here was complete. Not a single one of his observations but somehow fell into a place in it; not a breath of the cooler evening that wasn't somehow a syllable of the text. The text was simply, when condensed, that in *these* places such things were, and that if it was in them one elected to move about one had to make one's account with what one lighted on. (NY, XXII, 253–54)

In short, in this scene framed by the Lambinet, Strether comes to a full realization of the meaning of his decision not to urge Chad to return to Woollett. The Lambinet that he has missed owning recalls the constrictions and deprivations of his past existence, the pleasures of the spirit and senses that have been denied to him. Seeing the landscape through the picture heightens his awareness of the complexities of European experience. In a world which so gratifies the "lust of the eyes"[10] and stirs the imagination, and in which nature is so inextricably mixed with art, what is clearly seen as immoral in the sharp New England light may have a different aspect and meaning.

It is especially fitting that the picture through which he sees the landscape should have been a Lambinet. Guided simply by the desire to be true to history, James could have chosen any other of the Barbizon painters, for this was the French landscape school that discerning Bostonians were beginning to collect in the 1860's. James reviewed an exhibition in 1872 of privately owned paintings that included Rousseau, Daubigny, Diaz de la Peña, and Troyon and was held in the rooms of Messrs. Doll and Richards on Tremont Street.[11] Possibly this was the Boston gallery, as John L. Sweeney suggests, that James had in mind in describing "the sky-lighted inner shrine of Tremont Street" where Strether had his "aesthetic adventure."

What James said of place names applies to his choice of Lambinet: "to name a place, in fiction, is to pretend in some degree to represent it."[12] The naming of, say, Corot or Millet, two of the better-known Barbizonists, would have entailed description suggestive of the popular styles of those painters—the blurred foliage and misty groves of the former, the pathos and social message of the latter's reapers and gleaners. In effect, any other typical minor landscapist would have served his purpose just as well, as long as the name did not require the kind of doing that would interfere with the general impression James wished to convey. It is the generic quality of this landscape school—the delight of these painters in the quiet moods of nature and their intimate treatment of it—that matters. Slow moving rivers that reflect a luminous sky and tangled willows, gently undulating

meadows and winding forest paths, light filtering through trees—
these are their recurring motifs; this is the "picture" James evokes of
French "ruralism," and this is a typical Lambinet. Also, how much
more ironic is Strether's failure to obtain the work of a minor painter
like Lambinet than it would be if it had been a master like Corot.

To what extent James consciously sought the effect I am about to
describe probably cannot be determined, but it seems to me that
when Strether enters the village where he plans to have his dinner, it
is no longer a Lambinet which is being described but an impressionist
canvas instead. First of all, the setting—an inn by a river with a pa-
vilion "at the garden's edge" almost overhanging the water, "testify-
ing, in its somewhat battered state, to much fond frequentation"
(NY, XXII, 255)—is one which the impressionists were especially fond
of painting. The boating party on the river, the open-air dance place,
the crowd in a café or a public garden—these were some of their favorite subjects. (In the synopsis for *The Ambassadors* that James sent
to Harpers he refers to the setting as "a suburban village by the river,
a place where people come out from Paris to boat, to dine, to dance,
to make love, to do anything they like.")[13] When, at the opening of the
next chapter, Strether sees "a boat advancing round the bend" containing "a young man in shirt-sleeves" and a lady "with a pink
parasol," it seems to him "suddenly as if these figures, or something
like them, had been wanted in the picture, had been wanted more
or less all day" (NY, XXII, 256). Here, however, is no longer, say,
Lambinet's *Fishing on the Banks of the Seine*, but Renoir's *Canotiers
à chatou* or Manet's *En bateau*. Lambinet's figures are peasants, men
and women indigenous to the countryside, dressed in rough everyday garb and absorbed in their everyday tasks; Renoir's and Manet's
are city dwellers—the men relaxing in shirt sleeves and the ladies
stylishly dressed, wearing charming hats and holding parasols—
sophisticatedly enjoying the simple pleasures of the picnic excursion.

And it is not subject alone that suggests a difference. A comparison
of descriptive phrases in the first part of the chapter with those in the
last part and in the opening of the next chapter reveals a significant
change in Strether's vision: "sunny silvery sky, the shady woody
horizon," "the sky was silver and turquoise and varnish; the village
on the left was white and the church on the right was gray" (NY,
XXII, 247)—this is how Strether sees initially. Color is presented
through adjectives, and the light is represented as concentrated in the
sky, not diffused throughout. That the horizon is "shady woody" suggests a traditional aerial perspective in which objects at a distance
appear blurred. In contrast, the primary emphasis in the description

of the village where he stops for dinner is not on the thing modified by the adjective; instead, adjectives are converted into substantives, a grammatical shift which places the emphasis on the sensory quality of the visual experience rather than on the thing itself. "The village aspect" affects him "as whiteness, crookedness and blueness set in coppery green; there being positively, for that matter, an outer wall of the White House that was painted the most improbable shade." Madame de Vionnet's parasol makes "a pink point in the shining scene." Color details are rendered with greater precision: the church is a "dim slate-color" on the outside; the stream is "gray-blue." Distant objects are not described as in conventional perspective. "The valley on the further side was all copper-green level and glazed pearly sky, a sky hatched across with screens of trimmed trees, which looked flat, like espaliers" (NY, XXII, 254–57).

This subtle shift from the description of a Lambinet to that of an impressionist scene reinforces the thematic development of the episode. The movement of the chapter is from Strether's identification of the picture with the landscape to his grasp of the implications of the identity, from the past to the present. But his understanding and acceptance of its meaning are not tested until the encounter with Chad and Madame de Vionnet; he is confronted with the moral of his text, which, as he has just interpreted it, is that if "one elected to move about" in this kind of world, "one had to make one's account with what one lighted on." Strether actually makes his account the next evening in the "high, clear picture" of Madame de Vionnet's rooms; "he was moving in these days, as in a gallery, from clever canvas to clever canvas" (NY, XXII, 273). As may be seen, the movement from the "special-green vision" of a Lambinet canvas, low toned and idyllic, to the color nuances and pleasure-trip theme of the impressionist canvas corresponds to the evolution of Strether's experience which is climaxed by his discovery that after all "he was mixed up with the typical tale of Paris" (NY, XXII, 271).

Other instances of this kind of pictorialism, striking in its variety, richness, and subtlety, should come readily to mind to the alerted reader. The same progression from description to evocation and symbolization may be traced in James's treatment of art objects and background in general. Early "European" stories like "A Passionate Pilgrim" and "Travelling Companions" are so overloaded with art description that one almost wonders whether James intended their interest to be in the description or in the story as a whole. Even the more economically constructed "The Madonna of the Future" con-

Plate V   James Joseph Jacques Tissot: *The Gallery of the H.M.S. Calcutta.*
(Courtesy of the Tate Gallery, London.)

Plate VI William Holman Hunt: *The Scapegoat*. (Courtesy of the Trustees of the Lady Lever Art Gallery, Port Sunlight, Cheshire.)

Plate VII   *Farnese Palace*. Designed by Antonio da Sangallo; top story by Michelangelo. (Photograph by Alinari.)

Plate VIII   Antoine Louis Barye: *Jaguar Devouring Hare*. (Courtesy of the Corcoran Gallery of Art.)

tains unassimilated and overextended descriptive passages; Howells felt that one of the charms of the story was its "dissertations on pictures."[14] Nevertheless, even the works of James's apprenticeship show evidence of an attempt to assimilate art details and action. For example, in "Travelling Companions" the hero's purchase of a spurious Correggio from a poverty-stricken Italian family serves more than one thematic purpose: the madonna portrayed resembles Charlotte Evans, with whom the hero, influenced by the romantic atmosphere of Italy, imagines himself to be in love; and the incident in which the "so mendacious and miserable" but "so civil, so charming"[15] Italians sell it to him is worked in with another theme—the painful underside of Italian beauty and picturesqueness. Pictures are also used throughout as a sign of sensibility: Charlotte is moved to recite a dozen verses from the Gospel of Mark when standing before a Tintoretto *Crucifixion*; her father prefers watching the pretty women in the Milan cathedral to climbing to its top. *Roderick Hudson* marks a further advance in this direction. Unlike Hawthorne's *The Marble Faun*, it would make a poor guidebook to Italy; the descriptions of places and art objects are too well integrated with the action. The scene in St. Peter's, for example, in which Christina is seen kissing the bronze toe of the holy statue is not only a touch of local color but a sign of her capriciousness and flair for the dramatic. She has given no signs earlier of being devout. By the time of *The Portrait of a Lady*, James had become expert in conveying a great deal by a single stroke: when the again-rejected Lord Warburton bids Isabel goodby in Rome, the scene takes place in the gallery of the Capitol with the "lion of the collection"—*The Dying Gladiator*—in the background.

While James never exempted himself entirely, not even in his highly poetic and dramatic novels, from the novelist's obligation to satisfy the reader's visual imagination, he soon learned to practice a wise economy in fusing much of what is normally called background with action and characterization. The art object is an especially important means of achieving this desired fusion, for it may be used simultaneously as a visual detail and as a symbol of a culture, superficially as a plot device, and more profoundly as a means of revealing character or reinforcing a theme. When the allusion is to specific paintings by actual artists or to an artist's style or to that of a particular period, James's ideal of economical richness is most fully realized.[16]

The effectiveness of this kind of imagery in James depends of course on the reader's knowledge of the particular qualities of the

painting or of the style of painting alluded to. Moreover, as his references to art reflect his own assumptions about artists and styles,
which, of course, he by and large shared with his cultivated contemporaries, a knowledge of James's taste enhances appreciation of the
image. To know, for example, that he had a "sneaking relish"[17] for
Sassoferrato, "sneaking" because he considered him basically shallow, an essentially decorative artist, like Decamps, elucidates the
observation in *Roderick Hudson* of this being the one picture Christina Light and her mother own and display. Fond though he was of
the Dutch and Flemish school, James associated style in the grand
manner with French and Italian art. Thus, Maria Gostrey's "little
Dutch-looking dining-room" with its "ideally kept pewter" and
"specimens of vivid Delf" (NY, XXII, 319) speaks for the kind of
haven she has to offer Strether. Madame de Vionnet's "grayish-white
salon" with its "fine *boiseries*, . . . medallions, mouldings, mirrors,
great clear spaces" and "consular chairs," "mythological bronzes,"
"sphinxes' heads" and "faded surfaces of satin striped with alternate
silk" (NY, XXI, 243–44) symbolizes her quite different appeal to his
imagination. Similarly, as I shall develop in chapter 8, "The Connoisseurs and the 'Free Spirits,' " in *The Golden Bowl* Renaissance
imagery underscores the grand style of the Prince and Charlotte, and
that of classical antiquity, the idealism of Maggie and Adam, a reflection of what these art styles represented to James. Appreciation of
Italian Pre-Raphaelite painting is usually in a story or novel by
James a sign of cultivation or an aesthetic temperament: both the
diarist and the young man in "The Diary of a Man of Fifty" like the
early Florentines best of all; the painter-hero in "Mrs. Temperly"
thinks her daughter is "like a figure on the *predella* of an early
Italian painting" (NS, XXVI, 269). As an Englishman of his type
would, Sir Claude, the step-father in *What Maisie Knew*, regards a
taste for primitives as a "silly superstition" (NY, XI, 112). *Seicento*
art is generally admired by people without taste: the gentleman
painter of "The Sweetheart of M. Briseux" is doomed to fail if for no
other reason than that he admires Guido Reni and Caravaggio. No
one but a conventional English gentleman like Sir Arthur in "The
Siege of London" could feel indifferent to French painting and prefer instead the art exhibitions at the Royal Academy.

James's novelistic artistry and visual sensitivity are revealed in the
precision with which he selected particular art objects to express
shades of meaning. One is rather surprised at first that Henrietta
Stackpole's favorite painting should be the tender, almost senti-

mental *Virgin Adoring the Child* by Correggio in the Uffizi. On second thought, this unexpected preference may be seen as revelatory: for all her crisp, official feminism she has a more personal, even maternal side, as demonstrated in her loyalty to Isabel. Other examples of this kind of subtle expressiveness may be found throughout James's works. The specific pictorial references in *The Wings of the Dove* are perhaps the most richly allusive and most textural.

That the moment Milly Theale stands before the Bronzino portrait she is said to resemble marks a climax has been often critically analyzed. New insight may be gained by considering the qualities of Bronzino's portraiture. It is necessary first, however, to go back a few pages to the beginning of the fifth book, which opens with Milly's "agreeably inward response to the scene."

The great historic house had, for Milly, beyond terrace and garden, as the centre of an almost extravagantly grand Watteau-composition, a tone as of old gold kept "down" by the quality of the air, summer full-flushed but attuned to the general perfect taste. (NY, XIX, 208)

Carried throughout this chapter and the next is her sense of the occasion as a Watteau picture. "The largeness of style was the great containing vessel, while everything else, . . . became but this or that element of the infusion . . . . Everything was great, of course, in great pictures, and it was doubtless precisely a part of the brilliant life— since the brilliant life, as one had faintly figured it, just *was* humanly led—that all impressions within its area partook of its brilliancy." For Milly the Matcham reception is *"the* revelation" of her personal success—the "parenthesis" in her life beginning with the dinner three weeks before at Lancaster Gate and closing "with this admirable picture" (NY, XIX, 208–9). Evocative of the delicacy of Watteau, though by no means descriptive of his palette, is the interwoven blue and pink and lavender imagery: "they were all swimming together in the blue"; Lord Mark was "personally the note of the blue"; people "in your wonderful country" seem to be kept in "lavender and pink paper," Aunt Maud says to Milly; Lady Aldershaw "was all in the palest pinks and blues." And when Milly stands before the picture "the beauty and the history and the facility and the splendid midsummer glow" melt together in her consciousness: "it was a sort of magnificent maximum, the pink dawn of an apotheosis coming so curiously soon" (NY, XIX, 213–23).

The meaning and feeling of Milly's response to the Matcham festivity are resonantly conveyed by Watteau, whose special subject is the revels of an aristocratic society—the garden party and the feast of love. His settings represent the atmosphere of the park opening into the depths of a misty expanse; the mood evoked is one of gaiety and refined pleasure. In a review of the Wallace Collection in 1873, James comments on Watteau's "perpetual grace," his "elegance and innocence combined," his "irresistible air of believing in these visionary picnics." His canvases are peopled by "gentle folks all," and he "marks the high-water point of natural elegance."[18] In comparing the scene to a "Watteau-composition," Milly is seeing it as a picture of social intercourse at its highest pitch. Her vision of English society, the Watteau image suggests, is, of course, an idealization; from another point of view, for example, Densher's, instead of natural elegance, English society seems most to exhibit natural stupidity. And its predatory nature, based as it is on a system in which everyone "works" everyone else, is a theme running throughout the book. Milly is not unaware of the jungle aspects of the social struggle; even in the Matcham scene she perceives how Mrs. Lowder, "a natural force," is working Lord Mark; but it is the beauty of the scene, all of its elements fusing into a picture of high civilization, to which she responds.

While the Matcham occasion is for her "then and afterwards . . . a high-water mark of the imagination" (NY, XIX, 210), it is when she is brought by Lord Mark face to face with her "sister" in the Bronzino picture that she has her moment of supreme realization:

Perhaps it was her tears that made it just then so strange and fair—as wonderful as he had said: the face of a young woman, all splendidly drawn, down to the hands, and splendidly dressed; a face almost livid in hue, yet handsome in sadness and crowned with a mass of hair, rolled back and high, that must, before fading with time, have had a family resemblance to her own. The lady in question, at all events, with her slight Michael-angelesque squareness, her eyes of other days, her full lips, her long neck, her recorded jewels, her brocaded and wasted reds, was a very great personage—only unaccompanied by a joy. And she was dead, dead, dead. Milly recognized her exactly in words that had nothing to do with her. "I shall never be better than this." (NY, XIX, 220–21)

Lord Mark misunderstands, thinking that by "this" she is referring to the picture. But still, "It was probably as good a moment as she should ever have with him. It was perhaps as good a moment as she should have with any one, or have in any connexion whatever" (NY, XIX, 221). In spite of all of her richness and splendor, the personage in the picture is "unaccompanied by a joy" *and* dead. Through Milly's identification with her, she at one and the same time feels most fully and intensely the possibilities of life and has the strongest premonition of her doom. Paradoxically, the portrait of the dead woman that has itself endured also seems to urge her to assert her will to live: " 'But I can go for a long time.' Milly spoke with her eyes again on her painted sister's—almost as if under their suggestion. She still sat there before Kate, yet not without a light in her face. 'That will be one of my advantages. I think I could die without its being noticed' " (NY, XIX, 227–28).

In selecting a Bronzino portrait rather than, for instance, a Titian or a Vandyke, James again reveals his sensitivity to overtone and his preference for the "full-fed statement." A Titian portrait would suggest splendor, and a Vandyke, elegance and refinement, but with neither could Milly so readily have identified. It is very likely that James actually had in mind the portrait of Lucrezia Panciatichi in the Uffizi (see plate XIII);[19] his description in spirit and in detail is remarkably like it. The hair, the neck, the richness of dress, the large hands are all there. The "recorded jewels" may refer to the legend inscribed on her green beads—"Amour dure sans fin," not inappropriate as an inscription to *The Wings of the Dove*. As is generally true of Bronzino's portraits, the social position of the sitter is apparent: the long nose, the long thin fingers, the richness of clothing and jewels, the magnificent apartness created by placing the figure in front of a dark background with only a suggestion of an arch or niche—all these characteristics establish the high social status of the subject. However, the painting is not just a representation of a distinguished, cultivated, elegant woman. The arms gracefully follow the lines of the body, the right hand lightly touches an open book (as if the sitter has just looked up and is holding her place), the left rests on the arm of the chair. But there is a tautness in the fingers, a slight strain in the posture, giving an impression of repressed inner agitation; the repose is qualified by the imperfectly hidden tension. Almost all of Bronzino's subjects have this air of strain, reserve, containment—a general characteristic of the mannerists, who, in reaction to the High Renaissance celebration of the beauty and vigor of the human body, expressed in their works the spiritual unease, a lack of faith in mankind and matter. Typically mannerist, Bronzino's figures are elongated and distorted; his subjects appear overgraceful and ascetic, worldly and spiritual, elegant and sad. What has been said of his men may also be applied to the woman in the Panciatichi portrait: "It is an aristocracy alike of the intellect and of the senses that Bronzino has immortalized for us. These men of the Florentine decadence are no [not] representatives of a thin refinement of culture. They have known everything and felt everything. They are beyond good and evil."[20]

Coming after the Watteau image, which conjures up a delicious imaginary world exempt from time and pain, good and evil, the Bronzino becomes a symbol of mortality; the elegance and splendor incompletely mask an all-pervading sadness and sense of mutability.

The Veronese images in the Venetian chapters also illustrate the special economy and richness of particular art references. The descriptions of Palazzo Leporelli are largely of the Palazzo Barbaro, a fifteenth-century Gothic structure on the Grand Canal. James describes it as a "magnificent house—a place of which the full charm only sinks into your spirit as you go on living there, seeing it in all its hours and phases."[21] The owners were Mr. and Mrs. Daniel Curtis, with whom he stayed in 1887—a visit planned to last ten days extended to five weeks—as well as in the 1890's. Enshrined in *The Wings of the Dove* are James's impressions of its "pompous Tiepolo ceiling," Gothic windows, and court with a high outer staircase.[22] Perhaps through association the Veronese images sprang to mind; according to a painting representing the interior of one of the Palazzo Barbaro salons at the turn of the century, there were two Veroneses—*The Rape of the Sabines* and *The Continence of Scipio*—on its walls (see plate XIV).[23] There is no need to seek a specific source for the image; James was introduced to this painter of sumptuous feasts and splendid decorations on his first visit to Venice. "Never was a painter more nobly joyous, never did an artist take a greater delight in life, seeing it all as a kind of breezy festival and feeling it through the medium of perpetual success," James wrote of the Veronese wall paintings in the Doge's Palace. Of the famous *Rape of Europa*, he declares, "Nowhere else in art is such a temperament revealed; never did inclination and opportunity combine to express such enjoyment. The mixture of flowers and gems and brocade, of blooming flesh and shining sea and waving groves, of youth, health, movement, desire—all this is the brightest vision that ever descended upon the soul of a painter."[24]

It is in chapter 28, Milly's occasion in honor of Sir Luke Strett, that the Veronese allusions are clustered.[25] The association of Veronese with the scene contributes to the atmosphere of splendor in which Milly is making her life. As the Princess, she is "lodged for the first time as she ought, from her type, to be," according to Susan Stringham. "It's a Veronese picture, as near as can be—with me as the inevitable dwarf, the small blackamoor, put into a corner of the foreground for effect" (as in Veronese's *Feast at the House of Levi*, in which a jester, both a dwarf and a blackamoor, crouches on the staircase in the foreground). Densher wonders what part he is to play, "with his attitude that lacked the highest style, in a composition in which everything else would have it?" Mrs. Stringham informs him that he is "in the picture"—he is to be "the grand young man who surpasses the others and holds up his head and the wine-cup" (NY, XX, 206–7) (the pose of the cupbearer in the *Marriage at Cana* in the Louvre).[26] Later, after dinner, Densher feels "the effect of the place, the beauty of the scene" acting to transform the guests, "who during the day had fingered their Baedekers, gaped at their frescoes and differed, over fractions of francs, with their gondoliers," into figures not out of place in a Veronese canvas. "Milly, let loose among them in a wonderful white dress, brought them somehow into relation with something that made them more finely genial; so that if the Veronese picture of which he had talked with Mrs. Stringham was not quite constituted, the comparative prose of the previous hours, the traces of insensibility qualified by 'beating down,' were at last almost nobly disowned" (NY, XX, 213). Milly acquits herself as a hostess "under some supreme idea, an inspiration which was half her nerves and half an inevitable harmony" (NY, XX, 214) so well that the Veronese image is almost apt. But while Milly's festival represents an active affirmation of her desire and will to live, to live in the Veronese style, the climax of this scene is Densher's extortion from Kate at last of what it is Kate expects him to do—" 'Since she's to die I'm to marry her?'. . . 'To marry her.' 'So that when her death has taken place I shall in the natural course have money?' . . . 'You'll in the natural course have money. We shall in the natural course be free' " (NY, XX, 225). Veronese's huge pictures—described by Bernard Berenson as "cheerful," "simple," "displaying childlike naturalness of feeling" and "frank and joyous worldliness"[27]—are pitched in quite a different key. As may be seen, the association of Milly's occasion with a Veronese canvas is also highly ironic, an irony which becomes apparent only in the light of Veronese's meaning as a painter.

James's cultivation of his visual senses yielded him rich rewards as a novelist. His allusions to works of art, the framing of scenes through pictorial metaphor, evocations of natural scenery, cityscapes, and portraits testify to the precision and delicacy of his visual perceptions, the depth of his response to works of art, and the power of his visual memory. But the extent to which and the way in which particular painters influenced his writing are extremely difficult, if

not impossible, to determine. There are between the arts, as Wallace
Stevens notes, "migratory passings to and fro, quickenings, Pro-
methean liberations and discoveries,"[28] but the attempt to isolate an
unequivocal passage of painting into writing with regard to technique as well as to subject or theme more often than not results in
absurd analogizing. The inescapable fact remains that there are
definite boundaries between the arts.

James's imagery and descriptive passages occasionally are traceable
to specific paintings, as with the Bronzino. Other examples may be
cited. Hyacinth Robinson's vision of the plebian Millicent Henning,
"(if there should ever be barricades in the streets of London) with a
red cap of liberty on her head and her white throat bared so that she
should be able to shout the louder the Marseillaise of that hour" (NY,
V, 164), calls to mind Delacroix's famous *Le 28 juillet, La Liberté
conduisant le peuple aux barricades*, which James, who admired Delacroix above all other nineteenth-century painters, could not have
missed seeing in the Louvre. The red-capped figure of Liberty, as
Walter Friedlaender observes, "is no allegory, but a *femme du peuple*
with bared breast and blowing hair, holding a flintlock and waving
the tricolor."[29] Hyacinth hardly seems sensual enough even to
imagine Millicent with her bosom exposed, but the effect is suggested
by "white throat bared." The sentence that follows contributes
further to the likeness: "If the festival of the Goddess of Reason
should ever be enacted in the British Capital . . . who was better
designated than Miss Henning to figure in a grand statuesque manner
as the heroine of the occasion?" (NY, V, 164–65). (The sad, intro-
verted, rather delicately featured young man in the foreground, somewhat dwarfed by the monumental figure of Liberty, could be a representation of Hyacinth!)

Similarly, the narrator's allusion in *The Aspern Papers* to Sardanapalus—he fears that Miss Bordereau like that Eastern potentate will
burn her treasures before she dies—probably originated in James's
remembrance of Delacroix's *Sardanapalus*, which greatly impressed
him when he first saw it in 1876,[30] rather than Byron's. Likewise, this
image in *The Golden Bowl* may very well have had its source in a
recollection of a painting: Maggie sees "as in a picture" why she has
not given in to "the vulgar heat of her wrong." "The straight vin-
dictive view, the rights of resentment, the rages of jealousy, the protests of passion"—this "range of feelings . . . figured nothing nearer
to experience than a wild eastern caravan, looming into view with
crude colours in the sun, fierce pipes in the air, high spears against

the sky, all a thrill, a natural joy to mingle with, but turning off short before it reached her and plunging into other defiles" (NY, XXIV, 236–37). Oriental subjects were a staple of romantic literature as well as of painting, but I think the image came not from a source such as *Salammbô* but from James's memory of a work by Decamps (see plate IV). "The picturesqueness—we might almost say the grotesqueness—of the East no one has rendered like Decamps," James comments in an art review of 1873. He "paints movement to perfection; the animated gorgeousness of his famous 'Arabs Fording a Stream' (a most powerful piece of water-colour) is a capital proof."[31] The striking feature of the painting which connects it with James's image is its representation of a moving file of Arabs on horseback, bristling with spears, seeming to come directly at the spectator but in the foreground veering to their right in order to cross the stream at the ford.

William Rimmer's *Flight and Pursuit* (see plate XV), with its mysterious running figures, receding arches, elaborately decorated walls, could be taken as a visual analogue to James's "immense hallucination"—his "dream adventure" as recounted in his autobiography—and also to Spencer Brydon's stalking, and being stalked by, his alter ego in "The Jolly Corner." The autobiographical passage, the night scenes in the late story, and Rimmer's picture are strikingly similar in mood and detail: two figures ambiguously pursuing each other, open and closed doors, strange vistas and penumbral light. E. P. Richardson considers the painting "one of the most passionately convincing and disturbing visions of nightmare painted in this century."[32] The story and to a lesser degree the memory passage match it in eeriness. There is no actual proof that James saw the painting, dated 1872, but as Rimmer was well known in Boston and a teacher of La Farge and Hunt, the chances are he had seen it.

The evidence that James was recalling Tissot's *The Gallery of the H.M.S. Calcutta* (see plate V) in describing Daisy Miller's frock is, however, more tangible. As John L. Sweeney notes, the description of Daisy as "dressed in white muslin, with a hundred frills and flounces, and knots of pale coloured ribbon" corresponds with that of Tissot's "pretty woman" in James's criticism of this picture: "She wears a dress of frilled and fluted white muslin, set off with a great number of lemon-coloured bows, and its air of fitting her well, and, as the ladies say, 'hanging' well, is on the painter's part a triumph of perception and taste."[33] James's over-all authorial attitude toward Daisy diverges from his view of the women in the painting, demon-

strating the way in which the literary artist may use a pictorial detail
for purposes unrelated to the work from which it derives. In the review he implies, moreover, that the interest of the painting is limited
by Tissot's failure to characterize his women other than as merely
fashionable, "a stylish back and yellow ribbons." Contrastingly,
Daisy's clothes are more than a social notation: where and how she
has learned to dress in exquisite high fashion is a mystery; the verdict of her Europeanized American critics is that she has not acquired
correspondingly good, or even acceptable, taste in behavior. But her
innocence in the end is verified; her nickname Daisy, not her fashionable exterior, designates her essence: pure, naïve, a child of nature,
unable to compromise with or adapt to a sophisticated environment.

A reasonable case may be made for the visual sources of all of these
images and descriptive passages, but it should be noted that each
image, and description, necessarily seen with the mind's eye, is only
one stroke on James's canvas, whereas the assumed prototype may
have literary and historical meaning but is essentially self-contained
and appeals directly to the viewer's visual and tactile senses. Even
more important, despite James's remarkable ability to suggest the
spirit of individual works of art, it is the subject that is transposed
into fiction; the technique of describing a scene as a picture is intrinsically different from that of painting it.

In the analysis of the Lambinet passage, it is shown how James's
word choice and syntax are attuned to the conveying of sensation and
thus produce the effect of an impressionist vision of the scene. It
seems to me highly probable that James's knowledge of impressionist painting influenced his way of seeing but only indirectly his method of rendering in prose an impressionist scene or any other. His was
almost to begin with a picturesque vision, that is, he responded to the
play of light and shadow, color and movement detached from the
object. The impressionists, who carried to an extreme the tendency to
detach appearance from object and who rendered shadow not devoid
of color but only less bright, may have increased his awareness of
atmospheric effects and of the influence of light on color. Through
their treatment of contemporary life, he may have come to realize the
pictorial qualities inherent in certain settings. In addition to the
passages in *The Ambassadors* discussed, as F. O. Matthiessen suggests,
the scene in which Strether and Madame de Vionnet have luncheon
in the restaurant on the quay could, in terms of the treatment of
textures, light, and color and in the informality of Madame de Vionnet's pose, be a description of an early Renoir canvas.

Both William Morris Hunt and John La Farge had the impressionist eye, though they did not practice the technique of the color spot,
rainbow palette, broad brush stroke, and color perspective invented
by Pissarro, Monet, Renoir, and others of the school. Also, through
his associations with them in the Newport days, James was exposed to
their belief that "one should be alive to the crowding impressions
of life, instead of arranging one's ideas in any definite or schematic
way."[34] But the specifically impressionist characteristics of James's
style, for example, the conversion of adjectives into substantives so
that the quality, not the form, of the thing is emphasized, could not
have been precisely learned from the technique of painting anyhow.
The way in which James saw the physical world and apprehended
reality was shaped by pictorial experience, but his method of expressing his vision of reality, a method paralleled in, for example,
Flaubert, Daudet, and Loti, had to be developed within the possibilities and limitations of his own medium. What James had in common
with the impressionist painters was his view of the interrelatedness
of all experience, of consciousness as unfixed and unstable, and his
emphasis on the subjective aspects of experience. This summary of
the impressionist vision might be used to characterize one aspect of
James's:

A world, the phenomena of which are in a state of constant flux and transition, produces the impression of a continuum in which everything coa-
lesces, and in which there are no other differences but the various approaches
and points of view of the beholder. An art in accordance with such a world
will stress not merely the momentary and transitory nature of phenomena,
will not see in man simply the measure of all things, but will seek the
criterion of truth in the "hic and nunc" of the individual.[35]

But only one aspect, for as Ian Watt observes, "James's continual
need to generalise and place and order, combined with his absolute
demand for a point of view that would be plastic enough to allow him
freedom for the formal 'architectonics' of the novelist's craft, eventually involved him in a very idosyncratic kind of multiple Impressionism."[36] The characteristic tensions in James that set him apart
from a style of his period are intrinsic to a post-Renaissance style—
mannerism. His relation to mannerist painting and sculpture is an
instance of, in Henri Focillon's words,

affinities and accords far more subtle than those which preside over the
general historical groupings of mankind. There exists a kind of spiritual
ethnography which cuts across the best-defined "races." It is composed of
families of the mind—families whose unity is effected by secret ties, and who

are faithfully in communication with one another, beyond all restrictions of time or place. Perhaps each style, each state of a style, even each technique seeks out by preference a certain state of man's nature, a certain spiritual family. In any case, it is the relationships between these three values which clarify a work of art not only as something that is unique but also as something that is a living word in a universal language.[37]

The qualities of James's art which make him a member of the mannerist family should be apparent. The mannerist style developed in reaction to the High Renaissance ideal of isolation and balance of parts, as reflected most purely in the works of Raphael's mature period. Once thought merely to represent a decay of the Renaissance idea, it is now recognized as a separate style in painting which by 1520 was fully developed, by 1550 had degenerated, and by 1590 was sterile and conventionalized.[38] In High Renaissance art the object in nature was subordinate to established canons of proportion and harmony; it was to be treated not as an optical impression but as "heightened and idealized to something objective and regular."[39] In contrast, the mannerist approached nature subjectively, defying established rules of perspective, proportion, and composition. For the mannerist it was not a question of creating the object as one might or should or does see it, but as, to quote Friedlaender, "from purely autonomous artistic motives, one would have it seen."[40] Not attempting to represent the object according to what would be viewed as natural, the mannerist stretched limbs and fingers, broke up symmetry, dissolved figures in space—all for the sake of a particularly personal and rhythmic feeling for beauty. As exemplified by the works of Parmigianino, Tintoretto, Bronzino, and the Michelangelo of the Medici Chapel and of the anteroom of the Laurentian Library, mannerist art lacks the repose and stability of the High Renaissance as well as the turbulent struggle and triumphant resolution of the baroque. It is an art of preciosity, of intricate asymmetrical patterns leading to no final solution, of subjects treated from unexpected angles, of "rigid formality and deliberate disturbance, bareness and over-decoration."[41]

Various theories have been offered to explain the development of the mannerist style, but the most widely accepted seems to be that it was an expression not merely of dissatisfaction with the perfection of High Renaissance art but of the spiritual ferment of the times. As Hans Tietze observes in reference to Tintoretto's emphasis of material phenomena to express spiritual meanings: "The Renaissance affirmed and achieved reality both in life and in art. The period which followed it endeavored to discern in this dominated reality an image of metaphysical essence."[42]

The quality in James's art which has led to his being called a "romancier 'metaphysique' "[43] by T. S. Eliot, an "idealistic realist"[44] by Joseph Warren Beach, and a seeker of "the sacramental sensibility"[45] by R. W. B. Lewis is what relates him to the mannerist tendency to spiritualize the material world. Not born in a society rich enough in manners and social institutions to engage his imagination and unable to become immersed in the life of an alien culture, at least not in the sense that George Eliot and Balzac did in their own, he converted his preternatural sensitivity to surface appearances into an instrument for the revelation of moral meanings. In his preface to *The Tragic Muse* James mentions that in pondering over the problem of how to unify his two separate stories— "his political case" and "his theatrical case"—he asked himself, "Were there not . . . certain sublime Tintorettos at Venice, a measureless Crucifixion in especial, which showed without loss of authority half a dozen actions separately taking place? Yes, that might be, but there had surely been nevertheless a mighty pictorial fusion, so that the virtue of composition had somehow thereby come all mysteriously to its own."[46] But there is another sense in which, as shown in this quotation from an early essay, fusion in Tintoretto spoke to James's imagination:

Before his greatest works you are conscious of a sudden evaporation of old doubts and dilemmas, and the eternal problem of the conflict between idealism and realism dies the most natural of deaths. In Tintoret, the problem is practically solved, and the alternatives so harmoniously interfused that I defy the keenest critic to say where one begins and the other ends. The homeliest prose melts into the most ethereal poetry, and the literal and imaginative fairly confound their identity.[47]

The parallel in James's art to this mannerist characteristic of Tintoretto, who as Tietze notes, "makes form dissolve into matter and matter into form,"[48] is his masterly "interfusion" of psychological nuances with descriptions of things, so that through the inanimate thing the essence of the spiritual reality is revealed. However, both James's often tortuous, involuted late style and Tintoretto's twisted lines and tormented restless forms reflect an unresolved tension in their efforts to reconcile physical and psychical existence.

The irresoluteness of James's endings is suggestive of the mannerist style—the struggle for repose which lacks a final triumph. By irresoluteness I do not mean that James's works are not rounded-off, self-contained works of art, but rather that one is often left with a disturbed feeling because the solution is rarely presented with finality. Isabel Archer returns to Rome, but why and to what? Nick Dormer has, indeed, given up the political life for the artistic, but is his painting of Julia Dallow a sign that he will become the fashionable success that Gabriel Nash has predicted? In her renunciation of Owen Gereth and the spoils of Poynton, Fleda Vetch remains true to her finer instincts, but how is Owen's desire that she have a valuable object from Poynton to be regarded?

This ambiguity is partially attributable to James's approach to subject. In an essay on Flaubert, James states that the novelist may stand in two different relations to his subject and the treatment of it: "The more he feels his subject the more he *can* render it—that is the first way. The more he renders it the more he *can* feel it—that is the second way."[49] The second way is not only Flaubert's, but the evidence of the notebooks and the prefaces alone testifies to its being James's way as well.

Ever aware of the necessity for fiction to be in touch with life, James nevertheless created his motives for behavior as he worked out his subject, subordinating questions about human actions and emotions that other novelists might feel compelled to treat to his larger artistic purpose. In the detailed work sheets for *The Spoils of Poynton* in the notebooks, for example, Owen's marital fate is a foregone conclusion. As the focus is to be on Fleda's consciousness, whether he is subsequently happy or miserable is not revealed. As with the mannerist painter, it is not nature as seen by the ordinary person or by the conventions of another art style that was James's concern but rather nature as he would have it seen, hence, the superintelligence and hypersensitivity of James's characters, the probing dialectical conversations which in real life one cannot imagine sustained by even the most perceptive and highly cultivated beings, and the omission except through implication of drives and passions. What James said in an essay of 1892 about Tintoretto's *Marriage at Cana* at the Santa Maria della Salute is applicable here: "There could be no better example of the roving independence of the painter's vision, a real spirit of adventure for which his subject was always a cluster of accidents; not an obvious order, but a sort of peopled and agitated chapter of life, in which the figures are submissive pictorial notes."[50] For both painter and novelist, the schemata are first; the figures from life are treated as elements in the composition, subordinated to the prevailing artistic rhythm.

James's late style may be called either mannered or mannerist, depending on whether one views his hesitations and qualifications, his inversions and twisting of syntax, and his mingling of literary with colloquial language as artifice masking lack of content or as a mode of expression reflecting painstaking effort to communicate with precision refinements of feeling and thought. The mannered style is not always easily distinguished from the mannerist: when a figure in a painting is represented scratching his left ear with the right hand, his arm extended over his head, it may be a cliché of style and hence empty of meaning, or it may be the only possible way within a design to express a mood. One may point out instances in James in which the style is maddeningly overwrought, but on the whole his late style represents an effort to penetrate meanings deeply and subtly. But while this working out of detail "with a goldsmith's care . . . makes for an enormous gain in insight and precision . . . the total effect is frequently lost sight of."[51] James himself did not lose sight of the "total effect," but in spite of a classical feeling for balance and proportion, his tendency toward elaboration often resulted in works with the misplaced middle—overdevelopment in the first half necessitating radical foreshortening in the second. This asymmetry and preciosity in detail is characteristic of both mannerist architecture and painting.

Mannerist style, in the visual arts and correspondingly in literature, is the expression of a sensibility that cherishes the ideals of serenity and harmony but that, in an age of uncertainty and disruption of traditional values, must create out of its own consciousness order and beauty. To see James as belonging to this style family does not exempt him from negative critical judgment. Insofar as parallels between the arts may be pursued, however, this placement helps to account for, if not to justify, characteristics of language and structure that otherwise seem baffling and eccentric.

THROUGHOUT his career, from "A Landscape Painter" (1866) to "Mora Montravers" (1909), the visual artist, chiefly the painter, appears frequently in James's fiction. While the painter may be a secondary or minor character, in some works, such as "Madame de Mauves," "Four Meetings," *The Europeans*, and *The Ambassadors*, he is of crucial symbolic importance, standing for the possibilities of corruption or fulfillment in a way of life more hedonistic than the other characters have known or approve of. In numerous others, the artist is used more superficially: in many instances he is an amateur, his sketching and painting a sign of gentility or "niceness." Miss Frush in "The Third Person" and Mr. Bolton-Brown in "Lord Beaupré" fall into this category. At other times, the artist himself is less important than his studio: here persons, usually separated by national or class barriers, may easily meet. In *The Reverberator* Waterlow's studio provides a likely place for the socially unplaced American girl Francine Dosson to meet the aristocratic Gaston Probert and his sister Madame de Cliché. Beyond this kind of social notation, the artist serves as the narrator or center of consciousness, as in "A Landscape Painter," "The Impressions of a Cousin," "Glasses," and in part *The Europeans*. Or his portraits, expressions of his innermost feelings and insight, expose the character of the sitter and inadvertently himself, as in "The Story of a Masterpiece" and "The Liar." The identification of the artist with intelligence and moral perception is in James almost a reflex: though Fleda Vetch has studied impressionist painting in Paris, she is not depicted as an artist. She is shown as feeling the beauty of Poynton too strongly to be able to paint there. That she may be driven to try to sell her work to support herself adds indirectly to a sense of her vulnerability. Poor and apparently neither very talented nor inwardly compelled to paint, she can avoid dependence on her sister only by marriage. Perhaps by having her study impressionist painting, however, James wished to point up the contrast between her disinterested, open observer consciousness and Mrs. Gereth's creative but acquisitive collector's imagination. In his notes for *The Ivory Tower*, dealing with the problem of how to make his "Young Man. . . . *most* special," James expresses a desire "to steer clear of the tiresome 'artistic' associations hanging about the usual type of young Anglo-Saxon 'brought up abroad'; though only indeed so far as they *are* tiresome." With excruciating qualifications he works it out later: "Heaven forbid he should 'paint'—but there glimmers before me the sense of the connection in which I can see him as more or less covertly and waitingly, fastidiously and often too sceptically, conscious of possibilities of 'writing.' " As this quotation suggests, as much as James may have wished to avoid what he felt was by now a cliché, he could not help associating the " 'intelligent' . . . exposed and assaulted, active and passive 'mind' engaged in an adventure and interesting in *itself* by so being" with the artistic temperament.[1] Indeed, though James distinguishes between the artist and the artistic temperament, for example, Roderick and Rowland, Nick Dormer and Gabriel Nash, his observer characters with moral sensibility are endowed with the artist's vision and disinterestedness.

There is also a considerable body of fiction in which James deals directly with aesthetic problems. Through the depiction of the painter or sculptor, whose art is correlative to his own but whose media allow for more visually immediate and dramatic treatment, he deals with questions common to the artist generically: Should art be imitation or idealization of reality? What is the relation of craft to inspiration and of the necessity of experience to that of detachment? What are the artist's human responsibilities, and how is he to balance his needs as a man with the claims of his art? What part do social and physical setting play in furthering or hampering creativity? The link between the works in which aesthetic themes are treated directly and those in which the artist is a symbolic figure or the hero or heroine has the artistic temperament is ultimately epistemological, resting on James's conception of the artist as seer, not in the Emersonian religious sense, but in that expressed in the well-known phrases of "The Art of Fiction": "When the mind is imaginative—much more when it happens to be that of a man of genius—it takes to itself the faintest hints of life, it converts the very pulses of the air into revelations."[2]

Beginning with his earliest works James shows the successful artist as needing more than the gift of seeing the real in a visionary light. To be the greatest of artists one had to have it, but to be an artist at all one had to compromise the vision by descending to produce. This point is the central message of "The Madonna of the Future" and one of the conclusions, though more ambiguously arrived at, of *Roderick Hudson*, both works reflecting the tension in James's taste between the classical and the painterly, the idealized and the realistic.

In the parablelike story, Theobald, the American painter in Florence, has devoted his life to adding a thought to his conception of the perfect madonna which he expects someday to paint. As preparation, he spends his days communing with old masterpieces, especially Raphael's *Madonna of the Chair*, his "model at once and muse."[3] Similarly, "bending towards her in a sort of Platonic ecstasy" (p. 294), he worships Serafina, the woman whom he eventually hopes to use as a model because of her "divine" beauty. In reality, she is middle aged and coarse grained, but living as he does in a visionary world, Theobald does not perceive this. When the narrator forces him to see her and himself as they really are, Theobald realizes that he has wasted all of his powers in preparation for the masterpiece he will never paint. Although he has Raphael's brain, his hand is paralyzed. He is half a genius. "Where in the wide world is my other half?" he cries. "Lodged perhaps in the vulgar soul, the cunning, ready fingers of some dull copyist or some trivial artisan who turns out by the dozen his easy prodigies of touch!" (p. 319). He now sees that he has been too uncompromising; he has "taken it all too hard! Michael Angelo didn't when he went at the Lorenzo! He did his best at a venture, and his venture is immortal" (p. 318).

Theobald speaks better than he knows. His "other half" is lodged in the "vulgar soul" of Serafina's lover, who specializes in making figurines of cats and monkeys. Salacious caricatures of human beings, they illustrate "chiefly the different phases of what, in delicate terms, may be called gallantry and coquetry." The narrator finds these figures "cynical and vulgar" and "their imitative felicity . . . revolting." Symbolic of the artist's materialism, they are made of a new substance which he claims is indestructible, and his skill in reproducing physical likeness corresponds with his base view of human nature: "Truly, I don't know whether the cats and monkeys imitate us, or whether it's we who imitate them" (pp. 313–14).

The artist who tries to create only sublime art, by drawing his inspiration from masters supposed to have been truly inspired and waiting for a similar vision to descend, is stultified. Neither pushed by the public, as Michelangelo and Raphael were by their church and patrons, nor religiously inspired, Theobald fails because he does not realize that art requires craft and a more direct, immediate relation to life, his model. The conclusion that the artist can only do "his best at a venture" is not strange from the pen of a writer who kept the pot boiling when necessary and whose commercial works sometimes turned out to be minor masterpieces. On the other hand—and this point is equally important—the skillfully imitative materialistic artist who does not believe in intellectual beauty at all degrades reality. We are not cats and monkeys.

Theobald is portrayed as deluded, a victim of unbridled aspiration. Pathetic rather than heroic, he nevertheless has a kind of nobility and, as he admonishes the narrator, is "worthy of respect. Whatever my limitations may be, I'm honest. There's nothing grotesque in a pure ambition or a life devoted to it!" (p. 281). Further evoking sympathy for Theobald are society's loss of faith in him, as represented by Mrs. Coventry, and the crassness of his artistic opposite. Theobald's striving for the ideal has a poignancy comparable with that of Isabel Archer's desire to transcend the limitations of the conventional, socially defined self. That the artist must descend "into the vulgar effort and hazard of production" is a tragic limitation, but not an endorsement of a realism that denies the spirit. In portraying the realist as a cynical caricaturist and the romantic idealist sympathetically, James expresses his belief that while the artist must risk his ideal by immersion in the actual, without an ideal at all his work, no matter how clever or technically successful, will be base.[4]

The idealistic-realistic antithesis is further developed in *Roderick Hudson*. While James characterized Roderick as an "idealist," he was not himself enamoured of contemporary ideal sculpture. The visitor to the sculptor's studio in 1870 found mainly two kinds of works: either the ideal statue or the portrait bust, the former representing the victory of mind over matter, the latter the reverse. The titles of the ideal statues differed, but the statues were all bone white and smooth, all weak copies of poor Roman imitations of Greek statues. The portrait busts, mostly of politicians and rich American tourists, suffered not from idealization but from overelaborate detail or from the sculptor's efforts to combine the real and the ideal, as for example, Horatio Greenough's seminude Washington, draped in a sheet and posed as a Phidian Zeus. James did not have a high opinion of Gibson, the follower of Canova, the first of the neoclassicists, and one suspects that he thought even less of Gibson's pupil, the ebullient Harriet Hosmer, one of the last exponents of the pure neoclassical. Her friends, James remarked much later, were better than her work.[5] Through the character of Mr. Leavenworth, the rich widower "travelling to distract his mind," who orders from Roderick "an allegorical representation of Culture" for the morocco and gilt library of the "little shanty" he is having built, James broadly satirizes the crudity of patrons and the contemporary taste for the ideal.[6] Pausing before Christina Light's bust, Mr. Leavenworth presumes it is an "ideal head . . . a fanciful representation of one of the pagan goddesses—a Diana, a Flora, a naiad, a dryad?" (p. 272). He would not have had to ask that question of Hiram Powers' "ideal head," *Diana*; her fillet unmistakably identifies her as the goddess of the moon (see plate XVI).

Roderick, however, has higher aims than to make mere "fanciful representations" of pagan goddesses. Caring only for "perfect beauty," he hopes to create art in the grand style that will arouse "a kind of religious awe in the presence of a marble image newly created and expressing the human type in superhuman purity" (p. 107). Like Theobald, he views art as a high priesthood and himself as a kind of god. When Gloriani protests, "You don't mean to say you are going to make over in cold blood those poor old exploded Apollos and Hebes?", Roderick replies that their names do not matter: "They shall be simply divine forms. They shall be Beauty; they shall be Wisdom; they shall be Power; they shall be Genius; they shall be Daring. That's all the Greek divinities were." Furthermore he intends to do "all the Forces and Mysteries and Elements of Nature . . . . I mean to do the Morning; I mean to do the Night! I mean to do the Ocean and the Mountains, the Moon and the West Wind. I mean to make a magnificent statue of America" (p. 108).

Between Leavenworth's "Culture" and Roderick's colossal America squeezed into a classical form, there is not much choice. Treated to his theories at the dinner given in his honor, Roderick's listeners respond to his rhetoric with some skepticism: Madame Grandoni perceives similarities between his work and one of Overbeck's pupils, "a votary of spiritual art," who also had "highflown pretensions," which came to nothing. He married a buxom Roman model, who beat him and finally left him, and when last heard of he "was getting his living by painting views of Vesuvius in eruption on the little boxes they sell at Sorrento." Augusta Blanchard, painter of "dew-sprinkled roses, with the dew-drops very highly finished," or of peasants kneeling with their backs turned at wayside shrines ("She did backs very well, but was a little weak on faces") thinks Roderick's *intensions* "rather abstract." Gloriani predicts that he will not keep it up, because "passion burns out, inspiration runs to seed," the artist waits "in vain for the revelation to be made, for the Muse to descend. He must learn to do without the Muse!" (pp. 101–13).

But Rowland, who "had his apprehensions" about Roderick's theorizing, "for he knew theory was not his friend's strong point," is pleased to see him sitting there "in radiant ardor, defending idealism against so knowing an apostle of corruption as Gloriani" (p. 109). Roderick's extravagant defense of idealism is in part "mere magnificence of speech," and preposterous or quaint as his ambitions may seem contemporarily, clearly the reader is supposed to sympathize with the young man's aspirations to create sublime masterpieces, just as Theobald is meant to elicit pity, not ridicule. Roderick's lofty aims and innate powers are intended to make his destruction seem all the more tragic and wasteful. As was pointed out in the earlier analysis of James's aesthetic, he himself believed in the 1870's that the artist should consciously aim at the creation of beauty. He paid deference to the sculpture of antiquity, conventionally thought to embody ideal beauty, though he was most moved by the contorted, expressive art of Michelangelo and to a lesser degree by the realistic work of the early Florentines. And as for contemporary sculptors, he commented most favorably, not on the realists, but on academic artists, such as Dubois and later Saint-Gaudens, who worked in the Renaissance tradition. Dubois, James felt, at least had a vision of ideal beauty even though it was only imperfectly and even somewhat pedantically realized in sculptural form. The description of Roderick's Adam might apply to one of Dubois's works:

There was something especially confident and masterly in the artist's negligence of all such small picturesque accessories as might serve to label his figure to a vulgar apprehension. If it represented the father of the human race and the primal embodiment of human sensation, it did so in virtue of its look of balanced physical perfection, and deeply, eagerly sentient vitality. (p. 95)

Unlike Story's anecdotal statues or Rogers's groups, Roderick's are expressive through form itself, as James believed Dubois's to be. But this description hardly convinces us of Roderick's genius. James's contemporaries, especially if they could discriminate between the better and worse works of this type, might have been more easily convinced. For us, it requires suspension of our knowledge of art history. We must assume, as James did, that it is possible for a sculptor working in the academic tradition to produce vital art. At best, we can imagine Roderick's having the potentialities of a Saint-Gaudens.

To what extent are the artist characters in *Roderick Hudson* representations of the artist colony of the 1870's in Rome? At the beginning of his first visit to Rome in 1869 James complained of his isolation, but before he left he had become acquainted with some of the Americans and on subsequent visits renewed and extended his relationships in the Anglo-American colony.[7] From letters, memoirs by contemporaries, and his own reminiscences, we catch a glimpse of him at Mrs. Wister's, trapped with her husband and Mrs. Fanny Kemble into listening to William Wetmore Story reading his tragedy *Nero*, a torture for which James justly avenged himself later in an anonymous review of the published play. We see him visiting the Luther Terrys, who were installed in great frescoed rooms in the Palazzo Odescalchi, climbing the circular staircase in the even more famous Palazzo Barberini to the Gallery to see Guido Reni's *Beatrice Cenci*, immortalized in Hawthorne's *The Marble Faun*, and riding to the Villa Medici to partake of hospitality offered at the French Academy "under high *lambris* . . . in the presence of Poussinesque tapestries and an occasional bland great lady."[8] But though Rome even in the early seventies still had the character of a provincial town, its moss-covered ruins only beginning to be stripped by archaeologists and its quiet squares pierced by modern boulevards, everyone did not know everyone else: the greatest American sculptor of James's generation, Augustus Saint-Gaudens, was also in Rome from 1870 to 1875 (including the time of James's extended six-month visit in 1873), but apparently the two men did not meet until much later, not until James's 1904 visit to America.[9]

It has been assumed that in his portrayal of Roderick James had in mind Story, the most flashily successful sculptor of the Roman-American group. Actually, Roderick is modeled after him only to the extent that like Story he comes from New England and has studied law. The differences in background are sharper than the similarities: Story's father was a distinguished Supreme Court judge, and his son, far from being "superlatively primitive," as Roderick is, began his career abroad with the maximum of culture New England could provide. In contrast, Roderick's father is a Southern ne'er-do-well who drinks himself to death; the Southern strain in Roderick is apparently supposed to help account for his instability and flamboyance. Roderick, having wasted his brief college days, is shown as wonderfully receptive to culture in Rome but as initially crude and ignorant. Moreover, Roderick's best statues are decidedly not "clever"—an adjective James applied to Story's work and one not used ordinarily to describe what he considered to be deeply imaginative work—and are free from the fussy details and accessories of which Story was fond.

A much better case might be made for James's drawing on Story for Hudson's foil, Gloriani, and on William Morris Hunt's personal characteristics for Roderick. Hunt, it will be recalled, personified for James the artist: his powers of mimicry, his colorful turns of speech, his habit of contradicting himself through a kind of verbal exuberance, even his leanness have their counterparts in Roderick. An instance, perhaps, of life imitating art, Hunt, his strenuous social life apparently absorbing energies which could otherwise have been applied to his art, died, like Roderick, mysteriously—probably a suicide —and in the opinion of qualified critics, with his artistic promise unrealized.

The similarities between Gloriani and Story must not be pressed too far. It is Gloriani, not Roderick, to be sure, who is "consummately clever" and who loves the sensational subject so dear to Story's heart— Judas "nursing his money-bag and his treachery" (p. 106) and a "magnificent Herodias" (p. 172). James probably had Story in mind in his creation of Gloriani insofar as the latter is depicted as a superficial, successful, technically tricky sculptor who knows what will appeal to the public. But James associated his fictional character with French realism, whereas Story was completely out of sympathy with realist practices and doctrines.[10] Story had his *succès fou* at the 1861 London exhibition; his draped anecdotal figure of Cleopatra was just unusual enough in subject matter and conventional enough in treatment to appeal to Victorian taste. Gloriani's works, on the other hand, are "considered by most people to belong to a very corrupt, and by many to a positively indecent school. Others thought them tremendously knowing, and paid enormous prices for them; and indeed, to be able to point to one of Gloriani's figures in the shady corner of your library was tolerable proof that you were not a fool" (p. 98). Reviewing in 1875 an exhibition of realistic animal sculpture by Barye (see plate VIII), James remarked that "to have on one's mantel-shelf or one's library table one of Barye's businesslike little lions diving into the entrails of a jackal, or one of his consummate leopards licking his fangs over a lacerated kid," was the mark not "of a refined, but at least of an enterprising taste."[11] Likewise, "magnificent goldsmith's work," a phrase James applied to Gloriani's statues, could just as aptly have described Barye's, as they are at times overloaded with minute decorative detail. This is not to say that

Barye was the prototype of Gloriani but rather that in characterizing Gloriani's works James had in mind the realistic style initiated by Barye.

Moreover, Rowland, who is not enthusiastic about Gloriani's sculpture, expresses James's own mixed feelings about the antineoclassical sculpture of the time. Carpeaux's *La danse*, James said, in 1876, evoked in the visitor to Paris feelings of "mingled admiration and perplexity." "If to seize and imprison in clay or marble the look of life and motion is the finest part of an artist's skill, he [Carpeaux] was a very great artist," he observed. The strength of the "if" may be judged by his further comparison of Carpeaux's "undressed lady and gentleman" with the "unconsciously naked heroes and heroines of Greek art." Carpeaux's "poor, lean, individualized bodies," he felt, were "pitifully real."[12] James admired much more wholeheartedly the academic Paul Dubois.[13] Not Carpeaux, whose works James considered "the most modern things in all sculpture,"[14] nor Rodin (Barye's pupil), nor Rosso strove to create beauty of line but aimed instead at creating emotional or dramatic values through effects of light and surface movement. Moreover, Gloriani, whose sculpture is "quite the latest fruit of time," is a mouthpiece for orthodox realistic doctrine: according to him, "there is no essential difference between beauty and ugliness. . . . they overlap and intermingle in a quite inextricable manner; . . . there is no saying where one begins and the other ends; . . . hideousness grimaces at you suddenly from out of the very bosom of loveliness and beauty blooms before your eyes in the lap of vileness; . . . it is a sad waste of wit to nurse metaphysical distinctions, and a sadly meagre entertainment to caress imaginary lines; . . . the thing to aim at is the expressive, and the way to reach it is by ingenuity." Thus James, who chastised in 1876 the impressionists—ultrarealists, in his eyes—for considering the beautiful "a metaphysical notion" and for believing that "it will come at its own pleasure" and that the artist's "proper field is simply the actual,"[15] was hardly in sympathy with Gloriani's theory and practice. From what is known of his reactions in the 1870's to this school, it may be assumed that Rowland expresses James's own art views.

Foils to the neoclassic Roderick, neither the realist Gloriani nor the patient plodding watercolorist Singleton is capable of creating great art as neither has the combination of vision and skill which James felt was prerequisite. Gloriani in *Roderick Hudson* represents "art with a worldly motive, skill unleavened by faith, the mere base maximum of cleverness"; Singleton, "aspiring candor, with feeble wings to rise on"; while Roderick seems "the beautiful image of a genius which combined sincerity with power." The Ruskinian overtones are obvious: Gloriani, like the animal sculptor in "The Madonna of the Future," stands for the artist who can never produce art of the highest order no matter how great his skill, that is, his ability to create "speaking likenesses" of models or pleasing formal patterns of line, mass, and tone. James still assumed with Ruskin that motive or purpose in art was crucial: what distinguishes great from mean art in Ruskin's familiar words is the "nobleness of the end to which the effort of the artist is addressed." Gloriani has no faith, no transcendental intention; he merely seeks to create interesting aesthetic effects and to represent material reality. Roderick, on the other hand, has power, that is, not merely technical ability but the capacity to express noble emotions through formal design. He is, moreover, sincere, meaning that not only does he express through his art his own personality but he eschews formulas. An insincere artist ultimately is true neither to himself nor to natural appearances.

In *Roderick Hudson*, then, while James grants Gloriani talent and, more important, the will and craftsmanship Roderick lacks to make the most of his talents, Gloriani's art is clearly not of the highest order.[16] But it is questionable if Roderick's theory of art is really disproved by his destruction. Shortly after Gloriani's warning, the Muse does fail to descend, and Roderick has no other resources on which to draw. He starts on his road to destruction, Christina Light reappearing on the scene soon after to give him a good push. His conception of art is at fault insofar as he is encouraged by it to create only that which is positively beautiful: at the mercy of a divine influx to create divine beauty, he thinks he can do nothing at all during the intervals between inspirations. He refuses to compromise, to produce an art of effects which is empty of ideas, such as Gloriani's, or to plod along, learning what he is about by doing as Singleton has. But he does not suffer from the loss of skill which destroyed Theobald, and, in fact, his last statues are neither failures nor purely ideal works. These last works, the portrait busts of Christina Light and Mrs. Hudson, are supposedly exquisite. When he sees the latter, Gloriani congratulates Roderick and apologizes for his earlier predictions that he would not be able to keep it up. Neither statue, it should be noted, is completely realistic, as are the works of Gloriani and the cats-and-monkey artist. Roderick in each one succeeds in reproducing a likeness which yet transcends mere appearance. Each shows that "critical return upon reality,"[17] that elusive quality which for James distinguished truly imaginative works of art from the simply technically skillful or merely realistic. In these last efforts, Roderick has succeeded in embodying his vision of ideal beauty in the real. His failure ultimately is not so much the result of the weakness of his theory as of his character.

In one sense, in *Roderick Hudson* James was testing Ruskin's assumption that a bad or weak man could not make good art. Roderick's smashing of Striker's portrait bust in his Northampton studio is the first disturbing sign of his future destructiveness. Aware though he is of Roderick's character defects—his extravagance, self-indulgence, instability—Rowland believes in the "essentially good health of the sincere imagination. A man may be *all* imagination—if he *is* sincere." Roderick, after a fortnight in Rome,

gave Rowland to understand that he meant to live freely and largely, and be as interested as occasion demanded. Rowland saw no reason to regard this as a menace of dissipation, because, in the first place, there was in all dissipation, refine upon it as one might, a grossness which would disqualify it for Roderick's favor, and because, in the second, the young sculptor was a man to regard all things in the light of his art, to hand over his passions to his genius to be dealt with, and to find that he could live largely enough without exceeding the circle of wholesome curiosity. Rowland took immense satisfaction in his companion's deep impatience to *make something* of all his impressions. (p. 85)

Roderick, however, after his initial spurt of inspiration runs its course, seeks renewal in "experience," in gambling, drinking, and lovemaking in wicked Baden-Baden, and eventually justifies the continuation of his pursuit of Christina, even though he is betrothed to Mary Garland, on the grounds that men of genius are exempt from the moral rules that are binding on other men. He says to Rowland, "A mother can't nurse her child unless she follows a certain diet; an artist can't bring his visions to maturity unless he has a certain experience. You demand of us to be imaginative, and you deny us that which feeds the imagination. In labor we must be as passionate as the inspired sibyl; in life we must be mere machines. It won't do" (pp. 201–2). In short, artists must be allowed "to live on their own terms and according to their inexorable needs!" (p. 202). Having recovered some of his animation through an accidental encounter with Christina, Roderick asks Rowland for money in order to be able to follow her to Interlaken and gives as his reason that only she has the power to revive him. Roderick subscribes to the belief that his "inclinations" and his will are closely connected, that he can no more choose to work than decide to stop chasing Christina; presumably if his passion for her were gratified, his will to work would return.

Rowland initially disagrees with Roderick's view of his helplessness, but he comes to feel that there is a connection between the sculptor's failure as a human being and as an artist. Rowland is willing to grant Roderick as a genius larger moral leeway than is allowed the ordinary person, but when the artist ceases to invest his experience in his work, instead indulging in it for its own sake, both the artist and human being suffer. Unlike the painter Baxter in "The Story of a Masterpiece," whose "artist half . . . exerted a lusty dominion over the human half—fed upon its disappointments and grew fat upon its joys and tribulations,"[18] Roderick's human half asserts itself at the expense of his art, and he even uses his art to rationalize his self-indulgence. But it is Roderick's lack of moral awareness, his blindness and insensitivity to the feelings of others, more than any of his overt acts that shakes Rowland's belief in the "essential salubrity of genius." He comes to wonder if egotism does not make for the failure of the artist as it makes for failure of conduct. Only the "complete" man can be the "complete" artist, and it "dimly occurred to him that he was without a heart" (p. 198).

The theme of character and creativity is also carried out almost diagrammatically in the other artists. The contriver of clever, sophisticated, unconventional art, Gloriani is highly intelligent, frank, worldly. Unlike Roderick, he has converted his youthful wildness into art: having wasted a fortune in his youth, he has worked for the past fifteen years perfecting his talent. Even now his unconventional private life—Madame Gloriani is not his wife—does not interfere with his work; his type of work does indeed reflect his history and unorthodox relationship. Like her pictures, Augusta Blanchard is pedantic, old-maidish, overrefined. She abandons her conventional art for a conventionally good marriage. Singleton is shy, retiring, dependable: when filial and fraternal duty calls from Buffalo (his father and five unmarried sisters), he replies.

Near the end of the book, incongruously reminiscent of Natty Bumppo's heroic entry in *The Prairie*, Rowland and Roderick see projected on the slope in the Alps the giant shadow of small Singleton before he himself appears. Scarcely a person at all, colorless, patient, modest, single-mindedly devoted to his work, Singleton really is a successful artist. But his success is only relative. By making Singleton a water-colorist, James placed intrinsic limitations on his achievements. Because his genre is a minor one, James seems to imply that his was a minor although true talent. He does not have Roderick's potential for greatness, but he has made the most of his talent through patient industry and a self-abnegation of which Roderick is incapable.[19]

Similarly, suggesting the close relationship between the artist's character and his work, each of Rowland's statues marks a stage in his experience of life. His Waterdrinker represents Roderick himself in Northhampton: "youth, you know; he's innocence, he's health, he's strength, he's curiosity," and the cup symbolizes "knowledge, pleasure, experience" (p. 25). Roderick's first Roman statues, Adam and Eve, are symbolic of his almost godlike powers; his success with the Adam 'partook, really, of the miraculous" (p. 95). But his statue of the "listening" woman, made after his Baden-Baden interlude, is not "topping high art"; it is clever and superficial. Gloriani likes it, taking it as evidence that Roderick has come down to earth. He asks Rowland what has happened to the sculptor—"Has he been disappointed in love?" (p. 133).

If James intended to articulate his themes through the statues, the question might well be asked why the succeeding works by Roderick are not shown to be more degenerate as the sculptor grows increasingly more irresponsible and unfeeling. The last completed works mentioned are the artistically successful portrait busts of Christina and Mrs. Hudson. Christina awakens in Roderick his dormant vision of ideal beauty; his mother, his filial piety. The trouble is that he comes to think of Christina's beauty as his own property. He feels it is his because, as he says, "no one else had studied it as I had, no one else understood it" (p. 441). Instead of having "handed over his passions to his genius to be dealt with," he has allowed his passions to enslave his genius. (In James's other works, either the artist's relation to his model is impersonal, or the act of painting is a sublimation of the artist's feeling. In *The Tragic Muse*, for example, Nick Dormer's interest in Miriam as a subject precludes his falling in love with her. Probert, in *The Reverberator*, assumes that the painter Waterlow cannot have fallen in love with Francine because his portrait of her is exceptionally good.) Later, after a long sterile period, the sight of his mother's anxious and loving face awakens in Roderick a "plastic" idea, but the spell is momentary. Then Christina's marriage breaks some final spring of the will: by this time it is too late for him to try to follow Rowland's advice to "set to work and you *will* feel like it" (p. 210). It is in character that the artist who can be only either "ass" or "angel" should end with a crash, not dwindle away. There are no other works to symbolize his deterioration because it is marked by the absence of productivity itself.

While as a development of the ideas about art in the novel Roderick's cataclysmic end is justifiable and logical, the abruptness of his breakdown is not plausibly rendered, a criticism James himself makes in his preface: "We conceive of going to pieces—nothing is easier, since we see people do it, one way or another, all round us; but this young man must either have had less of the principle of development to have had so much of the principle of collapse, or less of the principle of collapse to have had so much of the principle of development."[20] But it is not alone the failure to suggest passage of time to allow for more gradual distintegration that is a weakness in the characterization of Roderick. The portrait of him as a genius would have been more convincing if it had been more of a sculptor and less of someone with the artistic temperament. Except for descriptions of his statues, Roderick could equally well have been a painter or a poet. Even when Roderick complains about the sculptor's dearth of subject matter as compared with the painter's wealth of opportunity, since the painter has only to respond to the visual aspects of a subject, this point is only made to show Roderick's rationalizations, his inability to exert his will. Granted that it would have been difficult to suggest qualities in Roderick's sensibility that differentiated him from any other artist, it is conceivable that with greater technical knowledge of the craft James could have done so. While James did Rome, he did not adequately represent the atmosphere of the studio or describe his works sufficiently in sculptural, nonliterary terms. Another self-criticism does not seem to me equally valid. James notes that "the determinant function attributed to Christina Light, the character of well-nigh sole agent of his catastrophe that this unfortunate young woman has forced upon her, fails to commend itself to our sense of truth and proportion."[21] Actually, as has been pointed out, the seeds of Roderick's destruction are present in his character to begin with. Christina is responsible only in a qualified sense. It is his incapacity to experience freely and objectively—his crippling egotism —that makes it possible for him to be destroyed by her.

The aesthetic questions in *Roderick Hudson* are not definitively answered. James subjects the romantic genius to the test of experience, and he fails. But none of the other artists has true genius, and none has the radiance with which James attempted to invest Roderick, whose face in death appears "indescribably, and all so innocently, fair."[22] What clearly emerges, however, is that the artist

must maintain a delicate balance between involvement in, and detachment from, experience. He must be allowed more than the usual
freedom from conventional moral codes, but abuse of this freedom
can destroy him.

On the other hand, respectability may also be death to the artist.
This belief is suggested in the character of the genteel Miss Blanchard
and her flower paintings. In other stories James underscores this idea
even more heavily. Harold Staines in "The Sweetheart of M. Briseux"
has all the hallmarks of gentility, good breeding, and decorum, but
his very conventionality prevents him from achieving artistic success.
It is the dirty, hungry, disreputable-looking Bohemian, M. Briseux,
who paints the masterful portrait of Staines's fiancée. Again, in the
much later "Mora Montravers" there is the contrast between the
would-be artist, the gentleman, who exemplifies middle-class propriety, and the real artist, who is socially outside but artistically very
much inside the pale. One of the lessons the artist in "The Real
Thing" learns is that "in the deceptive atmosphere of art even the
highest respectability may fail of being plastic" (NY, XVIII, 343).

II

According to his Notebooks, James intended in "The Real Thing" to
represent the ineptness of the impoverished society couple as models,
illustrating "once again the everlasting English amateurishness—the
way superficial, untrained, unprofessional effort goes to the wall when
confronted with trained, competitive, intelligent, *qualified* art—in
whatever line it may be a question of."[23] The superiority of the professional over the amateur in the "art" of modeling is, however, only
one facet of the completed story. More important is the treatment of
the artist's relation to his subject and of art to reality. By 1892, the
date of this story, James had discarded the Ruskinism of the Italian
art stories, had become more sympathetic to impressionism, and had
changed his art settings and art types, but he was concerned with
some of the same questions: the nature of inspiration and imagination; the artist's approach to his subject, whether generically or
specifically; his responsibilities to himself as an artist and as a moral
being. In "The Real Thing," however, there are significant changes
in emphasis: the "ideal" is clearly discarded in favor of the "actual,"
(the Monarchs are superseded by Oronte and Miss Churm); however,

the "actual" is not literal fact transcribed but what the artist perceives, what the fact stimulates him to see. Moreover, while the
artist's imagination nourishes itself on actuality, the produced work
of art is ultimately more real than the object represented.

Applying for work as models, the Monarchs assume that because
they are the genuine article, a real lady and gentleman, it will be to
the artist's advantage to use them for his illustrations of fictional
gentility. The artist is disappointed when he finds out that they have
come to apply for jobs as models because, in his words, "in the pictorial sense I had immediately *seen* them. I had seized their type—I had
already settled what I would do with it. Something that wouldn't absolutely have pleased them, I afterwards reflected" (NY, XVIII, 310).
They might make admirable subjects for one picture, their own, but
as models for others they prove to be failures. At first the artist thinks
Mrs. Monarch might be acceptable for the conventional stories of
society people; for the stereotyped fictional work, the real stereotype
of gentility might serve. But even for *Cheapside* illustrations of bad
novels, she will not do because she can only be the type of society
woman that the artist first perceives her to be. (Similarly, the artist in
"The Beldonald Holbein" assumes that the woman who looks like
a Holbein could sit for only one or two paintings but could not be a
model.) The model, like the actress, must be able to play different
roles; Mrs. Monarch has the "defect of the lack of representation."
In contrast, Miss Churm, the blowsy little Cockney girl, has a
"curious and inexplicable talent for imitation." "She was a meagre
little Miss Churm, but was such an ample heroine of romance. . . . she
could represent anything, from a fine lady to a shepherdess" (NY,
XVII, 321). In her line she is an artist, and therefore her representation of the lady is truer than any single example of one, such as Mrs.
Monarch.

The model has to have histrionic ability because the artist is afraid
of being dominated by a type, as he explains:

I cherished human accidents, the illustrative note; I wanted to characterise
closely, and the thing in the world I most hated was the danger of being
ridden by a type. I had quarrelled with some friends about it; I had parted
company with them for maintaining that one *had* to be, and that if the
type was beautiful—witness Raphael and Leonardo—the servitude was only
a gain. I was neither Leonardo nor Raphael—I might only be a presump-
tuous young modern searcher; but I held that everything was to be sacrificed
sooner than character. When they claimed that the obsessional form could
easily *be* character I retorted, perhaps superficially, "Whose?" It couldn't
be everybody's—it might end in being nobody's. (NY, XVIII, 327)

Unlike Roderick or Theobald, who aiming to represent ideal types place the "obsessional form" before empirical reality, this "young modern searcher" believes in working from the individual to the general. Characterize the individual, and the typical will take care of itself. When his Italian servant-model, Oronte, plays the part of a hero in a story, he is the individual character, but by virtue of his successful portrayal of the one he also represents the class. The artist's illustrations based on the Monarchs are bad because they themselves are typical, conventional, and generalized. He is attempting to represent what is already an abstraction. Reality is embodied in the concrete individual which Miss Churm or Oronte pretend to be.

Moreover, when the artist uses Mrs. Monarch, he finds himself trying "to invent types that approached her own" (NY, XVIII, 327), instead of making her own transform itself. The drawings of the Monarchs look exactly like them, except that they come out comically tall, whereas in the drawings of the professional models Oronte and Miss Churm are so transformed as to be unrecognizable. The artist does not attempt to, nor, in fact, can he, reproduce literal reality: "When I drew the Monarchs I couldn't anyhow get away from them—get into the character I wanted to represent; and I hadn't the least desire my model should be discoverable in my picture. Miss Churm never was, and Mrs. Monarch thought I hid her, very properly, because she was vulgar; whereas if she was lost it was only as the dead who go to heaven are lost—in the gain of an angel the more" (NY, XVIII, 334).

Nowhere more effectively than in this story does James demonstrate the "fatal futility of Fact."[24] Not aiming at copying the model line for line, the artist reproduces on paper or canvas his vision of reality; his subject is not life in the raw but his apprehension of life. As Étienne Gilson notes, "the origin of the creative process is not sensation itself, but, rather, the response of the imagination to the stimuli of the sense perceptions."[25] The artist paints the model as he sees her, and the function of the model is to stimulate the artist's vision. "A studio was a place to learn to see," the artist's friend maintains, "and how could you see through a pair of feather-beds?" (NY, XVIII, 340)—meaning the Monarchs. The finished work, moreover, is different in kind from the real thing; art clarifies, transforms, stylizes life. The real thing, as the artist points out, is indeed lost, but what is gained is truer and everlasting.

Nevertheless, the narrator's last words do not elevate art above life, understood in the sense of mental experience. In the opinion of Hawley, representing the pure artistic conscience, the Monarchs do

Plate IX Tintoretto: *The Last Supper*. San Giorgio Maggiore, Venice. (Photograph by Alinari.)

Plate X James Abbott McNeill Whistler: *Arrangement in Black,
No. 3: Sir Henry Irving in the Character of Philip II of Spain
in Tennyson's "Queen Mary."* (The Metropolitan Museum of
Art, Rogers Fund, 1910.)

Plate XI   John Singer Sargent: *Daughters of Edward D. Boit.* (Courtesy of Museum of Fine Arts, Boston; gift of the daughters of Edward D. Boit in memory of their father.)

Plate XII Émile Charles Lambinet: *Fishing on the Banks of the Seine.* (Courtesy, Museum of Fine Arts, Boston, Bequest of Ernest Wadsworth Longfellow.)

the narrator "a permanent harm, got me into false ways." That in fact his work is "harmed" is left in doubt; the narrator concludes the story with *"If it be true* I'm content to have paid the price—for the memory" [italics mine] (NY, XVIII, 346). What he has learned is that to save his talent he has to drop the Monarchs even though they desperately need him simply not to starve. Human good will does not make good art, and the artist is not portrayed as heartless in eventually getting rid of them, though the "law in virtue of which the real thing could be so much less precious than the unreal" is "perverse and cruel" (NY, XVIII, 345). That the narrator should have been satisfied to "pay the price" for the sake of the "memory" ends the story on an equivocal note, however. Perhaps it is only meant to round off the story, which *is* the memory. In view of the Monarchs' plight, it seems insensitive, for what is implied is that their existence is now significant only as an object for the mind to contemplate. But the question of the artist's human responsibility to the Monarchs has already been settled: only if he were a saint or a fool could he continue to use them in any capacity. What is at issue in this last exchange is, I believe, "consciousness"—the memory—as opposed to art; for the narrator, and one presumes James here, a gain in awareness could justify artistic loss.

Whereas one of the conclusions to be drawn from "The Real Thing" is that the painter's perceptions are his subject matter and may in themselves have a value beyond perfection in art, *The Sacred Fount* seems to deny the necessity of verifying the objective reality that is the artist's starting point. The action consists almost entirely of the perceptions of the narrator; from his observations at a country house where he is a visitor for the weekend, he constructs an elaborate theory about the relations among four other guests. He evolves his theory from the assumption that in a love relationship one person enjoys physical and mental life at the expense of the other. At the end, his theory, his "palace of thought," is declared by one of the four to be a "house of cards," but it is neither proved nor disproved by the facts of the case. The reader never learns what the facts are; the novel shows, by its very inconclusiveness, that the narrator's theory is no less real and true than the reality or truth of the existing relationships.

Neither the narrator's identity, nor his occupation, if he has one, is revealed, only that he is immensely clever, subtle, creative, vain, possibly mad. Significantly, however, the only other character who disinterestedly sympathizes with the narrator's pursuit of truth and who also constructs a theory, albeit in the opinion of the narrator, an inadequate one, is the painter, Ford Obert, R.A. In fact, it is Obert who assures the narrator when he expresses scruples about searching out other people's secrets that the search is "made not only quite inoffensive . . . but positively honourable, by being confined to psychologic evidence. . . . resting on psychologic signs alone, it's a high application of intelligence. What's ignoble is the detective and the keyhole" (NY, XXIX, 52) Obert has some of the narrator's own "constructive joy," and the narrator takes comfort in "the painter's sense deeply applied," though in this instance he thinks it falls short of his own insight.

The intellectual kinship between the narrator and the painter signifies that the narrator's quest is essentially the same as any artist's. Through this identification of the painter with the observant and, in this instance, obsessively percipient being, James suggests that creativity and perception are closely connected. In both *The Sacred Fount* and "The Real Thing," the facts are relevant only as a starting point; the artist constructs his work from his apprehension of facts, his consciousness of them. What matters, then, is the nature of the artist's perceptions, not the kind or amount of crude experience he enjoys or is exposed to. (Whether James loses more than he gains by so intellectualizing experience that he, in effect, denies all of the senses but one—the visual—is another question altogether.) The artist must live and live fully, but the degree to which he lives depends on the quality or reach of his imagination.

All of James's sensitive, perceptive characters are in effect artists, though they do not paint or write.[26] When Lambert Strether turns to little Bilham in that crucial scene in Gloriani's garden and passionately urges him not to miss life, as Strether feels he himself has missed it, what he means by life is the fullest development of consciousness: "It doesn't so much matter what you do in particular, so long as you have your life. If you haven't had that what *have* you had?" (NY, XXI, 217) Strether tells Bilham, and that Bilham has understood Strether in this sense is clear from what he says to Strether on a later occasion: "Didn't you adjure me, in accents I shall never forget, to see, while I've a chance, everything I can? and *really* to see, for it must have been that only you meant" (NY, XXI, 278). Similarly, in *The Europeans* in answer to Gertrude Wentworth's question, "What ought one to do? . . . To give parties, to go to the theatre, to read novels, to keep late hours?" Felix Young replies, "I don't think it's what one does or one doesn't do that promotes enjoyment. . . . It is

the general way of looking at life."[27] And just as the painter in that
early contrast between New England conscience and European
epicureanism seems most to enjoy life, the person who seems to
Strether to have lived the most is the sculptor Gloriani. In part,
Strether is dazzled by Gloriani's sheer success—the honors and ac-
claim which "crown him . . . with the light, with the romance, of
glory." The great artist is also a kind of natural aristocrat as he meets
a Duchess's "latent insolence" with "equal resources," is "beautiful"
to his *cher confrères*, and is the "same to everyone." His guests include, little Bilham tells Strether, "always artists" and "then *gros
bonnets* of many kinds—ambassadors, cabinet ministers, bankers, gen-
erals, what do I know? even Jews. Above all always some awfully nice
women—and not too many; sometimes an actress, an artist, a great
performer—but only when they're not monsters; and in particular the
right *femmes du monde*. You can fancy his history on that side—I
believe it's fabulous" (NY, XXI, 199).

But Gloriani's great artistic, worldly, even sexual success is but
the outer sign of that "terrible life," that "tigerishness" in him,
which makes Strether envious of him. It is not the quantity or variety
of sensations which constitutes the measure of Gloriani's aliveness.
What Strether is especially to recall in his meeting with the artist is

the penetrating radiance, as the communication of the illustrious spirit
itself, the manner in which, while they stood briefly, in welcome and response, face to face, he was held by the sculptor's eyes. He wasn't soon to
forget them, was to think of them, all unconscious, unintending, preoccupied though they were, as the source of the deepest intellectual sounding
to which he had ever been exposed. (NY, XXI, 197)

It is significant that Strether is struck by Gloriani's penetrating eyes.
"You've all of you here so much visual sense that you've somehow all
'run' to it" (NY, XXI, 206), Strether observes, and Gloriani as an
artist "runs" to it more than anyone else. Indeed, a keen visual sense
in James's work is a sign of a penetrative imagination. It is for this
reason that artists are extremely useful to James as narrators or
characters whose point of view is adopted. At the same time that they
take in impressions of the physical world, they see deeply into characters and human motives. They have the painter's special perspicac-
ity which makes them sensitive to the inner life as well as to physical
beauty. Florian Daintry, through whose painter's eyes James created
one of his best atmospheric pictures of Boston ("A New England
Winter"), is one of the few characters with trained visual powers who
is also shallow and even unfeeling. Daintry exhibits the inherent

limitations of impressionism; one of the dangers of the impressionist technique, James believed, was that in its emphasis on quick perception it sacrificed depth of feeling and meaning which emerge only through contemplation and familiarity with a subject.

After the previously quoted observation that Strether makes about the high development of the visual sense in Paris, he adds,

"There are moments when it strikes one that you haven't any other."

"Any moral," little Bilham explained, watching serenely, across the garden, the several *femmes du monde.* "But Miss Barrace has a moral distinction," he kindly continued; speaking as if for Strether's benefit not less than for her own. (NY, XXI, 206–7)

The implication is that surface beauty and "social beauty" (Christof Wegelin's phrase)[28] are not necessarily disconnected from morality: in order for the artist to see truly he must be free of prejudgments and preconceptions, "obsessional forms." The visual sense is opposed not to morality but to a narrow moral code. On the other hand, if a person does not have imagination, the life or work of art will be only superficially attractive. As Strether finally realizes, Chad, who speaks of Madame de Vionnet as he would of "roast mutton," lacks it and thus "moral distinction." Like Roderick, whose decline is dramatized through drinking, gambling, and women but whose basic flaw is egotism, Chad is unable to identify freely with others. Eventually, he acts according to the dictates of the Woollett code, though for his own reasons. His art is purely formal, and, as has been observed, it is especially fitting that he should return to take up advertising, the ultimate in form without content. In contrast, Strether comes to see more and more deeply and truly as he divests himself of his Woollett moral blinders. *The Ambassadors,* James notes, is a "demonstration of this process of vision."[29] In the end, it is probably more than his feeling for Madame de Vionnet that prevents his accepting the companionship offered by Maria Gostrey. He cannot allow himself to gain anything material because he makes a distinction between the rightness of his attempting to subvert his original mission and the rightness of profiting from the attempted subversion. From another point of view, however, Strether's reward has to be, as it is for all creative minds, immaterial; the artist's deepest satisfactions are intellectual, subjective, and Strether has the artist's imagination. Like the narrator in "The Real Thing," he is left with a memory; unlike John Marcher, he has lived. Strether "with his wonderful impressions," as Miss Gostrey puts it and not entirely facetiously, will have got a good deal—all, of course, within the value structure of the

Jamesian world. The emotionally spent atmosphere of the last pages, however, fully conveys the awareness of what Strether has missed and now sacrifices without the compensations of the artist whose medium is not life itself.

III

Even before *The Tragic Muse,* James had "a nursed intention" to " 'do something about art' . . . the conflict between art and 'the world' striking me thus betimes as one of the half-dozen great primary motives."[30] While in this novel of 1890 he treats this theme on the largest scale, paralleling the careers of the painter and the actress, he, in fact, touches on aspects of the conflict in earlier works, though as in Roderick's case, the "social" is not clearly separated from the personal. Given his own history of transatlantic movement before settling in England, it is not surprising that James should have cast the question in national terms. He defines the special problems of the English artists explicitly as follows:

In France the artist finds himself, *ex officio,* a member of a large and various society of fellow-workers; whatever may be his individual value, his basis or platform is a large and solid one, resting upon social position and public opinion. He has to make a work a success, but he has not, as happens in England, where the vivacity of the artistic instinct appears to have been checked in a mysterious manner by the influence of Protestantism, to justify and defend his point of view. His point of view is taken for granted, and it may be said that his starting-place is the point at which, after much superfluity of effort, the artist in other countries arrives.[31]

The American artist's difficulties went beyond that of the necessity "to justify and defend his point of view." Deprived of that familiar list of items from castles to Eton which the Englishman could take for granted, the American artist had to overcome more than Philistinism and Protestant hostility to art. According to contemporary orthodox opinion, Rowland in offering to take Roderick to Italy is providing him with what he needs to develop as a sculptor.

Until about 1876 (the date of the Philadelphia Centennial Exposition, after which Paris and Munich became the dominant training centers for all American artists) a year in Italy was generally considered a necessity for American sculptors; in 1859 William Cullen Bryant counted thirty such expatriates in Rome.[32] Their reasons for going were numerous: partly they went in search of atmosphere and community, for according to Henry T. Tuckerman, one of the leading American art critics of the period, while American artists were better paid than ever before, they suffered from a "lack of enlightened public sympathy and extensive accesable [*sic*] resources for self-culture."[33] In America there were neither schools for sculptors nor competent critics and enlightened patrons; the horror of the nude and suspiciousness of art displayed by Mrs. Hudson and Striker, the lawyer, were typical of the times. How bleak Boston or New York seemed compared with Rome where one could, as noted by William Wetmore Story, hear a single soprano voice chanting the lamentations of Jeremiah "floating out like a glass thread in the great interior"[34] of St. Peter's or spend a quiet afternoon at the Baths of Caracalla! The artist's life, as James himself described it, was full not only of "solitary" but of "social joy." That "there is inspiration in the very atmosphere of Italy, and that there, one intuitively becomes artistic in thought,"[35] in the words of Harriet Hosmer, was the common view of artist expatriates and students. Other attractions of Rome for the American sculptor—also as reflected in James's novel—were the trained craftsmen available to translate clay models into marble and bronze, easy access to the only marble considered aesthetically pleasing, and "celestially cheap" rents even in a Bernini palace or "the luck of a lodging that was a minor masterpiece of early eighteenth-century *tarabiscotage*."[36]

But even in *Roderick Hudson* doubts are expressed about expatriation: on the verge of departure for Europe, Rowland Mallet, looking at the "far-spreading" view in a Connecticut River valley, is filled with a "strange feeling of prospective regret. . . . 'It's a wretched business,' he said, 'this practical quarrel of ours with our own country, this everlasting impatience to get out of it. Is one's only safety then in flight? This is an American day, an American landscape, an American atmosphere. It certainly has its merits, and some day when I'm shivering with ague in classic Italy, I shall accuse myself of having slighted them' " (pp. 29–30). With this, Roderick launches into a characteristic defense of American art, but he soon forgets about "National Originality" when Rowland makes it possible for him to go to Rome. In time, he becomes, like Theobald, guilty of that "superstitious valuation of Europe" which James felt Americans had to fight against. Significantly, it is Singleton, who looking at a photograph of the Waterdrinker, says to Roderick, "If you could do as well as this there [Northampton] . . . one might say that really you had only to lose by coming to Rome" (p. 110).

Whether or not Roderick would have succeeded at home and the extent to which his downfall may be attributed to the heady Roman atmosphere are moot points. Roderick's Waterdrinker evokes in Rowland the same response as the classical sculpture he has seen in the Louvre and the Vatican, and the Waterdrinker is described in words very similar to those James used to characterize *Jeunesse* by the contemporary academic French sculptor Mercié. Singleton goes home to Buffalo apparently to paint not New York State scenery but the Roman campagna and Swiss valleys; he returns with a suitcase bulging with sketches of European landscape and scenery to be used as a basis for future works. Similarly, the artist in "A Landscape Painter" dreams, as Roderick has, of creating a national masterpiece, but he visualizes it as a Renaissance *fete champêtre*, not, say, as a Winslow Homer:

One of these days I mean to paint a picture which in future ages, when my dear native land shall boast a national school of art, will hang in the *Salon Carré* of the great central museum, (located, let us say, in Chicago), and remind folks—or rather make them forget—Giorgione, Bordone, and Veronese: A Rural Festival; three persons feasting under some trees; scene, nowhere in particular; time and hour, problematical. Female figure, a big *brune*; young man reclining on his elbow; old man drinking.[37]

As the American artist's work is conceived by James as ideally a continuation of European styles and subject matter, then obviously the artist stands to gain by the European experience.[38] The choice between Europe and America as far as art training alone is concerned is scarcely presented as a real dilemma in *Roderick Hudson*, but James, habitually undogmatic, allows for the wisdom of skepticism. Striker, the man most unsympathetic to Roderick's art aspirations, makes the most "pregnant sense" on the subject: "Well, if our young friend's booked for fame and fortune, I don't suppose his going to Rome will stop him. But, mind you, it won't help him such a long way, either. . . . The crop we gather depends upon the seed we sow. He may be the biggest genius of the age: his potatoes won't come up without his hoeing them" (p. 58).

James also touched on the problem of expatriation in other contexts. He expressed the view in an 1890 essay on the illustrator Charles S. Reinhart that cosmopolitanism may be detrimental to the artist as it deprives him of a characteristic style or stamp, but in the story "Collaboration" one of the characters asserts that "in art there are no countries—no idiotic nationalities, no frontiers, nor *douanes*, nor still more idiotic fortresses and bayonets. It has the unspeakable beauty of being the region in which these abominations cease."[39] Consisting mainly of a mulling over of the conflict between art and patriotism, the story takes place in an American painter's Paris studio, which has an air, the painter narrator maintains, "as international as only Parisian air can be" (p. 100). He has to warn the American journalist Bonus, whose main interest is the progress the American "boys" are making in Paris, against writing criticism which is more "American" than "critical." Patriotism is put in its place most dramatically by the penniless French writer Vendemer and the German composer Heidenmaur, who decide to join forces to compose an opera. The collaboration costs Vendemer his anti-German fiancée—she and her mother have lost "husband, father and brother" in the Franco-Prussian war—and his public as well. Heidenmaur, in turn, loses his allowance from his brother, who is anti-French. "The really damnable, the only unpardonable, sin" against "the religion of art," according to Vendemer, is "the hideous invention of patriotism" (p. 132).

In the Story biography James again takes up the question of expatriation, noting that in Rome the artist lapsed "from the strenuous . . . in spite of an Overbeck, of an early Ingres, of other academic phantoms, unless stiffened, as in the case of the Niebuhrs and even of the Ampères, for some effort of the quite heroic sort" (I, 329). Rome, James thought, was an antidote to the "dryness and dreariness" of "Anglo-Saxondom," but "the medium was one, in fact, in which that hard grain [of concentration] was apt richly to dissolve" (I, 331). What was really crucial, however, was not place but "artistic insistence": "the act of throwing the whole weight of the mind, and of gathering it at the particular point (when the particular point is worth it) in order to do so. This, on the part of most artists—or at least on the part of those who are single in spirit—is an instinct and a necessity, becomes in fact the principal sign we know them by" (II, 216–17).

In short, while James does not deny that some places are more conducive to creativity than others, concentration is what matters most. In practice, this means that the artist really worthy of the name must be not only willing but in some sense impelled to sacrifice national interests, material gain, and love when they interfere with his work.

The Tragic Muse sums up all of the lures of the world which a man must resist in order to be an artist. Earlier works touch on the world's, that is, polite society's, lip service to art: for Mrs. Coventry in "The Madonna of the Future" it has meaning mainly as tea talk; like Eliot's women who "come and go/talking of Michelangelo," she wears on her bosom a "huge miniature copy of the Madonna della Seggiola" and "enjoyed the dignity of a sort of high priestess of the arts" (p. 286). Similarly, Cousin Maria in "Mrs. Temperly" decorates her salon with chic contemporary French art but refuses to allow her daughter to marry an artist because of the low status of his profession. When Nick Dormer gives up his seat in Parliament, he sacrifices not merely a brilliant political career and his chance to serve his country and "grow old in a national affection" (NY, VII, 292) but marriage to Julia Dallow, her fortune, and an inheritance from Mr. Carteret. He gains nothing but everything—self-identity. In the role of politician he feels like a humbug; he nominally "represents" Harsh, but what does "*it* represent," he asks, "poor stupid little borough with its strong, though I admit clean, smell of meal and its curiously fat-faced inhabitants?" (NY, VII, 243). According to Julia, he represents the idea of his party, but Julia's political philosophy boils down to keeping the Tories out.

However, when Nick closes his studio door on the world in order to find self-realization in his work, he is not abstaining from life but dedicating himself more seriously to it. Having made his decision, Nick at first finds his spirit checked. What lies ahead of him is dullness, obscurity, and work. His career is not to have the immediate, worldly, tangible rewards which Miriam's has. On a visit to the National Gallery in this mood, he finds himself "calling the whole exhibited art into question." Looking with a "lustreless eye at the palpable polished 'toned' objects designed for suspension on hooks," he "blasphemed if it were blasphemy to feel that as bearing on the energies of man they were a poor and secondary show. The human force producing them was so far from one of the greatest; their place was a small place and their connexion with the heroic life casual and slight. They represented so little great ideas, and it was great ideas that keep the world from chaos." He resists his revulsion, for "to do the most when there would be the least to be got by it was to be most in the spirit of high production." His conclusion is that "art was doing . . . which politics in most cases weren't" (NY, VIII, 265–67). Somewhat later, standing before the portraits in the gallery, he feels that it is the pictures which in the end

seemed far most to prevail and survive and testify. . . . The perfection of their survival often struck him as the supreme eloquence, the virtue that included all others, thanks to the language of art, the richest and most universal. Empires and systems and conquests had rolled over the globe and every kind of greatness had risen and passed away, but the beauty of the great pictures had known nothing of death or change, and the tragic centuries had only sweetened their freshness. The same faces, the same figures looked out at different worlds, knowing so many secrets the particular world didn't, and when they joined hands they made the indestructible thread on which the pearls of history were strung. (NY, VIII, 390–91)

As this passage indicates, the opposition is between the "world" which is material but transitory and that which is "made," eternal, and universal. In developing the theme of art versus the world, James in effect claims for art a long-run utility as an extension of man's limited self. "Art is an embalmer, a magician, . . ." he says in his essay on Daumier, "It prolongs, it preserves, it consecrates, it raises from the dead."[40]

Each character in the novel is related to the others and subtly judged by his attitude toward the usefulness of art. At one end of the scale are Nick's mother, Lady Agnes, and his sister Grace, Mr. Carteret, and Julia Dallow; at the other end is Gabriel Nash. Lady Agnes feels that "art's pardonable only so long as it's bad—so long as it's done at odd hours, for a little distraction, like a game of tennis or of whist." She urges Nick to "go in for a great material position" (NY, VII, 18). Julia, Nick observes, doesn't "care a rap about art. It's a fearful bore looking at fine things with Julia" (NY, VII, 8). She is extremely ambitious to be the mistress of a great political salon. According to Lady Agnes, she will be the "perfect companion" for a public man. "She's made for public life—she's made to shine, to be concerned in great things, to occupy a high position and to help him on" (NY, VII, 247). Nick feels that she lives very publicly, that she lives for the impressions she makes on the world outside of herself. When he thinks of her and the part she has played in his successful political campaign, "what had happened met his eyes as a composed picture—a picture of which the subject was inveterately Julia and her ponies: Julia wonderfully fair and fine, waving her whip, cleaving the crowd, holding her head as if it had been a banner, smiling up into second-storey windows, carrying him beside her, carrying him to his doom" (NY, VII, 264). Someone else aptly characterizes her as "the surface so delicate, the action so easy, yet the frame of steel" (NY, VII, 257). Julia is of the same sisterhood as Mona Brigstock in *The Spoils of Poynton*, Mrs. Lowder in *The Wings of the Dove*, and Mrs. Temperly: they are all steely will power, successful by nature in their undertakings, against whose faculty perceptive artistic people are defenseless.

The irreconcilability of the public and the private life, of the world and art, and of Nick and Julia is brought out in the scene in which

Nick asks Julia to marry him. The scene takes place in the eighteenth-
century temple of Vesta on an island in the middle of a lake on Julia's
estate. The temple is charming, delicate, and ornamental; it has been
the plaything of a man of taste, an "architectural pleasantry," which
Julia's husband, an art collector and connoisseur, had amused himself by restoring. Nick is fond of it "because it was absurd," but Julia
"had never had a particular esteem" for it. She doesn't mind visiting
it in order to see "how they keep it up." She is insensitive to its charm
and thinks it

> ridiculous to withdraw to an island a few feet square on purpose to med-
> itate. She had nothing to meditate about that required so much scenery and
> attitude.
>   "On the contrary, [Nick says] it would be just to change the scene and
> the *pose*. It's what we have been doing for a week that's attitude; and to
> be for half an hour where nobody's looking and one hasn't to keep it up
> is just what I wanted to put in an idle irresponsible day for." (NY, VII, 268–
> 70)

Like the praetors, consuls, and dictators of ancient Rome who sacrificed to the Vesta at Lavinium before taking office, Nick offers marriage to Julia in the beautiful, useless temple of Vesta before assuming
his office, sacrificing his private ambitions for the sake of her hand and
the useful public life in which she is in her element.

The third major character aligned with the world is Mr. Carteret,
the interior of whose home, full of Landseers, oilcloth, woodwork
painted and grained, "expressed a whole view of life" (NY, VII, 288).
Unlike Julia and even Lady Agnes, who are driven by desires for
personal power and place, Carteret represents the dedicated public
servant. Nick likes to think of his father as the same general type—
"a type so pure, so disinterested, so concerned for the public good"
(NY, VII, 294). Carteret has a "rare simplicity," which is the main
source of his personal value.

> It was as if experience, though coming to him in abundance, had dealt
> with him so clean-handedly as to leave no stain, and had moreover never
> provoked him to any general reflexion. He had never proceeded in any
> ironic way from the particular to the general; certainly he had never made
> a reflexion upon anything so unparliamentary as Life. . . . Life, for him,
> was a purely practical function, not a question of more or less showy phras-
> ing. (NY, VII, 295)

His very imperviousness to experience, his innocence and rigidity
of mind, which give him his characteristic tone and make him rep-

resentative of a "departing tradition of manners," preclude his being responsive to art or an artistic career. " 'The pencil—the brush? They're not the weapons of a gentleman,' Mr. Carteret pronounced" (NY, VIII, 171).

At the other end of the scale, directly opposite Lady Agnes, Julia, and Mr. Carteret, is Gabriel Nash, who has given up practicing art to make an art of life. His "little system," as he calls his philosophy of life, is to seek pleasure wherever he can find it, avoiding the "dreary" in life whenever possible, to be the same to all people, and in short, to live exclusively for himself by gratifying his refined senses. He considers any expression of the self through art as bound to be imperfectly representative and hence a vulgarization of self, of one's style. Art, according to his view, is only less utilitarian than politics; the shaping of the aesthetic impulse into form is to be avoided because the result is bound to be a caricature of the perfect idea. Nash's system requires complete detachment from the world; in fact, he is so much the observer of life that when Nick begins to paint him he becomes so uncomfortable and irritated because he perforce has become a subject and an ingredient in life that he eventually fades away, just as the portrait grows dim and blurred. When Nick asks him what he will do when he grows old, he replies:

> "Old? What do you call old?" Nash had replied bravely enough, but with another perceptible tinge of irritation. "Must I really remind you at this time of day that that term has no application to such a condition as mine? It only belongs to you wretched people who have the incureable [*sic*] superstition of 'doing'; it's the ignoble collapse you prepare for yourselves when you cease to be able to do. For me there'll be no collapse, no transition, no clumsy readjustment of attitude; for I shall only *be*, more and more, with all the accumulations of experience, the longer I live."

In response to Nick's, "Then you need never die," he says, "Certainly; I dare say I'm indestructible, immortal" (NY, VIII, 411). By desiring to be only in himself "a fine consequence," he denies himself the possibility of achieving the kind of immortality open to creators of works of art. (He has written "a sort of novel . . . with a lot of good writing" and presumably could have been a writer.) Nick is not sure that in ranking "himself among imperishable things" Nash "hadn't at last, balancing always on the stretched tight-rope of his wit, fallen over on the wrong side" (NY, VIII, 412). But whether or not he is mad, in cultivating himself as if he were an art object and thus detached from the vicissitudes and obligations of human, and therefore necessarily social, existence, he is paradoxically in spite of his extreme individuality without tangible identity. There is the "air" about him "as of the transient and occasional, the likeness to curling vapour or murmuring wind or shifting light" (NY, VIII, 402).

Nash is an antidote to British Philistinism, and he gives Nick the courage to be true to himself. "To be what one *may* be, really and efficaciously," he says at one point, "to feel it and understand it, to accept it, adopt it, embrace it—that's conduct, that's life" (NY, VIII, 26). But Nick knows that his friend does not entirely approve of his having become a painter, though Nash has been in favor of his abandoning his political career. Nick says to Miriam: "Indeed he'll probably tell me frankly the next time I see him that he can't but feel that to come down to small questions of action—to the small prudences and compromises and simplifications of practice—is for the superior person really a fatal descent" (NY, VIII, 395). Viewed in this light, Nash is seen to be an idealist, an absolutist of the imagination, blood brother to Theobald and Roderick. Art necessarily involves compromise, the bringing of the ideal down to earth; it is also in an ultimate sense deeply functional; it is art which makes order out of chaos and rescues life from that "waste" which, according to James, is "life sacrificed." James cared too deeply for art and was too socially responsible to fail to see the emptiness of the ideals of the Wilde dandy—of the soul, independent, mentally austere and fastidious, superior to art and to the honor accruing to its creators, dedicated to an absolutely useless, aimless, and asocial existence.

The artists, then, fall between, on the one hand, those who live for the world, worshipping material gain, power, and practical results, and, on the other hand, the person who stands completely outside of society, preoccupied as he is with essences and pure forms; two other principals, Biddy and Peter Sherringham, have yet to be placed. Biddy, one of James's many amateur artists, is paired off appropriately with Sherringham, who is unable at the crucial time to commit himself to art. Peter says, "I'm fond of representation—the representation of life: I like it better, I think, than the real thing" (NY, VII, 78). But when art in the form of Miriam, "instead of making all the concessions . . . proceeds to ask a few," he is unable to sacrifice the "real thing." "Where is the virtue of his high interest," James asks in his preface, "if it has verily never *been* an interest to speak of and if all it has suddenly to suggest is that, in face of a serious call, it shall be unblushingly relinquished?"[41] Peter's reluctance to put art first, as Nick does, irrevocably aligns him, no matter what his professions and sympathies, with his sister and Lady Agnes.

The Tragic Muse is in many respects an admirable work. The social surface is rendered as having depths: Lady Agnes may be Britannia incarnate in her self-assured stupidity and ambitiousness, but she evokes pity as well as amusement. In Miriam, James explores the mysteries of the histrionic temperament without sacrificing her vitality and immediacy as a person. The scenes saturated with "the very odour of Paris . . . the rich rumble of the Rue de la Paix"[42] are at least as evocative as similar ones in other works. The note of dry literalness and absolute integrity in the character of Mr. Carteret resounding through his richly hideous house is perfectly pitched. James justifiably prided himself on the "preserved and achieved unity and quality of tone" as the best thing about the book. "The appeal, the fidelity to the prime motive, is, with no little art, strained clear (even as silver is polished) in a degree answering—at least by intention—to the air of beauty."[43] Miriam herself, as James notes in the preface, is in her person only one link joining the two plot strands of the separate struggles of the painter and actress. The title after Sir Joshua Reynold's portrait of Mrs. Siddons as "the tragic muse" epitomizes the perfect fusion of the two strands achieved by James: every incident, every character, and every detail seem to play a part in developing the "prime motive."

In spite of its real virtues, I do not find it an ingratiating work; it is thin and bloodless, even in comparison with more obviously flawed novels such as *The Bostonians*. The fault lies, to extend James's metaphor, in its very sheen and lack of resonant roughness. Characters seem to have been manipulated to illustrate the central theme rather than the theme arising from the fullness of created life. The choice demanded of Peter Sherringham is absolute and decisive according to the thesis but so abstractly conceived that he, in fact, does not seem to have a choice. Julia on the Kate Croy and Charlotte Stant worldly pattern has none of their rich appeal; one can hardly understand why Nick would be attracted to her. It fails thus in psychological reality and complexity, and, as a novel of social-artistic documentation, it succeeds partially, only in the depiction of Miriam's struggles to become an actress. A crucial flaw is the characterization of Nick.

Upon mature reflection James found Nick "not quite so interesting as he was fondly intended to be . . . he has insisted in the event on looking as simple and flat as some mere brass check or engraved number, the symbol and guarantee of a stored treasure." This flatness is attributed by James to the impossibility of depicting the artist at work: "any presentation of the artist *in triumph* must be flat in proportion as it really sticks to its subject—it can only smuggle in relief and variety. . . .'His' triumph, decently, is but the triumph of what he produces, and that is another affair." But if the artist as artist cannot enjoy the privileges of hero, the "artist deluded, diverted, frustrated or vanquished"[44] can. Having ceased to function as an artist, he becomes human and hence raw material for fiction.

One cannot quarrel with James that the artist at work cannot be fictionally interesting, but neither can the lawyer nor the school teacher per se. But even before Nick Dormer forsakes the world for the studio, he is uninteresting. If it were not for different outer signs, Nick and Peter might be the same bland nonentity, they are so basically alike —*the* type of the civilized, sensitive, upper class young man. Even more important, James inadvertently portrays Nick's problems as factitious ones. From the details given he could be exactly the kind of painter who would win the "honours and emoluments," their bestowal in England, as James remarked, being "more than a custom, . . . on occasion almost a fury."[45] Nick's taste in art seems conventional; he admires the current works in the Salon. He is "bent . . . on working in the modern" (NY, VIII, 390), but the only portrait painters mentioned are Sir Joshua Reynolds and George Romney. While the pose in which he places Miriam for the first painting is not that of Mrs. Siddons in the Reynolds portrait, the idea of painting her allegorically is closer in spirit to the eighteenth than to the nineteenth century. That he spends six weeks in Paris—"a Paris of the Rue Bonaparte and three or four professional friends . . . a Paris of studios and studies and models, of researches and revelations, comparisons and contrasts, of strong impressions and long discussions" (NY, VIII, 417)—suggests that he is in touch with contemporary art movements, but the two portraits he paints of Miriam, judging from James's description of them, would win a place on the line at the Academy. To be sure, he is afraid that he will be tempted to work for easy success at the Academy, but there is no indication that he aims at standards different in kind from the academic. James's purpose in the novel is to show that society only pays lip service to art, confining "its attention to vanities and frauds,"[46] but does not understand or respect really serious work. Nick's work seems to have the conventional qualities that society does respect. James's authors, his "supersubtle fry," represent writers who, according to James, do not exist but should; Nick should not but seems to represent mediocrities who do (or did) exist.[47]

In stories such as "The Liar" and "Glasses," a few metaphors and a sprinkling of art terms are enough to prevent embarrassing questions about truth to life from arising. In earlier works, such as "A Landscape Painter," "The Story of a Masterpiece," and "The Sweetheart of M. Briseux," artists are drawn sharply enough to be recognizable as contemporary types. In *The Reverberator* and "A New England Winter," James's conception of impressionist method and art (through not entirely valid) is solidly worked into the structure and meaning of each story. In *The Tragic Muse* James fails, on the one hand, to create in Nick a character wih vitality whose alternatives provide genuine conflict or the challenge of complex moral choice— the political career does not seem to offer any but the most abstract of gratifications—and, on the other, to draw a convincing particularized picture of a painter in conflict with the world. Nick actually seems to have no need to "justify and defend his view" before getting to work; his work is precisely the kind that would guarantee fame and social success in his society. It is not a matter of rendering the artist's craft with a precision that would satisfy a painter[48] but rather of providing the kind of detail that Zola does in his characterization of Charles Lantin in *L'Oeuvre*, Proust in Elstir, and Cary in Gulley Jimson which distinguishes the painter from a person with an artistic sensibility and which thus when the narrative emphasis is on artist *qua* artist is convincing. James's dependence on associational values rather than purely aesthetic ones may be blamed for the vagueness and contradictions in his treatment of Nick as a painter.

To point out that James's portraits of the artist are at times sketchily or too conventionally executed is not to deny their significance in his work. Directly as a central subject and indirectly as a symbolic figure the artist in confronting the conflicting claims of art and life expresses his deepest sense of art as redemption from the waste and chaos of life. Even a pathetic failure like Theobald affirms his vision of the artist as tragic yet triumphant. A vision having its beginnings in James's experience in the Louvre, it is manifest in his mature meditations on Tintoretto's poignant self-portrait in the Louvre:

The old man looks out of the canvas from beneath a brow as sad as a sunless twilight, with just such a stoical hopelessness as you might fancy him to wear if he stood at your side gazing at his rotting canvases. It isn't whimsical to read it as the face of a man who felt that he had given the world more than the world was likely to repay. Indeed before every picture of Tintoret you may remember this tremendous portrait with profit. On one side the power, the passion, the illusion of his art; on the other the mortal fatigue of his spirit. The world's knowledge of him is so small that the portrait throws a doubly precious light on his personality; and when we wonder vainly what manner of man he was, and what were his purpose, his faith and his method, we may find forcible assurance there that they were at any rate his life—one of the most intellectually passionate ever led.[49]

I

JAMES'S use of the visual arts to frame scenes and of specific art allusions to create a symbolism both precise and reverberative has been explored. Finally to be considered is the question central to James's fiction thematically: What are the moral implications of art appreciation and possession?[1]

In spite of the sophisticated Jamesian criticism of recent years, the popular assumption that the equation of moral sense and aesthetic sense in James is one for one dies hard. So usually discerning a critic as John Henry Raleigh states, for example, that for James "the individual who most appreciates the beauty of a Renaissance painting is also the most moral."[2] This assumption is valid if one interprets "appreciates" in the light of James's own aesthetic, which, as we have seen, was far from formalistic. Responsiveness to art, even if taste is untutored, is almost always a given in James's sensitive, intelligent, morally scrupulous characters, from the passionate pilgrim Clement Searle to the heroes of the unfinished novels. Just as obviously, bad taste or insensitivity to art objects and décor is almost always a sign of impervious, power-seeking, morally suspect, or limited characters—Paul Muniment, Mrs. Lowder, Tom Tristam, Julia Dallow, Casper Goodwood, to name a few. Within this range of character, taste is as much a touchstone as politeness is in Hemingway. But there is also a class of characters who, appreciating beauty or surrounding themselves with beautiful objects, are nevertheless sinister and cruel (Urbain de Bellegarde, Gilbert Osmond, Dr. Sloper), egotistic (Roderick Hudson, Mrs. Gereth), or morally ambiguous in their acquisitiveness (Maggie and Adam Verver). Taste as an index to moral values is over-all only roughly accurate; once beyond the radical division between those who have it and those who do not, other signs come into play, those that decisively distinguish the free spirits from the connoisseurs, namely, disinterestedness (here the artist and the art lover are alike) and an associative aesthetic. Thus, art is identified with moral refinement only insofar as the viewer responds to the historical, spiritual, psychological qualities of the Renaissance painting and does not seek to possess it or use his aesthetic knowledge for self-aggrandizing purposes. Those for whom art is a means of exercising power or who disengage it from its historical, human context, valuing it chiefly as part of an aesthetic design, are not necessarily malignant or egotistical, though some are, but are at least in some way lacking in moral awareness.

So closely linked are the aesthetic sense and the historical imagination in James's thinking that the question of the relation of aesthetic to moral values is inevitably bound up with that of the proper place of the past in the present and hence of the museum in contemporary life. Owing much of his education to the museum and living in an age of encyclopedic collecting, *bibelot* hunting, museum founding and expansion, and archaelogical excavation, James viewed the art object as an embodiment and a revelation of civilization but was also aware of the inherent dangers in the museum world of the estrangement of art from life. A storage house for the past, the museum serves an indispensable purpose in preserving works of art and in making them available to the public. However, the museum setting is necessarily artificial, and in it the art work loses an essential connection with human life. In becoming a part of a collection, public or private, the object changes in function: taken out of its original context, the portrait becomes a picture; the goddess or saint, a statue; the household object, an *objet d'art*. James did not, to my knowledge, express directly any views on the principle of the museum in his time, though, as I have shown in Chapter 2, he expressed preferences for seeing works in their own contexts. In his fiction he does treat this question in his frequent characterization of the individual as a collector or in relation to the museum world. Art objects and backgrounds primarily appear in relation to the individual, but the broader question of national cultural values is also frequently involved, as in Densher's response to the "heavy horrors" of Mrs. Lowder's drawingroom: "He couldn't describe and dismiss them collectively, call them either Mid-Victorian or Early—not being at all sure they were rangeable under one rubric. It was only manifest they were splendid and were furthermore conclusively British" (NY, XIX, 78).

In the earlier fiction in which the contrast between American and European national types and morality is central and in which, as the titles *The American* and *The Europeans* indicate, James is specifically concerned with national identity, there is more emphasis on art as revelation of national traits. As America was a country without art (or of relatively little and mostly inferior in James's view) and without a storied past, and as Europe meant "art, history, beauty," the contrast in types could be dramatically projected through placing characters in alien settings: the American in the museum of Europe; the European in pastoral America. In *Roderick Hudson* the European-American confrontation is presented more through Mary, Roderick, and Christina Light than through the collector Rowland. Rowland, given his mixed Dutch and American-Puritan ancestry, is, to begin with, a semi-Europeanized American; he has received his European initiation but is not expatriated and is divided between his sensuous pleasure in beauty and his utilitarian Puritan conscience. His vision of endowing a museum in his native city and his patronage of Roderick are expressions of his desire to satisfy his conscience and fulfill himself imaginatively and likewise to convert the passive observer self into a creative active one in the world. That his collection is as Christina notes, "an odd jumble. . . . Some things are very pretty—some are very ugly" (p. 151), indicates that he is not guided by the principles of good taste alone; unlike Roderick he does not aim for the ideal. As a Western, and hence "American," American, Christopher Newman is another type. His collecting—and it is of copies, not originals—is not philanthropically motivated, though he does eventually try to make a dot for Noémie as a patron. Initially, he seems to turn to the buying of pictures as a cure for his "aesthetic headache." Comparable to Waymarsh in *The Ambassadors*, when faced with a Europe he cannot fathom, he expresses himself through the "sacred rage" of purchase; he can own it even if he cannot adequately know it, an ironic foreshadowing of his attempted purchase of Madame de Cintré. However, though Newman blandly finishes off an order for five copies of masterpieces in the Louvre with one of the series in Rubens's *Marriage of Marie de Medicis*, he is no mere innocent abroad. He is guilty of admiring copies as much as originals, and copyists even more, and of examining with equal thoroughness the street cars and cathedrals of a country, but his conclusion after his grand tour that he has been seeing a "very rich and beautiful world and that it had not all been made by sharp railroad men and stock-brokers"[3] shows that he is not the prototypal Western barbarian. Harking back to the uncultured, unpolished American businessman in "Travelling Companions," he has not only Evans's "substance in character, keenness in perception, and intensity in will"[4] but also the capacity to respond to the old and the beautiful. His mistakes in taste are comic and crude, but the "inward tremor" he feels before unstarred items in the guide book—"some lonely, sad-towered church, or some angular image of one who had rendered civic service in an unknown past" (p. 84)—reveals the inherent sensitivity in his character which makes him capable of appreciating Claire de Cintré's fineness and his winning of her hand plausible.

The attitudes toward art of other characters significantly contrast with Newman's. The introduction of the young Unitarian minister Babcock, who accompanies Newman for part of his grand tour, gives James a chance not only to satirize the Ruskinian moralistic view of art but to define more sharply Newman's own easy way of taking life. Babcock admonishes Newman to remember that "Life and Art *are* extremely serious" (p. 91), and to him taking them seriously means categorizing and labeling them. He goes back to Milan for another look at Luini because he is afraid that he has made a mistake in his original judgment. "I am afraid I overestimated him. I don't think that he is a painter of the first rank," he explains to Newman.

"Luini?" Newman exclaimed; "why, he's enchanting—he's magnificent! There is something in his genius that is like a beautiful woman. It gives one the same feeling."
Mr. Babcock frowned and winced. (p. 90)

Newman feels that "an undue solicitude for 'culture' " is "a proceeding properly confined to women, foreigners, and other unpractical persons" and that it is "slightly contemptible to feel obliged to square one's self with a standard" (pp. 82–83). He thinks at the end of his tour that after all "he had seen the great things, and he had given his mind a chance to 'improve,' if it would. He cheerfully believed it had improved" (p. 93).

Tom Tristram, a sketch of the American from still another angle, not only feels no obligation to "improve" but is immune to culture. He pays his first visit to the Louvre on his own, though he has lived in Paris for six years, because he happens to be strolling by "rather hard up for amusement." "But if I hadn't found you there," he tells Newman, "I should have felt rather sold. Hang it, I don't care for pictures; I prefer the reality!" (p. 24). Newman rather priggishly disapproves of Tristram, who in his opinion is a "degenerate mortal," a "very light weight," who only aspires "to hold out at poker at his club, to know the names of all the *cocottes*, to shake hands all round, to ply his rosy gullet with truffles and champagne" (p. 40). If Mr. Babcock's categorical approach to art shows him to be narrow minded and unimaginative, Tristram's preference for good living over high thinking is a token of his shallowness and frivolity.

Clearly, Newman comes off best of the Americans, and in spite of his comically deplorable admiration for inferior works, he is genuinely receptive to art, an openness that is a sign of his largeness of character, But that he has never before in his life followed "the line of beauty" becomes evident when he meets the Europeans. Both Valentin and Urbain de Bellegarde have inherited a sense of discrimination with their names. The charming insouciance of the one and the polished offensiveness of the other are conveyed through their relations to art. Valentin, an "insatiable collector," lives in the midst of his bric-a-brac: "his walls were covered with rusty arms and ancient panels and platters, his doorways draped in faded tapestries, his floors muffled in the skins of beasts." The curious objects which fill his "low, dusky, contracted" apartment are not on display but are as much a part of the atmosphere as the "odor of cigars, mingled with perfumes more inscrutable." His is not a perfect collection, like the spoils of Poynton, each piece complementing the other. His possessions are in "picturesque disorder," and his furniture has a "fragmentary character" (p. 128), indicating that collecting is a pleasurable activity, not a dominating passion of this amiable and somewhat aimless Frenchman.

In contrast to Valentin, in whom traditions are "muffled in sociability and urbanity, as an old dowager in her laces and strings of pearls" (p. 122), his brother Urbain insists on the purity of his lineage and the superiority of his race and uses art to set himself apart from others. Afraid of conversation with Newman that might lead to "startling personal revelations," he utters "polished aphorism upon the flesh-tints of Rubens and the good taste of Sansovino" (p. 198). Although there is no indication that his taste is any less cultivated than Valentin's, it is associated with his sinister suavity and arrogance. But while Urbain's aesthetic is an expression of his deification of the past, his aristocratic pride, and authoritarian attitudes, the inadequacies of Newman's artistic sense are a sign of the very limitations in him that make him vulnerable to Urbain's treachery. His experiencing Raphael, Titian, and Rubens as a "new kind of arithmetic" (p. 6) which he was unequipped to master has its counterpart in his bafflement in the fact of the European social order. His instincts of civilization do not prove to be enough for him to understand and to cope with a complicated society and its tortuous behavior; his inability to grasp the significance of forms, though he has exquisite natural tact, is at the heart of his failure to understand the Bellegardes' betrayal of him. His very belief that Europe is made for him, not he for Europe, while freeing him from the ludicrous anxieties that torture Babcock on the grand tour, does not prepare him sub-

sequently for dealing with it. His contempt for the conscious striving
for standards in art and fine discriminations, signifying his large
easiness of character, also helps to explain not only why he finally
gives up his revenge, but why he has only a limited understanding of
his enemies. The large uneasiness, moreover, carries with it some imperviousness: When Valentin mentions his lack of "quarterings" as
standing in the way of marriage to Claire, Newman answers: " 'Ah,
your quarterings are your little local matter!' Valentin just hesitated.
'But aren't we all—isn't my admirable sister in particular—our little
local matter?' "[5]

The old and neglected stir his imagination, but when Valentin
jokingly offers to take him through the Bellegarde house, the young
man is aware that if indeed as a family they are a curiosity, Newman
would see them almost simply as museum pieces. Revealing an
absence of a sense of historical continuity, Newman's attitudes toward
houses have important implications. He is impressed by the age of
the Bellegarde house in the Faubourg Saint Germain, but he feels
it is mean and inelegant; the Marquise's salon strikes him as "rather
sad and shabby" (p. 171). His conception of magnificence is satisfied
by the modern apartment with mechanical devices on the Boulevard
Haussmann that Tristram found for him: "a first floor," consisting
of "a series of rooms, gilded from floor to ceiling a foot thick, draped
in various shades of satin, and chiefly furnished with mirrors and
clocks" (p. 100). It is not so much that his taste in interior decoration
is for the garish and the grandiose but that he dissociates beauty from
history, object from context, the past from the present. This attitude
is shown in several ways. While he submits to the humiliation of being patronized by the Bellegardes for Claire's sake, he thinks that
she was "a woman for the light, not for the shade" (p. 218), and that
he can relieve the hereditary gloom. He imagines that after their
marriage they can live anywhere, not perceiving that her setting is
an inescapable part of her. He thinks of a wife as "a beautiful woman
perched on the pile" of his financial success "like a statue on a monument," wants "the best article on the market" (p. 48), and, though
there is no doubt that he values Claire for herself, the "world's
admiration" of her pleases him as adding to "the prospective glory of
possession" (p. 165). Of course, that he expresses his blameless, altogether humanly understandable, and even admirable intentions
through commercial metaphors cannot be held against him. After
all, though he has manufactured washtubs, *he* is not crude and grasp-
ing as, for all their quarterings, the Bellegardes are. My point is that
the commercial flavor of his language is a sign that even though he

has given up his commercial enterprises, he cannot divest himself of them; they are an ineradicable part of him. In London, after the Fleurières episode, asking himself whether "he *was* more commercial, than was pleasant," he comes to the conclusion that "if he had been too commercial, he was ready to forget it, for in being so he had done no man any wrong that might not be as easily forgotten. . . . If there was any reason in the nature of things why his connection with business should have cast a shadow upon a connection—even a connection broken—with a woman justly proud, he was willing to sponge it out of his life forever" (p. 461), but contrary to his belief, "ingenuity and energy" cannot "arrange everything." One may stand "in an attitude of general hospitality to the chances of life" (p. 7), but the chances may go against one. The past lives on into the present, as it does in Claire de Cintré. Newman's reasons for believing he could eradicate his own past are why he is finally unable to understand his failure.

Art and artfulness, manners and mannerisms, the social fib and the calculated lie—how is one to tell them apart? Richard Poirier penetratingly shows how James in *The Europeans* handles the paradox that to be natural one needs the subterfuge of art.[6] Eugenia is comically out of place, but there are tragic overtones in the failure of the Wentworth world to assimilate her. What Poirier overlooks, however, is that Eugenia's artistry in life shades into actual deception: her lies about Clifford and the famous paper releasing her from her morganatic marriage are in the context of a human drama in which she plays for material stakes, not of the social play-acting that James considers enriching and valid self-expression. Felix, who wishes only to win Gertrude, succeeds; Eugenia, though she carries off her part to the end superbly, goes back to Europe empty hearted and empty handed. The answer to her question "Was she to have gained nothing—was she to have gained nothing?"[7] is a negative "yes," as she has come essentially to make her fortune.

As in *The American*, though even more importantly as the American scene is devoid of art, the house and interiors project not only the differences between the European and American types but also individual moral sensibility. The Wentworth's "large square house" with its windows open to admit the sunshine so that it seems to Felix lighter inside than outside, its white wainscots and highly placed old engravings of biblical subjects, speaks for the life of its inhabitants, a life which Eugenia is imaginative enough to appreciate for its perfection of kind: it is "wonderfully peaceful and sunspotted," Quaker-like in its "quietude and benevolence" (pp. 78–89) but based on material abundance. Its starkness, bareness, and lack of dark corners are also suggestive of the Wentworth's naïvete, literal mindedness, dry provinciality—that sincerity which Stendhal says is the death of wit. No less does Eugenia's decoration of the little white house put at her disposal indicate her European propensity to improve upon nature, to put up screens for privacy and introduce modulations and halftones into relationships. But Eugenia's properties—the India shawls and exotic fabrics draped on the backs of chairs and suspended as portieres, the pink silk blinds which "strangely bedimmed" the room, the "remarkable band of velvet, covered with coarse, dirty-looking lace" (p. 80) on the mantelpiece—also give the effect of a cluttered and slightly tawdry atmosphere, the correlative of her equivocations and shadiness.

Robert Acton's sensibility is also reflected in his house and possessions. He has made a fortune in China, or rather "quintupled" one, knows a "great deal about porcelain and bric-a-brac (p. 132), has a "handsome library" and is "also very fond of pictures" (p. 116). Of the Wentworth circle, he correctly assesses himself as having "most adequately gauged her capacity for social intercourse." However, the library is "handsome" in comparison with Mr. Wentworth's and as for his pictures, "it must be confessed, in the fierce light of contemporary criticism, that his walls were adorned with several rather abortive masterpieces" (p. 116). These are signs of his provinciality, but he knows that "he was by no means so much of a man of the world as he was supposed to be in local circles; but it must be added that he knew also that his natural shrewdness had a reach of which he had never quite given local circles the measure" (p. 116). He is a match for Eugenia and the only one capable of detecting the duplicity in her behavior with regard to Clifford and to him. His "experimentation" with her after the farcical episode in which Clifford blunders through her parlor deepens our sympathy for Eugenia, who is acting within the traditions of her world and has only the resources of her own talent to make her way. As with some of the other Jamesian characters in quest of knowledge, his "curiosity" about her is off-putting. However, there are other signs that we are not to take Eugenia as a victim of the narrowness of the American world: Felix has a sense of honor she does not have; he has the delicacy to fear that in wooing Gertrude he is violating his uncle's hospitality. Eugenia dislikes Lizzie: "It was a source of irritation to the Baroness that in this country it should seem to matter whether a little girl were a trifle less or a trifle more of a nonentity; for Eugenia had hitherto been conscious of no moral pressure as regards the appreciation of diminutive virgins" (p. 132). For a nonentity, Lizzie has considerable perception: she knows how to appreciate Eugenia's compliments as the following reveals:

Clifford told Lizzie Acton that the Baroness thought her the most charming girl she had ever seen. Lizzie shook her head. "No, she doesn't!" she said. "Do you think everything she says," asked Clifford, "is to be taken the opposite way?"
"I think that is!" said Lizzie. (p. 181)

Ironically, Lizzie's "influence upon her husband was such as to justify, strikingly, that theory of the elevating effect of easy intercourse with clever women which Felix had propounded to Mr. Wentworth" (p. 281). Finally, that Acton's "trophies of his sojourn in the Celestial Empire" are an integral element in his house, "large and square and painted brown," suggests that he has assimilated his experience in the outer world and yet has not lost the rigorous New England standards of probity. Eugenia thinks his house "a very good one" and the impression it gives is of "material comfort," spaciousness, and gleaming order. The "delightful *chinoiseries*" are not excrescences and merely on display: they are "scattered all over the house" and "though it was almost a museum, the large, little-used rooms were as fresh and clean as a well-kept dairy" (p. 131). The blending of the old and the new, the Eastern and the Western, the strange and grotesque with the homely and plain supports the view that his moral judgment is trustworthy.

Clearly, those with an aesthetic sense are more open to life than those who, like Brand and Wentworth, feel that to enjoy beauty is to sin, but it is also evident that form is more liberating and life enhancing when one prefers the work of art or the window to the mirror, as the amusing opening scene contrasting the two Europeans hints: While Felix is working on his sketches, Eugenia paces up and down.

She never dropped her eyes upon his work; she only turned them, occasionally, as she passed, to a mirror suspended above a toilet table on the other side of the room. Here she paused a moment, gave a pinch to her waist with her two hands, or raised these members—they were very plump and pretty—to the multifold braid of her hair, with a movement half caressing, half corrective. An attentive observer might have fancied that during these periods of desultory self-inspection her face forgot its melancholy; but as soon as she neared the window again it began to proclaim that she was a very ill-pleased woman (p. 2).

All of the possibilities for imbalance in the finely adjusted ideal relations between the aesthetic and moral sense in the works just discussed are fully explored and of strategic importance in Isabel Archer's engagement to "see" life. Not only do art objects furnish the setting and project characters' perceptions and moral qualities, but recurring art metaphors support and extend their significance. The relation of the "self" to "things" is the central issue—"things" coming to represent fate and form, the inevitable limitations on freedom and the constructive possibilities for self-realization. The issue is explicitly set forth in the exchange between Madame Merle and Isabel, beginning seriously and ending, perhaps so as not to appear as an undigested lump of "philosophy," in badinage.

"When you have lived as long as I you will see that every human being has his shell, and that you must take the shell into account. By the shell I mean the whole envelope of circumstances. There is no such thing as an isolated man or woman; we are each of us made up of a cluster of appurtenances. What do you call one's 'self'? Where does it begin? where does it end? It overflows into everything that belongs to us—and then it flows back again. I know that a large part of myself is in the dresses I choose to wear. I've a great respect for *things!* One's self—for other people—is one's expression of one's self; and one's house, one's clothes, the book one reads, the company one keeps—these things are all expressive."

This was very metaphysical; not more so, however, than several observations Madame Merle had already made. Isabel was fond of metaphysics, but was unable to accompany her friend into this bold analysis of the human personality. "I don't agree with you. I think just the other way. I don't know whether I succeed in expressing myself, but I know that nothing else expresses me. Nothing that belongs to me is any measure of me; on the contrary, it's a limit, a barrier, and a perfectly arbitrary one. Certainly, the clothes which, as you say, I choose to wear, don't express me; and heaven forbid they should!"

"You dress very well," interposed Madame Merle, skilfully.

"Possibly; but I don't care to be judged by that. My clothes may express the dressmaker, but they don't express me. To begin with it's not my own choice that I wear them; they are imposed upon me by society."

"Should you prefer to go without them?" Madame Merle enquired, in a tone which virtually terminated the discussion.[8]

Madame Merle's words have a dubious wisdom if she is to be taken as exemplifying her ideas. Her brilliant piano playing, her skill in sketching, her remarkable embroidering, her letter writing, her fondness for pictures, her rich conversation express her as the most ripely civilized of beings. But she has so assiduously cultivated her shell that even at the Gardencourt stage of their relationship, Isabel feels that "if . . . she had a fault, it was that she was not natural . . . she had become too flexible, too supple . . . too finished, too civilized . . . too perfectly, the social animal that man and woman are supposed to have been intended to be. . . . Isabel found it difficult to think of Madame Merle as an isolated figure; she existed only in her relations with her fellow-mortals. Isabel often wondered what her relations might be with her own soul" (p. 167). Ralph expresses his reservations about Madame Merle similarly: "she pushes the search for perfection too far . . . her merits in themselves are overstrained." It is not her having perfected the social arts that makes her morally suspect, but her having expended herself in polishing the social surface she presents to the world. Motivating her great drive for social perfection are her ambitions: Isabel thinks she has "aspired to a crown"; Ralph is sure that she has been "richly ambitious. . . . She had got herself into perfect training, but she had won none of the prizes." Her great natural talents, in short, have not been so much cultivated for themselves as for the prestige and social position which she has hoped to win for herself, and which, having to admit failure—the fact that she is after all only "plain Madame Merle, the widow of a Swiss *négociant*, with a small income and a large acquaintance, who stayed with people a great deal, and was universally liked" (p. 220)—she then tries to win for Osmond and Pansy. In the light of her later actions, her statement that she has "a great respect for things" takes on another meaning. She respects but does not love. There is missing in her relations with things a feeling for them which if lacking makes having a refined aesthetic sense worse than not having one at all. She admits to Rosier, when he asks her to help him win Pansy, that she has "some very good things," but she says, "I hate them." Rosier answers that he loves his things but that he cares "more for Miss Osmond than for all the *bibelots* in Europe!" (p. 314). And though he is at different times likened to his "sprigged porcelain" and a lace pocket handkerchief, he heroically gives up the things—his chief value in the eyes of the world—he loves, hoping by the money raised to win Pansy. Rosier's feeling for Pansy, whom he thinks of as a Dresden shepherdess, is similar to his feeling for his things, in that his tenderness is for the thing and the person itself, not for the use to which each may be put to increase his prestige. He appreciates Pansy aesthetically, but he is not confused as to which—a thing or a person—has the higher value. Not having a real reverence for things, Madame Merle makes a convenience of them and of people alike and in the process damns the very self of which her shell is supposedly an expression.

Gilbert Osmond is even guiltier than Madam Merle of arranging his "cluster of appurtenances" to impress the world. "As cicerone in your own museum you appear to particular advantage" (p. 212),

Madame Merle tells him, and it is a museum world in which choice objects will speak for him that he tries to create. His place "told of habitation being practised as a fine art" (p. 198), his beard, "cut in the manner of the portraits of the sixteenth century, . . . gave its wearer a somewhat foreign, traditionary look, and suggested that he was a gentleman who studied effect" (p. 199). Isabel thinks that "he was fine, as fine as one of the drawings in the long gallery above the bridge, at the Uffizi" (p. 216); his features are "overdrawn, retouched" (p. 228). His belief that one's life should be a work of art is not in itself pernicious, but he literally tries to subdue all of life to form. Moreover, at the heart of his wish to make his life beautiful is his desire to make others envious of him. He treats human beings and art objects indiscriminately as things to be manipulated in order to extract from the "base, ignoble world" he professes to despise "some recognition of his own superiority" (p. 376). He comes to hate Isabel because she refuses to become an inert piece in his collection. Before marrying her, he thinks of her intelligence as a "silver plate . . . that he might heap up with ripe fruits, to which it would give a decorative value, so that conversation might become a sort of perpetual dessert. He found the silvery quality in perfection in Isabel; he could tap her imagination with his knuckle and make it ring" (p. 307), but she proves to have an indestructible will and an independent imagination. If Isabel fails him as a silver plate, he succeeds only too well in forming Pansy into a crystal goblet, responding thinly but faithfully to his taps. Isabel's pledge to Pansy to return is surely in no small part a pledge to prevent her selfhood, minute as it is, from being completely reduced to an abject ornamental utility.

That "the self overflows into everything that belongs to us" is actively demonstrated in *The Portrait* by the way in which all the art objects—Madame Merle's porcelain cups and old damask, Ralph's Turners, Constables, and Watteau, Osmond's Italian primitives and especially the houses—speak for their possessors. One can hardly think of a scene in which the spirit of the house does not loom large. First and last there is Gardencourt, its name embodying the harmony of civilization and nature; the house in its relation to the surroundings epitomizing the picturesque which James responded to so enthusiastically upon his initiation into Europe. One does not easily forget the opening scene on the velvety lawn of the old English country house—the ritual of tea, the figures in the foreground, the "long gabled front of red brick . . . with its patches of ivy, its clustered chimneys, its windows smothered in creepers" (p. 2), not a mere backdrop but an inseparable background. It is a picture of a mode of life characterized by deep privacy, a reverence for ancient privileges and decencies and human continuities. Gardencourt's most recent owner is an American, but Daniel Touchett has grown to love it without having lost his identity, individual or national. The young men contrastingly appear somewhat displaced, in a mood of low-keyed restlessness and ennui. They are ready to appreciate Isabel's spontaneity and eagerness when she makes her entrance. It is to Gardencourt, moreover, that Isabel must return to complete the circle, no longer seeing the house as "a picture made real" (p. 45) and a ghost as a necessary romantic appendage. Walking about, unannounced, she reminds herself of her aunt wandering about still another house, her grandmother's in Albany, which was the real beginning. The difference between the two persons is marked: the reality beneath picturesque surface has been revealed to Isabel: her long tutelage to pain and suffering has qualified her to see the ghost which, according to Ralph on first visit, only those who have been unhappy are privileged to see.

Then, there are Gilbert Osmond's hilltop villa, the front of which seems like the "mask of a house," having "heavy lids, but no eyes" (p. 197), and which "looked somehow as if, once you were in, it would not be easy to get out" (p. 221), and the Osmond residence in Rome, "a dark and massive structure," which is "mentioned in 'Murray' and visited by tourists who looked disappointed and depressed" (p. 319). The prisonlike parlor of the convent, looking more like Philadelphia than Rome, where Pansy is to benefit by the "old ways," and the garish hotel parlor in which Osmond confesses his love to Isabel, the violent colors and cheap fabrics a comment on his essential tawdriness —also come to mind as places rich in allusiveness.

Extending the thematic significance of places and things are numerous art and architectural images; for example, Ralph says to Isabel, as an explanation of his humorous attitude toward everything except his father:

> "I keep a band of music in my ante-room. . . . It has orders to play without stopping; it renders me two excellent services. It keeps the sounds of the world from reaching the private apartments, and it makes the world think that dancing is going on within." It was dance-music indeed that you usually heard when you came within earshot of Ralph's band; the liveliest waltzes seemed to float upon the air. Isabel often found herself irritated by the perpetual fiddling; she would have liked to pass through the ante-room, as her cousin called it, and enter the private apartments. (p. 50)

This image is further carried out, first gaily in the Watteau[9] Ralph shows Henrietta Stackpole in which he compares himself to the gentleman "in pink doublet and hose and a ruff, leaning against the pedestal of the statue of a nymph in a garden, and playing the guitar to two ladies seated on the grass" (p. 76), and then as a frivolous counterpoint in the somber scene in which Ralph makes his single effort to dissuade Isabel from marrying Osmond. It takes place in the garden of Mrs. Touchett's villa where Ralph sits at the "base of a statue of Terpsichore—a dancing nymph with taper fingers and inflated draperies, in the manner of Bernini" (p. 298). The plan Ralph had conceived for Isabel in his "private apartment" leads to her entrapment in actuality, not to the high amusements of the idealized worlds of Watteau and Bernini.

The Gothic imagery employed in Isabel's recognition scene conveys with dramatic intensity her spiritual claustropobia. This imagery does not seem melodramatic nor she hysterical in context because it is a part of the larger pattern of houses in settings and as metaphors. The house in Albany, Gardencourt, Osmond's high windowless Florentine villa, and fortresslike Palazzo Roccanera prepare for "a house of darkness, the house of dumbness, the house of suffocation. Osmond's beautiful mind gave it neither light nor air; Osmond's beautiful mind, indeed, seemed to peep down from a small high window and mock at her" (p. 375). Isabel's discovery that she is trapped in a "dark, narrow alley, with a dead wall at the end" (p. 371) harks back to the fear that Ralph has expressed in his mother's garden that Isabel would be "put into a cage." The architectural imagery is hard to separate from the architecture itself; it is the interlocking of metaphor and real objects which gives this novel its special quality of poetic truth growing out of the rich soil of actuality.

Closely linked to the question of the relation of the self to things is that of the relation of the individual to the past and to the forms of the aristocratic life. Osmond exemplifies the museum consciousness at its worst; his relation to the past is arbitrary, artificial, and lifeless. Not having inherited traditions, he has picked up a "large collection" of them, from where Isabel does not know. "The great thing [for him] was to act in accordance with them." Just as he consciously strains for aesthetic perfection in his collection, he views the aristocratic life as "altogether a thing of forms, a conscious, calculated attitude." Isabel conceives of the aristocratic life as "simply the union of great knowledge with great liberty; the knowledge would give one a sense of duty, and the liberty a sense of enjoyment." Her attitude toward traditions is that "to serve for another person than their proprietor, traditions must be of a thoroughly superior kind" (p. 377). Her own relation to the past is personal, empathic; among the Roman ruins she finds ease:

She rested her weariness upon things that had crumbled for centuries and yet still were upright; she dropped her secret sadness into the silence of lonely places, where its very modern quality detached itself and grew objective, so that as she sat in a sun-warmed angle on a winter's day, or stood in a mouldy church to which no one came, she could almost smile at it and think of its smallness. Small it was, in the large Roman record, and her haunting sense of the continuity of the human lot easily carried her from the less to the greater. (p. 454)

Her fondness for the old house in Albany because, as she tells Mrs. Touchett, "the place has been full of life. . . . full of experience—of people's feelings and sorrows" (p. 22), indicates an innate sensitivity to the continuity and relatedness of human experience as embodied in things. The old is meaningful insofar as one feels in it common human experience.

In his relations to the past and to forms, to things and moral values, Ralph represents the ideal civilized consciousness. Unlike Osmond, he has no pretensions whatsoever to the title of the "first gentleman of Europe," but in a world in which Gardencourt is not passed on to an heir, he comes close to deserving it.

" 'It has not been a successful life,' " Ralph's mother says to Isabel just before his death. Her answer is " 'No—it has only been a beautiful one' " (p. 500), "beautiful," of course, in the sense of the moral imagination, which is, indeed, in James rarely not opposed to "success" in Mrs. Touchett's terms. No less subtle in intellect and knowing about the arts and amenities of civilized life than Osmond, Ralph has not used art egotistically. Seen against an art background and presented through art imagery, again unlike Osmond, who is expressed through his "small, odd, elaborate" water colors and his copy of "the drawing of an antique coin," he is not delimited by these associations. Only Madame Merle, presumably speaking with exaggeration but actually with more malice than Isabel at the time realizes, defines Ralph through his collection—she cites him as an example of the expatriate American whose identity is his "very pretty collection of old snuff-boxes"—and unwittingly gives herself away.

To return to my initial quotation, the true wisdom of Madame Merle's words is ultimately understood by Isabel. Isabel's life has been a web of relationships rather than the ship with wind in its sails. In returning to Osmond at the end, she affirms her commitment to life, not joyously (how could she?) but nevertheless positively. In resisting the temptation of freedom, which in the past she has both feared and desired, and thus in accepting the choice of Osmond as her own, though she knows it is not absolutely so, she accepts actuality and necessity. By acting as if she has been free, she arrives at the knowledge that is the essence of Strether's speech on "moulds" and "freedom" to little Bilham.

There is the problem of the "white lighting" imagery of Casper Goodwood's famous kiss in the last scene at Gardencourt, as it makes sexual fear seem crucial in showing Isabel the "very straight path" to Rome and makes the freedom of her choice illusory. Moreover, her choice of an older man for a husband after her rejection of likelier suitors and other indications of sexual coldness suggest sexual-psychological determinism at work. Whether James intended it or not, Isabel is thus seen as a victim of her own sexual nature, which conflicts with the view of her as having gained in awareness. This ambiguity is partially James's fault: he says more than he probably means to imply. As is true elsewhere in his work, he fails to treat sexual experience deftly or fully. One senses that he is not aware of the psychological issues he has introduced. Partially, the difficulty may be attributed to the differences between an essentially pre-Freudian and post-Freudian frame of mind. Modern readers habituated to thinking of behavior as primarily unconsciously motivated tend to single out imagery in James's work that supports a psychological interpretation and thus they overlook other significant patterns.

Ironically, echoing the earlier Miltonic phrasing applied to Isabel after seeing her sister off ("The world lay before her—she could do whatever she chose" p. 282), Casper ends his plea with,

"The world's all before us—and the world's very big. I know something about that."

Isabel gave a long murmur, like a creature in pain; it was as if he were pressing something that hurt her. "The world's very small," she said at random; she had an immense desire to appear to resist. She said it at random, to hear herself say something; but it was not what she meant. The world, in truth, had never seemed so large; it seemed to open out, all round her, to take the form of a mighty sea, where she floated in fathomless waters. She had wanted help, and here was help; it had come in a rushing torrent. I know not whether she believed everything he said; but she believed just then that to let him take her in his arms would be the next best thing to her dying.[10]

Then, another drowning, dying image: as he kisses her, "she felt each thing in his hard manhood that had least pleased her, each aggressive fact of his face, his figure, his presence, justified of its intense identity and made one with this act of possession. So had she heard of those wrecked and under water following a train of images before they sink" (NY, IV, 436). Earlier, on her journey from Rome to London, she had

Plate XIII   Bronzino: *Lucrezia Panciatichi.* (Uffizi.)

Plate XIV Walter Gay: *Interior of Palazzo Barbaro*. (Courtesy of Museum of Fine Arts, Boston, Charles Henry Hayden Fund.)

Plate XV William Rimmer: *Flight and Pursuit.* (Courtesy of Museum of Fine Arts, Boston, Miss Edith Nichols Fund.)

Plate XVI Hiram Powers: *Diana*. (Courtesy of the Corcoran Gallery of Art.)

desired death itself but at the same time had had a feeling that "life would be her business for a long time to come" (NY, IV, 392).

The images of drowning and death in association with Casper imply within the intellectual pattern of the novel that with her final rejection of him she has indeed returned to the beginning at Gardencourt but with the difference that she realizes that the "self" is a "whole envelope of circumstances" and that "there is no such thing as an isolated man or woman." The self needs the shell, though some (Osmond, Madame Merle) wrongly consider the shell as primary. It is an illusion to suppose that one can live separately from others and that one is free to disavow one's commitments, relations, and things.

The conclusion is meant to be tragically affirmative. It is true that at the end of the novel we feel indeed that "character is fate"—that Isabel could not have acted in any other way. But one of the triumphs of *The Portrait* is that we make this judgment after the fact; corresponding to our own sense of life as we live it, we feel in the course of the novel that she is "affronting her destiny" rather than succumbing to it—that though we see the net tighten she does have options. Passion and moral choice come into conflict in James more than once: there is the carriage scene, for example, in *The Golden Bowl* in which Maggie has to resist the Prince's overtures in order to pursue the clues in their moral labyrinth. The title, *The Portrait of a Lady*, is not meant to be commiserative. Isabel is not trapped within a frame. In accepting the limitations of a frame, she becomes in herself, in her acceptance of the imperfect world in its materiality, a representation of the ideal in the real, which is what James looked for in great portraiture.

II

In the works from *The Portrait* to *The Wings of the Dove* (1902), James registers a continuing belief in the evil of divorcing aesthetic from human values, but art imagery and art objects play, with a few notable exceptions, a less prominent role in the definition of character and clarification of moral conflicts. To some extent, the decreased significance of art is due to James's temporary abandonment of the international theme. When not invaded by perambulating Americans, the museum world recedes into the background. Another explanation for this change lies in the nature of the new subjects and techniques, in the social criticism of the novels of the late 1880's and in the technical experimentation in the works of the later 1890's, especially with the dramatic method in *The Awkward Age* and *What Maisie Knew*. The shifting points of view in the former are incompatible with consistency in art imagery, and dialogue subordinates visual detail. In *What Maisie Knew*, the child's point of view largely precludes extensive use of art imagery. Nevertheless, even in these works, art objects and imagery function in the assessment of character and mark degrees of awareness. For example, in *What Maisie Knew* as what the child understands becomes commensurate with what she sees, the process traced in the novel, her aesthetic judgment is modified by the increased complexity of her social and moral judgment; the Countess's drawing room that impressed Maisie before meeting her seems contaminated by the "queer expression" of her face and by Maisie's realization that she is a woman whom no one else she knows "could possibly have liked" (NY, XI, 196).

While aesthetic values are of some importance in *The Bostonians*, mainly negatively as in Olive Chancellor's suppression of her taste, they are crucial in *The Princess Casamassima*. The central conflict is between civilization—the "monuments and treasures of art, the great palaces and properties, the conquests of learning and taste"—and radical forces aimed at redressing social evils—"the despotisms, the cruelties, the exclusions, the monopolies, and the rapacities"—on which this civilization rests. The irreconcilability of beauty and social justice, taste and egalitarianism, is demonstrated in the hero's case: half-aristocratic, half-plebian, torn between his radical opinions and his artistic sensibility, abandoned by friends from both political sides and classes, he takes his own life because he is unwilling either to help destroy "the fabric of civilisation" or to be disloyal to those who wish to bring about a new social order. It is through a series of broadening exposures to the arts of civilized life that Hyacinth's natural taste is educated and his imagination awakened to the splendor and beauty of the old order: Sholto's room decorated with trophies of wide travel; the Princess's London house appointed to befit her high station and reflecting her superb taste; Medley, the English country house, the most exquisite product of English culture, a harmony of humanized landscape, history and art; and, finally, Paris and Venice, the former revealing to Hyacinth the meaning of style and the latter crystallizing his awareness of "the great achievements of which man has been capable . . . the splendid accumulations of the happier few, to which doubtless the miserable many have also in their degree contributed" (NY, VI, 145).

The insight, however, which leads to Hyacinth's defection—in attitude, not in action—from the radical cause is not merely that civilization is worth saving, but that at bottom the revolutionists are motivated by an "insidious jealousy," a "grudging attitude—the intolerance of positions and fortunes that are higher and brighter than one's own" (NY, VI, 146). Poupin, after hearing Hyacinth's praise of Paris, remarks: " 'Ah yes, it's very fine, no doubt, . . . but it will be finer still when it's ours'—a speech which caused Hyacinth to turn back to his work with a feeling of sickness. Everywhere, everywhere he saw the ulcer of envy—the greed of a party hanging together only that it might despoil another to its advantage. In old Eustache, one of the 'pure,' this was especially disenchanting" (NY, VI, 158). Similarly, in Muniment and the Princess, instead of considering the objective political or social basis of their radicalism, James explores their private, partially unconscious motivations, which, as they are not disinterested, compromise the radical position itself. Muniment wants to be prime minister. He hardly seems to care that Hyacinth may lose his life; without her husband's money, he has no use for the Princess. Insensitive to color and form, he wears a necktie, Hyacinth observes, which is a "crude false blue" (NY, V, 114) and admires the gimcrackery in the Madiera Crescent house. One might wish that James had not included these touches which come across as cultural snobbery, but Hyacinth prizes his friendship nevertheless, and it is not Muniment's bad taste, a premonition of what the new democracy prizes, which damns him but his desire to get what he considers beautiful and tasteful into his own hands for his own use. Significantly, the plural of his name means a document or documents serving as evidence of title to property. At bottom, the difference between Hyacinth and Muniment is the difference between the disinterested imagination and the ambitious power seeker.

The Princess is the obverse of Muniment in cultivation, but, though more complexly and sympathetically portrayed, her idealism is likewise egotistic. Her sacrifices of taste to humanitarianism are perverse and self-deceiving: she moves into the Madiera Crescent house with its "stuffed birds in the window, alabaster Cupid, the wax flowers on the chimney-piece, the florid antimacassars on the chairs, the sentimental engravings on the walls" (NY, VI, 181) on the "theory that the right way to acquaint oneself with the sensations of the wretched was to suffer the anguish of exasperated taste" (NY, VI, 182). Restless and eager, vain and sincere, she descends into Philistia, but she keeps in her pocket her passport out. She "confesses" the admirable sentiment that "when thousands and tens of thousands haven't bread to put in their mouths" she "can dispense with tapestry and old china," but Hyacinth notices "she couldn't dispense with a pair of immaculate gloves which fitted her to a charm" (NY, VI, 168–69). The sacrifice of her love of beautiful things to the people is both factitious and gratuitous; like Madame Merle, Osmond, and Urbain she misuses things; she gives them up for the same reason they acquire them—to create a self-gratifying image. Though Hyacinth too blandly accepts the suffering of "the miserable many" as the price for civilized life, he at least realizes, as the revolutionists do not, that every great achievement must be paid for in some way. But even more important, like Ralph and Isabel, he has no desire to possess the wonders of the world in order to increase his own power or to exclude others from enjoyment. Responding to the voices of memory speaking through things, he instinctively allies himself with the class committed to their preservation.

Although contemporary in his literary culture, James glorified the visual arts of the past, created in an aristocratic society. Fearing that the rise of the masses would result in a debasement of cultural values, if not actual destruction of the relics of civilization, he viewed social radicalism as a threat, yet he also considered the existing social order to be corrupt. He was not under the illusion that the aristocracy was fulfilling its obligations, even in the narrow sense of art preservation. In *The Outcry* (1911) he deals overexplicitly with the question "of the degree in which the fortunate owners of precious and hitherto transmitted works of art hold them in trust, as it were, for the nation, and may themselves, as lax guardians, be held to account by public opinion."[11] A nouvelle—originally a play—*The Outcry* is chiefly interesting as a statement of James's attitude toward the responsibilities of aristocratic owners of paintings.

The impoverished Lord Theign, whose name speaks for the venerability of his house, is willing to sell a painting, about which there is some doubt as to attribution though not of period authenticity, to the American millionaire Breckenridge Bender. Hugh Crimble, a man without great ancestors, one of the new connoisseurs who like Bernard Berenson are upsetting the old standards of evaluation and classification, nevertheless upholds the aristocratic ideal of keeping treasures intact in their setting. He knows that the Rubens in the Dedborough library is a fake, but he will not "expose" the Theigns if they "go straight,"[12] that is, do not break up their collection. Except for Lady Grace, none of the members of the aristocracy has this reverence for continuities, of the rightness of the ancestral portrait in the ancestral house, or accepts his view of their roles as guardians for the public good of these treasures. The values of Lady Grace's suitor, Lord John, are pecuniary; pictures to him are a means of raising cash. He stands to gain a commission on Bender's purchase. Lady Sandgate is less reprehensible than Lord John, but she, too, strikes a modern note and *sub rosa* tries to persuade Bender to buy her great-grandmother's portrait by Lawrence. Lord Theign apparently stands for the old sanctities, but in him these mainly take the form of pride and exercise of personal power. He thinks he is exercising his traditional English rights in doing whatever he pleases with his own possessions. But both Lady Grace and Crimble think he is disloyal to England in disposing of the picture. According to their view, he is not a free agent but is "great" because he meets "tests" and "opportunities" with "greatness." Theign, Crimble thinks, takes care of his greatness in a cheap way by refusing to have anything to do with him rather than in the great way by refusing to have anything to do with Bender. The warning is sounded that the aristocracy will not continue to be seen "in the grand glamour of their greatness" (p. 241) by their inferiors unless they fulfill their social obligations. Theign eventually does fulfill his, but not quite for the reasons Crimble and Lady Grace would wish. He is willing to sell the picture to Bender only for a "decent, sufficient, civilised Dedborough price" (p. 262), but not for the hundred thousand dollars Bender wants to buy it for: Bender cares not at all about the picture's identity or aesthetic qualities; he only wants it to be made known that he has paid a fabulous price for it. Theign is in the end forced to act greatly and grandly in spite of himself; Lord John tricks him into giving the picture to the National Gallery.

To return to *The Princess*, one of the weaknesses of the novel is that Hyacinth seems too special a case and too passive to bear the burden of meaning he is meant to carry. In attempting to dramatize social injustice through the pathos of a refined sensibility excluded from the artistic riches of the civilized world and in assessing the radicals almost entirely by their characters rather than by their politics, James, in effect, undertook to write a novel with broad social implications while committed to a highly individualistic attitude and a subjective narrative method. And, indeed, what is most moving in the work is the opening up to Hyacinth of the beauty of the world, not the human suffering which at least partially underwrites its creation. It is the treatment of the hereditary leisure class as not fulfilling its responsibilities as the devoted keeper and transmitter of civilization that saves the work from a fatal one-sidedness. Although the Princess does not speak for James generally, her judgment of the venality and spiritual emptiness of the English aristocracy is his own, as is evident from his other fiction—*The Outcry*, most blatantly—and his biography. The envy at the bottom of the social ladder is matched by the stupidity, immorality, and irresponsibility at the top. The bias is in favor of conservatism, but in the portrayal of Hyacinth's dilemma and suicide, James does not gloss over the impasse in the conflict between civilization and of social justice. Both the old and the new order are condemned in his death.

The Spoils of Poynton begins with a marshaling of forces in what seems will be clear-cut conflict between insensibility and civilization, will and imagination, the new and the old. Mona Brigstock of the awful Brigstocks of Waterbath, whose wallpaper keeps Mrs. Gereth awake at night, is the barbarian, who, according to James, "is *all* will, without the smallest leak of force into taste or tenderness or vision, into any sense of shades or relations or proportions."[13] She has none of Fleda's wasteful perceptions and scruples or Mrs. Gereth's passion for beauty. The purity of bad taste at Waterbath is the clue to her power: The house is

smothered . . . with trumpery ornament and scrapbook art, with strange excrescences and bunchy draperies, with gimcracks that might have been keepsakes for maid-servants and nondescript conveniences that might have been prizes for the blind. They had gone wildly astray over carpets and curtains; they had an infallible instinct for gross deviation and were so cruelly doom-ridden that it rendered them almost tragic. . . . The house was perversely full of souvenirs of places even more ugly than itself and of things it would have been a pious duty to forget. (NY, X, 7)

As for the beautiful things at Poynton, she thinks that "they're all right!" (NY, X, 29). She is incapable of feeling their beauty, but she does not want Owen without them. That she and Owen afterward stay away confirms that she has wanted possession alone. The servants Mona leaves behind prove to be poor caretakers of the great treasure; the fire, it is implied, is due to neglect.

But long before the end, the question of sides becomes almost intolerably obfuscated, for Mrs. Gereth is not a "free spirit," as James also notes in his preface. That having Adele Gereth as a mother, Owen should choose Mona for a wife is not as much a marvel as Fleda thinks. Mrs. Gereth is admirable in her energy and the boldness of her stratagems, "masterful and clever," but is lacking in "the imagination of loving," the generosity of spirit and openness to life of a Ralph Touchett, to whom the phrase was applied. Fleda feels that

She had no imagination about anybody's life save on the side she bumped against. Fleda was quite aware that she would have otherwise been a rare creature, but a rare creature was originally just what she had struck her as being. Mrs. Gereth had really no perception of anybody's nature—had only one question about persons: were they clever or stupid? To be clever meant to know the "marks." Fleda knew them by direct inspiration, and a warm recognition of this had been her friend's tribute to her character. (NY, X, 138)

While she has great gifts—in her way, she is a creative artist—her devotion to beauty has supplanted her respect for human feelings. Fleda soon perceives that she has a "strange, almost maniacal disposition to thrust in everywhere the question of 'things' . . . . 'Things' were of course the sum of the world; only, for Mrs. Gereth, the sum of the world was rare French furniture and oriental china" (NY, X, 24). Hers is not, however, a "crude love of possession"; she is willing to relinquish the treasures to one who will love and appreciate them. She is as splendid and sublime as any great martyr in her "need to be faithful to a trust and loyal to an idea" (NY, X, 46), and indeed her devotion to the beauty she had created is fanatically religious. She can hardly be made to understand why Fleda resents being offered to Owen as a wife who would be worthy of Poynton, for she seems to care at first for Fleda "only as a priestess of the altar" (NY, X, 37) and thinks only of how to use Fleda's feeling for Owen "not only with the best conscience in the world but with a high brutality of good intentions" (NY, X, 131). In short, "the truth was simply that all Mrs. Gereth's scruples were on one side and that her ruling passion had in a manner despoiled her of her humanity" (NY, X, 37).

Mrs. Gereth is a victim of the English custom in accordance with which Owen is to inherit the house and all of its contents and Mrs. Gereth to receive a maintenance and Ricks, the dower house. (In James's original plan for *The Spoils*, the inequity of the English practice was to be fully developed.) "No account whatever had been taken of her relation to her treasures." Her husband "appeared to have assumed that she would settle questions with her son and that he could depend upon Owen's affection and Owen's fairness" (NY, X, 15–16). Though she is a victim of a social law, she is also responsible for her situation. It is strongly intimated that she has devoted her energies to creating the perfection of Poynton at the expense of cultivating her son's potentialities and an affectionate relationship with him. "What a strange relation between mother and son," Fleda thinks, "when there was no fundamental tenderness out of which a solution would irrepressibly spring!" (NY, X, 44). From the beginning, in fact, Mrs. Gereth shows that she does not really understand Owen; she continually misjudges him and imagines him to be abusing her, when, in fact, he behaves decently and thoughtfully, and to be insensitive to the treasures of Poynton, when he has cared for and felt pride in them. Such slowness of mind and utterance, such simplicity and clumsiness in a son of Mrs. Gereth's suggests that she has neglected to bring out the best values in the human material she has been given to work with.

Yet, with her free manner, high insolence, and buccaneer spirit, she is one of the most likable, strongly colored women in James's gallery. In the scene in which she comes to Fleda to announce her return of the spoils expecting that Fleda *has* Owen only to find that she has made him return to Waterbath, her angry outspokenness is a relief from Fleda's subtleties and qualifications. Fleda

exclaimed with a certain hard pride: "He's enough in love with me for anything!"

"For anything apparently save to act like a man and impose his reason and his will on your incredible folly. For anything save to put an end, as any man worthy of the name would have put it, to your systematic, to your idiotic perversity." . . . She paused. . . . then exclaimed with the very best of her coarseness: "Any one but a jackass would have tucked you under his arm and marched you off to the Registrar!" (NY, X, 219–20)

What she calls a spade, however, is not quite a spade. In fact, her failure to know Fleda precipitates the marriage. She does not consider the possibility that Fleda might not act as she herself would. Assuming that Fleda has secured Owen, Mrs. Gereth returns the things to Poynton. Somehow, Mona hears of it. When she "has let herself go," Owen succumbs. After there is no doubt her life's work is lost, Mrs. Gereth is generous with Fleda and otherwise bears the loss with dignity and fortitude. Just as she momentarily reveals to Fleda "the showy side of truth, . . . a blinding glimpse of lost alternatives" (NY, X, 219), Fleda educates Mrs. Gereth in the associative beauty of Ricks: "Mrs. Gereth's face showed the dim dawn of an amusement at finding herself seated at the feet of her pupil" (NY, X, 249). Through her loss Mrs. Gereth is not converted to Fleda's idealism, but she is notably humanized; in turn, she helps Fleda to see the consequences of her prideful idealism.

Fleda's moral scruples seem an "incredible folly" not only to Mrs. Gereth but also to many critics. In allowing Owen to marry a woman whom he supposedly hates and who is obviously a terrible person, Fleda is judged guilty of pride, self-deception, and pernicious idealism. I think, however, that her refusal to assist Owen "save in the sense of their common honour" (NY, X, 106) is intended to be taken as moral heroism in spite of its consequences and Fleda's muddlement and self-idealizing tendencies. For an act to be heroic a serious risk must be involved, and Fleda is aware of the risk: "Even in the ardour of her meditation Fleda remained in sight of the truth that it would be an odd result of her magnanimity to prevent her friend's shaking off a woman he disliked." Fleda does not pursue moral heroism, however, without hope of eventual happiness. The authorial voice enters to make this clear: "We may not perhaps too much diminish the merit of that generosity if we mention that it could take the flight we are considering just because really, with the telescope of her long thought, Fleda saw what might bring her out of the wood. Mona herself would bring her out; at the least Mona possibly might" (NY, X, 108). She is idealistic but not quixotic. Her aspirations, like Theobald's and Isabel's, are doomed from the start, given Mrs. Gereth's misconception of her, Owen's weakness and sexual susceptibility, and Mona's unqualified will to possess, but there appears to be a possibility that she can be perfectly honorable *and* successful. Again, as with Theobald and Isabel, one sympathizes with her. Her downfall (whether it is also Owen's is unknowable) arises from generosity of spirit, inconsistent and deluded as she may be; it is, in the end, for that spirit that she is loved.

Her relation to objects distinguishes her from both Mrs. Gereth and Mona. The love of the beautiful plays almost as much a part in her life as in Mrs. Gereth's, but the girl's "was somehow the larger for it" (NY, X, 25). Her taste is inborn, not a matter of acquired knowledge. "The museums had done something for her, but nature had done more" (NY, X, 23). As she does not live by aesthetic criteria, she feels Mrs. Gereth "imprisoned her in that torment of taste" when she stays with her at Ricks furnished with the stolen things from Poynton. Taken out of their rightful setting, they seem to Fleda to "suffer like chopped limbs" (NY, X, 78–79). When she waits to learn whether Owen has in fact returned to Mona, her one consolation is that Poynton is again a splendid whole:

That they might have been, that they might still be hers, that they were perhaps already anothers, were ideas that had too little to say to her. They were nobody's at all—too proud, unlike base animals and humans, to be reducible to anything so narrow. It was Poynton that was theirs; they had simply recovered their own. (NY, X, 235)

Her consolation is short lived. When Owen writes asking her to accept from him "the thing in the whole house that's most beautiful and precious," she does not need to understand what his request means: "what determined her was the simple strength of her impulse to respond" (NY, X, 258, 260). Imagining her hour in the great rooms of Poynton, "she should be able to say to herself that, for once at least, her possession was as complete as that of either of the others whom it had filled only with bitterness" (NY, X, 260). She is not allowed her moment of possession, nor the precious thing, which probably would have been the Maltese cross. In the later stories "The Tone of Time" and "The Special Type" the sensitive deprived women, who have been used by rapacious successful people, are each left with a presumably consoling portrait of the man loved. Neither the symbolic recovery of Poynton nor the precious object that Owen wishes her to have is to be Fleda's. "Mixed with the horror, with the kindness of the station-master, with the smell of cinders and the riot of sound was the raw bitterness of a hope that she might never again in life have to give up so much at such short notice." The loss of Owen's tribute to her underscores the finality of her loss of him and, possibly, the loss of the cross represents the temptation she must resist of seeing herself as martyr to an ideal. "She heard herself repeat mechanically, yet as if asking it for the first time: 'Poynton's *gone*?' The man faltered. 'What can you call it, miss, if it ain't really saved?' " (NY, X, 266). The logic is irrefutable: extended it means that if Owen and Poynton have not been really saved, they are really gone. What is left to her is not, however, nothing. The fire and the loss of the cross would seem to imply that she must be stripped of lingering illusions as to the consequences of her idealism. But the last line is "I'll go back." And what she goes back to is Ricks, which represents the humanized beauty that James consistently in his works contrasts with formal beauty divorced from the accidents and rough and tumble of life. (In "The Beldonald Holbein" of this same period an ironic contrast is drawn between the shallow vain Lady Beldonald, who has preserved her conventional beauty by means of a plate-glass imperviousness to others, and Mrs. Brash, whose exposure to life has made her beautiful in old age; "every wrinkle was the touch of a master." "Time and life were artists" the painter observes, "who beat us all, working with recipes and secrets we could never find out" [NY, XVIII, 394].) Fleda Vetch recognizes the beauty of the uncollected and the unarranged, the beauty that has nothing to do with marks or periods but that arises from the human life of which the relics have been a part. It is this kind of beauty that she from the first responds to in Ricks: she feels in the house "crowded with objects of which the aggregation somehow made a thinness and the futility a grace" (NY, X, 54) the spirit of the maiden aunt who gathered them. They convey her history and to Fleda give an impression, "the impression in which half the beauty resides—the impression somehow of something dreamed and missed, something reduced, relinquished, resigned; the poetry of, as it were, of something sensibly *gone.*" Little undistinguished Ricks has a "kind of fourth dimension . . . a presence, a perfume, a touch. It's a soul, a story, a life." The only fault of Poynton with its handsome and finely sifted collection was that, like any other magnificent museum, it was "too splendidly happy" (NY, X, 249–50) to have had a ghost. Time and suffering enrich places as well as persons; they thus acquire a grace, a luster, which transcends surface beauty.

III

In James's late international novels,[14] things play an even greater role than in the fiction of the middle years in defining character and themes. As his Americans once more confront their destinies in Europe, the museum world is the arena and test it had been in the earlier phase: Lambert Strether's succumbing to old world charms, the softening-up process having begun in the shadows of the "wicked old Rows of Chester," recalls Mary Garland's discoveries through Roman rides of greater possible mixtures of good and evil than New England ever dreamed of. Milly Theale, the American princess in a Venetian palace, is the apotheosis of all of her predecessors, all the Isabel Archers who sought life among the ruins and relics of a decaying Europe. Maggie Verver's acquisition of the Prince for his family history as much as for his private self goes back to the little American Martha who fell in love with the last of the Valerii as much for his ancient villa as for his personal attractions.

The individual threads that James weaves together to create his most elaborate and cunningly complex tapestry, *The Golden Bowl*, are familiar: recognizable in Adam Verver are some of the collector traits of Gilbert Osmond, Rowland Mallet, and Mrs. Gereth; in him the lineaments of Christopher Newman's good faith and innocence may also be traced. Without arrogance and without awareness of the disruptive power of their wealth, both seek the best of European culture. The Prince Amerigo also has his predecessors. Like Madame de Vionnet, he embodies transmitted history, and like Merton Densher, he learns, in R. P. Blackmur's words, "a new possible, impossible (James's phrase) mode of love in which conscience and moral beauty are joined."[15] Charlotte Stant is the Jamesian socially adept, worldly woman, like Kate Croy and Madame Merle, with a talent for life that makes her great but not good. And Maggie Verver, the little princess, is the inevitable American girl, not, however, seeking life, as Isabel Archer and Milly Theale do, but forced to seek it against her inclinations. In short, the novel may be viewed as James's fictional *summa* of the interrelations of morality and aesthetics, inherited and acquired culture, European experience and American innocence. As it is a self-contained work although most of its elements have been encountered before, one of the main questions to be answered is, Does it also reflect a belief that art should be a mode of knowledge arising out of human life and referable to it, not a means of escape or insulation from it?

The crux of the problem is Adam Verver. As he has some of the connoisseur's traits associated with egotism in other works, some critics view him as essentially an inhumane aesthete. Others see him as essentially beneficent if not the incarnation of wisdom.[16] What, indeed, is to be made of him, "the incredible little idealist" in his inveterate frock coat and pale blue cravat with his incalculable millions and motives?

First of all, the plan of the novel requires that Verver's knowledge of the intrigue between the Prince and Charlotte should remain a mystery. Maggie, in the scene in her room in which she confronts the Prince with the evidence of the golden bowl, flings at him the challenge to " 'find out the rest!' " (NY, XXIV, 203), that is, to find out whether or not her father knows what she knows. Charlotte's and the Prince's punishment, their cage, is partially that they cannot find out how much, if anything, Verver knows about their relationship. Maggie herself never openly discusses it with him, but the evidence of three remarkable scenes between her and her father—that in the park near Portland Place, the talk under the tree at Fawns in which Maggie leads him to understand that she is sacrificing him, and the visit before Charlotte's and Adam's departure for America—leaves no doubt that while neither says anything overtly, each is aware of what the other knows. Furthermore, Verver's feelings for Charlotte are unknown even to Maggie and therefore to the reader. (More will be said about the significance of this point later.) Verver, then, is the most enigmatic of the four principal characters, not only because he is seen more often in a reflected light but also because the suspense and resolution of the "general embroglio"[17] depend on his having for the others an "unfathomable heart."

A second point to bear in mind is that James is aiming here for a kind of ultrapsychological realism, "for the process and effect of representation, my irrepressible ideal."[18] He attempts to convey only what could be known from two perspectives about a situation as it develops in which four (five counting Fanny Assingham) people become embroiled and in which, as happens in actuality, no one of the involved persons is entirely guiltless, though degrees of responsibility vary, and all do not achieve the same level of awareness. Maggie Verver is the heroine nominally and actually, but she has no opposite; neither Charlotte nor the Prince is villainous. It is debatable who initially is more culpable: the Ververs with their money and goodness or the Prince and Charlotte with their opportunism and good faith.

The Ververs' acquisition of the Prince is hardly crass—Maggie is genuinely in love with her idea of him, and he in turn considers Verver a *"real* galantuomo" (NY, XXIII, 6) and her charming and beautiful in the Jamesian sense. But the brute fact behind the civilized agreement is that he is selected and purchased for his marks and signs of value, as if he were an old master, the Luini, for example, which Adam verifies at the same time that he checks the Prince's credentials. Maggie jokes about his being a "morceau de musée" (NY, XXIII, 12), but jokes have a way of expressing deeper truths than their tellers sometimes realize. Similarly, Adam is attracted to Charlotte because she has social gifts on a grand scale. After Charlotte has cleared out the Miss Lutches and Mrs. Rance, Fanny Assingham points out to Adam that she has succeeded because she is the "real thing";

The note of reality, in so much projected light, continued to have for him the charm and the importance of which the maximum had occasionally been reached in his great "finds"–continued, beyond any other, to keep him attentive and gratified. Nothing perhaps might affect us as queerer, had we time to look into it, than this application of the same measure of value to such different pieces of property as old Persian carpets, say, and new human acquisitions; all the more indeed that the amiable man was not without an inkling, on his own side, that he was, as a taster of life, economically constructed. He put into his one little glass everything he raised to his lips, and it was as if he had always carried in his pocket, like a tool of his trade, this receptacle, in a little glass cut with a fineness of which the art had long since been lost, and kept in an old morocco case stamped in ineffaceable gilt with the arms of a deposed dynasty. . . . It was all, at bottom, in him, the aesthetic principle, planted where it could burn with a cold, still flame; where it fed almost wholly on the material directly involved, on the idea (followed by appropriation) of plastic beauty, of the thing visibly perfect in its kind; where, in short, despite the general tendency of the "devouring element" to spread, the rest of his spiritual furniture, modest, scattered, and tended with unconscious care, escaped the consumption that in so many cases proceeds from the undue keeping-up of profane altar-fires. (NY, XXXIII, 196–97)

The implication of the passage is that Verver judges both human beings and things according to aesthetic standards but that his connoisseurship and acquisitive instincts have not corrupted his moral values. And, indeed, Verver is neither a heartless aesthete like Gilbert Osmond nor a futile one like Gabriel Nash. Collecting for him is an intellectual passion and is directed toward a philanthropic end; it is not a means of gaining personal prestige or of exerting power over others. There is also evidence that he has separated, even when they impinge, his love of art from his personal relations. Art objects given as gifts of love are exempt from critical appraisal: Maggie looks for a birthday gift for Adam in the shabby unpromising Bloomsbury antique shop (where she comes upon the golden bowl) only because she does not try to find something really good. She knows his "sweet theory that the individual gift, the friendship's offering, was by a rigorous law of nature a foredoomed aberration, and that the more it *was* so the more it showed, and the more one cherished it for showing, how friendly it had been" (NY, XXIV, 156). From the beginning of their marriage, Charlotte seems to work his love of beauty as if it were the only love of which he were capable. Adam's memories of his first wife's taste are not happy ones—"the futilities, the enormities, the depravities of decoration and ingenuity, . . . she had made him think lovely!" (NY, XXIII, 143). In contrast, Charlotte "had probably not so much as once treated him to a rasping mistake or a revealing stupidity." But possibly Charlotte overdoes this "fortunately natural source of sympathy" between them: "she abounded, to odd excess, one might have remarked, in the assumption of its being for her, with her husband, *all* the ground, the finest clearest air, the most breathable medium common to them. It had been given to Maggie to wonder if she didn't in these intensities of approbation too much shut him up to his province" (NY, XXIV, 286–87).

In an almost Dantesque matching of penance to sin, abandoned by her lover and fearful of the doom her husband is preparing for her, Charlotte has during those terrible last days at Fawns only one way to present an image of herself as a faithful wife. Demonstrating her "cheerful submission to duty," she acts as cicerone to Adam's collection and coerces bewildered, "semi-scared" visitors into listening to pointless lectures on garlands of "the finest possible *vieux Saxe*" in a voice which sounds to Maggie "like the shriek of a soul in pain" (NY, XXIV, 291–92).

Though Verver keeps "his spiritual furniture" intact, his collector's passion for "the thing visibly perfect in its kind" applied to "human acquisitions" has nearly calamitous consequences. Judging by the "aesthetic principle," he neglects the relatedness of the object or person to the social and historical context. Most perniciously innocent is his assumption—which Maggie initially shares—that one's life, like one's museum, may be perfectly arranged, "a triumph of selection."

There is a touch of megalomania in Verver's philanthropic schemes and confidence in his connoisseurship, as several passages dealing with his "monomania," James's phrase, suggest. His realization "that he had in him the spirit of the connoisseur," a revelation which he compares to Cortez's discovery of the Pacific in Keats's poem, transforms his life: he perceives that "a world was left him to conquer and that he might conquer if he tried." His awareness "of the affinity of Genius, or at least of Taste, with something in himself," makes him feel "equal, somehow, with the great seers, the invokers and encouragers of beauty—and he didn't after all perhaps dangle so far below the great producers and creators" (NY, XXIII, 140–41). His confidence in his own taste "represented it must be allowed his one principle of pride." His "divination of his faculty most went to his head" in Rome, "where the princes and Popes had been before him," but where not one of them, it is his belief

> had read a richer meaning . . . into the character of the Patron of Art. He was ashamed of them really, if he wasn't afraid, and he had on the whole never so climbed to the tip-top as in judging, over a perusal of Hermann Grimm, where Julius II and Leo X were "placed" by their treatment of Michael Angelo. Far below the plain American citizen—in the case at least in which this personage happened not to be too plain to be Adam Verver. Going to our friend's head, moreover, some of the results of such comparisons may doubtless be described as having stayed there. (NY, XXIII, 149–50)

That Adam considers himself superior as a patron to Renaissance popes is not without irony, for unlike the patrons who mistreated Michelangelo, Verver apparently does not collect contemporary works at all, nor is there any suggestion that he is in touch with any living artists whatsoever. In his search for treasures he goes to some strange, out-of-the-way places, but concentrating on old masters, tapestries, ancient tiles, and antique furniture, he is hardly venturesome as an art collector.

That art collecting breeds, or at any rate fosters, in the Ververs a superficial, romantic view of history and fails to teach them the importance of ambience and continuity in a culture is evident in their acquisition and subsequent treatment of the Prince. Adam Verver is himself a modern merchant prince, but his incalculable riches and extraordinary taste cannot provide him with a venerable family tree. His given name almost too obviously suggests not only his innocence and necessary fall but his lack of antecedents. In contrast, the Prince exists, at the beginning, almost in virtue of his family name and archives. Maggie's interest in him is first aroused when she hears a friend greet him by the name that he has inherited from his explorer ancestor—Amerigo Vespucci. The Prince warns her before their marriage that she does not know him personally.

"There are two parts of me. . . . One is made up of the history, the doings, the marriages, the crimes, the follies, the boundless *bêtises* of other people. . . . But there's another part, very much smaller doubtless, which, such as it is, represents my single self, the unknown, unimportant–unimportant save to *you*—personal quantity. About this you've found out nothing." . . . [But Maggie declares she is] "not afraid of history!" . . . "What was it else," Maggie Verver had also said, "that made me originally think of you? It wasn't —as I should suppose you must have seen—what you call your unknown quantity, your particular self. It was the generations behind you, the follies and crimes, the plunder and the waste—the wicked Pope, the monster most of all, whom so many of the volumes in your family library are all about. . . . Where, therefore"–she had put it to him again–"without your archives, annals, infamies, would you have been?" (NY, XXIII, 9–10)

The limitations of the romantic view of history are shown up in Maggie: her imagination is aroused by the wickedness and plunder in the Prince's background, but she does not see his past as an integral part of him or him as a person. The habit of lifting things out of their historical contexts, of "rifling the Golden Isles," for the sake of an ideal—the recreation of civilization in a city west of the Mississippi—makes it natural for the Ververs to wrest the Prince out of his context, divorce him from his setting, while ignoring historical continuity and social place.

One of the reasons the Prince is vulnerable to Charlotte's advances is that he is not only morally but socially a displaced person. He expects through his marriage to make "new history," as he feels he is allying himself with "science," which he defines as "the absence of prejudice backed by the presence of money." But his hopes of "not being at all events futile" (NY, XXIII, 17) are not realized, for he becomes an appendage to the Ververs, not an ally. He is cherished by them as if he were a rare, eminent specimen of his class, a privilege to possess but too bright for use. As Colonel Assingham (whose opinions are not altogether to be discounted, though James makes much of the limitations of his imagination) observes, "The man's in a position in which he has nothing in life to do" (NY, XXIII, 278). The Prince feels himself to be an outsider in English society, even though "he was one of the modern Romans who find by the Thames a more convincing image of the truth of the ancient state than any they have left by the Tiber" (NY, XXIII, 3). He outwardly conforms to what is expected of him on English country visits, but "something of him, he often felt at these times, was left out: it was much more when he was alone, or when he was with his own people—or when he was, say, with Mrs. Verver and nobody else—that he moved, that he talked, that he listened, that he felt, as a congruous whole." Chosen by Lady Castledean to stay behind with Charlotte to "cover" for her "quiet morning with Mr. Blint" at Matcham, the Prince has no objections whatsoever but nevertheless has the sense of what "during his life in England, he had more than once had reflectively to deal: the state of being reminded how, after all, as an outsider, a foreigner, and even as a mere representative husband and son-in-law, he was so irrelevant to the working of affairs that he could be bent on occasion to uses comparatively trivial." Well able to rise above his reduced state—he goes off with Charlotte to Gloucester—he nevertheless feels that "it kept before him again, at moments, the so familiar fact of his sacrifices—down to the idea of the very relinquishment, for his wife's convenience, of his real situation in the world; with the consequence, thus, that he was, in the last analysis, among all these so often inferior people, practically held cheap and made light of" (NY, XXIII, 352–53).

Though officially the Prince's wife, Maggie is still Maggie Verver. Adam has "relieved him of all anxiety about his married life in the same manner in which he relieved him on the score of his bank-account." The Prince does not have to worry about a lack of intimacy with Maggie, for the "community of interest" that Maggie and Adam share has created a "deep intimacy" (NY, XXIII, 292–93) between them which in effect renders a personal relationship with Maggie unnecessary. Even as a father, having provided Maggie with a son, he has abdicated in favor of Adam:

It was of course an old story and a familiar idea that a beautiful baby could take its place as a new link between a wife and a husband, but Maggie and her father had, with every ingenuity, converted the precious creature into a link between a mamma and a grandpapa. The Principino, for a chance spectator of this process, might have become, by an untoward stroke, a hapless half-orphan, with the place of immediate male parent swept bare and open to the next nearest sympathy. (NY, XXIII, 156)

That the Prince is for Maggie after several years of marriage still a kind of valuable inheritance providing the Ververs with the needed consecration of the past is suggested in the very phrasing of the following passage. After visiting the British Museum to read further into the Prince's family history, Maggie feels greater ease about their marriage: "It was as if she hadn't come into so many noble and beautiful associations, nor secured them also for her boy, secured them even for her father, only to see them turn to vanity and doubt" (NY, XXIII, 155).

In his plan to "release from the bondage of ugliness" the people of his "adoptive city and native State," Verver is beneficent and inspired, yet fanatical and naïve. The museum is to be "a monument to the religion [Adam wishes] to propagate, the exemplary passion, the passion for perfection at any price" (NY, XXIII, 145–46). And it is this "passion for perfection" carried over into their personal lives which makes Maggie and Adam almost as responsible as Charlotte and the Prince for the failure of the marriages. They attempt to be kind, unselfish, morally worthy of their wealth, but they try too consciously to make an art of life, as if it were a plastic material capable of being shaped into a perfect form. They want to have everything—beautiful things, clear consciences, happy marriages, an undisturbed father and daughter relationship—without sacrificing anything.

Having learned the truth about the relations between Charlotte and the Prince, Maggie becomes aware of the hideousness that often exists side by side with beauty, the "awful mixture in things" of good and evil, and of the price that must be paid for happiness. " 'It's as if her unhappiness,' " she says of Charlotte to the Prince, on the eve of the final departure of Adam and his wife, " 'had been necessary to us—as if we had needed her, at her own cost, to build us up and start us' " (NY, XXIV, 346). Having awakened from the sleep of her "benighted innocence," she acts boldly, imaginatively, and compassionately to hold together the broken pieces of the golden bowl for the sake of "love." It is not the perfect work of art, but the flawed one, she acts to preserve.

Though Maggie comes to realize that for love one must be prepared to suffer and sacrifice, her faith in her father ultimately rests on her belief in him as a great man—"the 'successful' beneficent person, the beautiful bountiful original dauntlessly wilful great citizen, the consummate collector and infallible high authority" and above all in his self-confidence that "had somehow never appeared more identical with his proved taste of the rare and the true" (NY, XXIV, 273–74).

In the leavetaking scene, he and Maggie review her possessions:

She had passed her arm into his, and the other objects in the room, the other pictures, the sofas, the chairs, the tables, the cabinets, the "important" pieces, supreme in their way, stood out, round them, consciously, for recognition and applause. Their eyes moved together from piece to piece, taking in the whole nobleness–quite as if for him to measure the wisdom of old ideas. The two noble persons seated in conversation and at tea fell thus into the splendid effect and the general harmony: Mrs. Verver and the Prince fairly "placed" themselves, however unwittingly, as high expressions of the kind of human furniture required aesthetically by such a scene. The fusion of their presence with the decorative elements, their contribution to the triumph of selection, was complete and admirable; though to a lingering view, a view more penetrating than the occasion really demanded, they also might have figured as concrete attestations of a rare power of purchase. There was much indeed in the tone in which Adam Verver spoke again, and who shall say where his thought stopped? *"Le compte y est. You've got some good things."* (NY, XXIV, 360)

This passage is often cited to indicate that Maggie and Adam have not been cleansed of the collector's acquisitive taint. "Rare power of purchase" is the crucial phrase, in its literal and metaphorical meanings. It refers not only to the Verver wealth without which the scene with its "human furniture" could not have been assembled, but also to human resources: Charlotte's making the most of the dignity which Maggie has helped her to preserve; the Prince never blighting "by a single false step the perfection of his outward show" and achieving a new informed vision of goodness; Maggie's will, imagination, discipline, and ideal of love enabling her to reconstruct the marriages. Adam's "power of purchase" is both the most blatant and the most ambiguous. Maggie parts with her father on the basis of Charlotte's "value." " 'Charlotte's great,' " (NY, XXIV, 364) meaning in the sense of social presence, not in the sense of having "a great imagination" and "a great conscience" (NY, XXIII, 182), phrases Maggie had much earlier used in attempting to define her greatness to Adam. Verver's acuity in judgment is apparent in proposing that Charlotte would be "great for the world that was before her" (NY, XXIV, 365), that her highest talents would be put to use. Though American City seems unlikely to offer social promise to a woman who has attracted the attention of Royalty at a London diplomatic reception, the Prince is probably accurate in predicting that Charlotte will make a life for herself. Indeed, she has already begun: "Her mission had quite taken form—it was but another name for the interest of her great opportunity: that of representing the arts and graces to a people languishing afar off and in ignorance" (NY, XXIV, 357). The Prince and Charlotte are reduced in this scene to looking like "a pair of effigies of the contemporary great on one of the platforms of Madame Tussaud" (NY, XXIV, 360–61). Re-enacting the roles which they have previously been cast in and have accepted on their own terms, they momentarily exist because of the actual changes that have taken place as eerie facsimiles of themselves. But they have proved themselves to be rarities worth their price: they have behaved throughout in a manner so as not to destroy the possibility of recreating relationships so that the inner reality could be brought to correspond to the surface appearance. It also should not be forgotten that beneath the surface of mutual self-congratulation on the soundness of their original ideas, Maggie and Adam are attempting to reconcile themselves to a separation. The breaking of this tie is the highest price for her happiness with the Prince which Maggie must pay.

To some extent Verver, however, remains an enigma. Sifting all of the evidence, I think it is impossible, for example, to ascertain his real feelings for Charlotte. That he marries her because she is "the real thing" and because through the marriage he will relieve Maggie of anxiety about him is apparent. But to what extent is he motivated by other personal feelings and desires? In the scene at Fawns in which Adam arrives at the decision to ask her to marry him, he has the idea of asking her *before* he feels justified in doing so, before it comes to him as a kind of revelation that his marrying will benefit Maggie. Clearly, he is glad that Charlotte likes him, but after they have been married for some time, Charlotte tells Fanny that she has done her best to make him love her, but that he is inaccessible. Is he incapable of loving Charlotte because of his feelings for Maggie? Charlotte explicitly tells the Prince that she and Adam will never have children, but not why they will not. Besides, is Charlotte trustworthy, especially when she is justifying herself to Fanny or to the Prince? In the last scene, when Maggie praises Charlotte to him, a light comes into Adam's eyes which he cannot conceal, but then he speaks of her as "beautiful, beautiful," as if in appreciation of her as a fine work of art. His voice moreover sounds a note of "possession and control" which gratifies Maggie. Is this the husband who has asserted his rightful masculinity, or is this the father who is dragging his wife away from his son-in-law to save his daughter's marriage? It may be both, of course, and there is no way of knowing. One of the images that persists is that of Verver, as Maggie perceives it, his hand on the "long, fine cord" around Charlotte's neck, leading her back to America. She is, indeed, a valuable human animal who "wasn't to be wasted in the application of his plan" (NY, XXIV, 365). One's view of Verver's greatness of spirit in appreciating Charlotte's style depends on whether one feels the emphasis is on his intention that her talents be given a wide field for expression or whether the phrase "in the application of his plan" strikes one as the predominant note.

By concentrating on the implications of the Ververs' aestheticism and therefore on the first book of the novel, I have not given corresponding attention to the Prince's and Charlotte's contribution to the failure of the marriages. Their adulterous relationship is partially accounted for but not justified by Maggie's and Adam's seemingly implacable innocence and perfectionism. Irony pervades the presentation of the case for Charlotte and the Prince, to which the first book is devoted. A distinction is made between Charlotte and Amerigo: she is driven by passion and is the initiator; his is the undeveloped conscience and consciousness. Both are guilty of a betrayal of trust, self-deceiving about their rights and obligations, and deceived in not realizing the complexity of the Ververs' simplicity.

The golden bowl—a mysterious talisman which links and separates characters, a wedding and a birthday gift that is not a gift and yet proves eminently valuable, flawed but seemingly perfect—contributes to the parabolic, fairy-tale quality of the work. The other art imagery in conjunction with images of violence, unrest, and the exotic (the caravan, the pagoda, the broken neck, the sacrificial goat) helps to create the strange atmosphere of the novel—of surface decorum and lurking tensions and of confined, elaborated detail and the emptiness of vast spaces. Particular clusters of images, mainly architectural, emphasize the conflict between the private and the public life and between spiritual and worldly values. The very proliferation of art metaphors underscores the asocial historical position, possibly plight, of the characters.

When Edith Wharton asked James what his idea had been "in suspending the four principal characters in *The Golden Bowl* in the void," painfully surprised, he answered "in a disturbed voice: 'My dear,—I didn't know I had!' "[19] I suspect that James was considerably more aware of his own practice and intentions than Mrs. Wharton realized, for the presentation of his characters not through realistic descriptive detail but largely through art metaphors, creating the effect of a formal, highly civilized world removed from the forms of any particular society, is entirely in keeping with two of the basic assumptions of the novel: first, that the Ververs, as Americans from west of the Mississippi, individualistic, unreligious—Maggie, though a Catholic, throughout the crisis depends on herself, not on the guidance of her priest or the precepts of her religion—and intensely home-bound, private people, have only a vague conception of a hierarchical social order as a fact of existence, and, second, that existing society, represented in the novel by a stratum near the top of the English pyramid, Matcham, is corrupt.

Neither Maggie nor Adam has public presence: on the occasion of a Verver dinner party, Maggie seems to the Prince to have 'in perfection her own little character, but he wondered how it managed so visibly to simplify itself . . . to the essential air of having overmuch on her mind the felicity, and indeed the very conduct and credit, of the feast" (NY, XXIII, 322). Unlike Charlotte, who needs only the Verver money to demonstrate her mastery of the art of personal arrangement, Maggie lacks a clothes sense, taking refuge on this occasion in "bedizenment" when simplicity and fewer jewels would be more appropriate. Similarly, unimpressive in appearance and bearing, Adam as the host "at the top of his table" looks "like a little boy shyly entertaining in virtue of some imposed rank" (NY, XXIII, 324).

It is through art imagery that the contrast between the public personalities of the Prince and Charlottte and the essentially private dispositions of Maggie and Adam is dramatized. The Prince's eyes resemble "the high windows of a Roman palace" (NY, XXIII, 42); Adam thinks of him as a "great Palladian church" which had been dropped into "some pleasant public square, in the heart of an old city," that is, his and Maggie's "old-time union" (NY, XXIII, 135), and also compares the Prince's smoothness with the "little pyramidal lozenges" (NY, XXIII, 138) on the side of the Doges's Palace in Venice. When Charlotte sees the Prince on the grand staircase (the opening of chapter XIV), coming back from seeing Maggie to her carriage, she has the impression "of all the place as higher and wider and more appointed for great moments; with its dome of lustres lifted, its ascents and descents more majestic, its marble tiers more vividly overhung, its numerosity of royalties, foreign and domestic, more unprecedented, its symbolism of 'State' hospitality both emphasised and refined" (NY, XXIII, 247).

Charlotte is also presented in images associating her with the grand style of the Renaissance: her arms remind the Prince of the "completely rounded, the polished slimness that Florentine sculptors, in the great time, had loved" (NY, XXIII, 47). Charlotte marches Maggie into the great empty drawing room at Fawns, which had the look "with all its great objects as ordered and balanced as for a formal reception, been appointed for some high transaction, some real affair of state," to wrest from her the admission that she has not wronged her. For her great scenes, Charlotte needs an appropriate setting; her histrionic talents require the witnesses of "old lustres of Venice and the eyes of the several great portraits, more or less contemporary with these" (NY, XXIV, 246). Later, she seeks refuge in a summer house, "a sort of umbrageous temple, an ancient rotunda, pillared and statued, niched and roofed" (NY, XXIV, 309); it is here that her second great scene with Maggie takes place. And in the leave-taking scene at Portland Place, Charlotte's superior style, her mastery of the mask, is expressed through an image that refers back to the enclosure of the garden temple: "The shade of the official, in her beauty and security, never for a moment dropped; it was a cool high refuge, the deep arched recess of some coloured and gilded image" (NY, XXIV, 357).

The art and architectural images associated with Adam and Maggie are of another order: classical and domestic. To Adam, Maggie at times has

the appearance of some slight, slim draped "antique" of Vatican or Capitoline halls, late and refined, rare as a note and immortal as a link, set in motion by the miraculous infusion of a modern impulse and yet, for all the sudden freedom of fold and footsteps forsaken after centuries by their pedestal, keeping still the quality, the perfect felicity, of the statue; the blurred, absent eyes, the smoothed, elegant, nameless head, the impersonal flit of a creature lost in an alien age and passing as an image in worn relief round and round a precious vase. She had always had odd moments of striking him, daughter of his own though she was, as a figure thus simplified, "generalised" in its grace, a figure with which his human connexion was fairly interrupted by some vague analogy of turn and attitude, something shyly mythological and nymph-like. (NY, XXIII, 188)

Maggie reminds the Prince of "the transmitted images of rather neutral and negative propriety that made up, in his long line, the average of wifehood and motherhood" (NY, XXIII, 322), an image which goes hand in hand with the "impersonal, smoothed, elegant, nameless head," and "simplified, 'generalised'" in Adam's picture of Maggie as a classical nymph. Needless to say, the Prince thinks of Maggie in this way before the breaking of the golden bowl, and indeed she only gains identity after she has been confronted with evil and been forced to accept its existence.

The domestic imagery is consonant with the classical: Adam's "neat, colourless face, provided with the merely indispensable features, suggested immediately, for a description that it was *clear*, and in this manner somewhat resembled a small decent room, clean-swept and unencumbered with furniture, but drawing a particular advantage, as might presently be noted, from the outlook of a pair of ample and uncurtained windows" (NY, XXIII, 170). The "suggestion of the swept and garnished" in Maggie's splendid room, reflects, we are told "her small still passion for order and symmetry" (NY, XXIV, 152).

As may be seen, the association of the Ververs with classical art and domestic settings and of the Prince and Charlotte with Renaissance art and with ornate monumental architecture objectifies the basic temperamental and ethical differences between them. The Renaissance meant to James the pleasures of the senses, delight in earthly life, pageantry, pomp, and ceremony. Classical art stood not only for order, restraint, balance, and clarity but also for ideal in opposition to the real, the spiritual to the material, the general to the particular.

High civilization, according to James's view of it, combines the attributes of both of these art styles, just as in the highest art the quarrel between idealism and realism is meaningless. Moreover, isolated civilized cultivated people do not make a civilized society; there must be social intercourse, continuity, and a past. Thus, a civilized society cannot be manufactured but must develop; a past cannot be assembled or collected. As the richest culture is one which goes back the furthest and which maintains a living relationship with its past, the individual born without a past or in a society without one must resist the temptation to form an arbitrary relationship with the history and traditions of an older society. Art collecting becomes a sign of a wrong, an arbitrary relationship to the past if the collector or connoisseur views art purely aesthetically and acquisitively, not as an expression of human life.

Maggie's union with the Prince at the end (their marriage is only then truly consummated) represents the marriage of the spirit and the senses, of American conscience and the European cultural heritage, of the private sensibility and the public personage. Furthermore, there is a Principino to inherit the best of two worlds, a human vessel to perpetuate James's ideal civilization. That James's vision of high civilization could only be realized in this symbolic sense goes without saying. He could not have embedded his novel more firmly in English society because one of the requirements for an ideal civilization, as James conceived of it, was moral refinement. Though the Prince has a new moral vision, English society as represented by Matcham gives no sign of regeneration. The last glimpse of Adam and Charlotte is of them in their carriage leaving Portland Place, heading for an unimaginable American City bearing with them the spoils of Europe. The new world is to receive what it notably lacks—an infusion of formal beauty in the person of Charlotte and in works of art. Beyond the idea of some merging of American idealism and European style, it is difficult to project the significance of Adam's plan; its meaning as the potential realization of an ideal society lies outside the work. The exit of the new Ververs leaves us with Maggie and the Prince and the ending: " 'See? I see nothing but *you*.' And the truth of it had, with this force, after a moment so strangely lighted his eyes that, as for pity and dread of them, she buried her own in his breast."

Even though Maggie succeeds in welding together the fragments of the golden bowl, a feat suggesting the possibilities of the triumph of goodness when it accepts human limitations and dares imaginatively to work within given forms, one cannot help feeling beneath the reconciliation and promise unresolved strain. The irresoluteness, the elusiveness, the ambiguities—especially in the portrayal of Adam —may be seen as the characteristic lack of final clarification in mannerist art. The lack of clarification is a sign not of a purely relativistic or anarchic view of life but of a mind seeking to be absolutely true both to its sense of the multitudinous facets of any moral dilemma and to its belief in the existence, outside the framework of a formal religious, ethical, or social system, of transcendent values, of which the empathic imagination is the supreme. The result is an art of unease and precariousness, having neither the balance and harmony of classical form nor the exhilarating openness of a work of organic romanticism. Recognizing the possible genesis of tension and inconclusiveness within his art and seeing it as a trait of a general style do not, of course, resolve the question of aesthetic evaluation or of interpretation, except insofar as this particular style requires from the reader a high degree of tolerance for ambiguity. There is a difference between justifiable ambiguity and obscurity: the difference between an artistic representation of a vision of life embracing complexity and a failure of artistic communication, the result of which is a baffled irritation. The ending of *The Golden Bowl* seems to me to exemplify justifiable ambiguity: clearly both Maggie and the Prince have achieved an awareness of themselves, of each other, and of the heart of man that is a positive good. That the final reconciliation should be tinged with strangeness, that Maggie should feel "pity and dread" of what perhaps suggests the Prince's now absolute commitment to her conveys the strangeness of the mixture of bliss and bale in life as James envisions it. In the treatment of Adam, however, as I have suggested, James's narrative pattern—Adam's motives are to

be hidden from the other characters except for Maggie and to her
they are unexpressed—and hence adherence for the most part to an
indirect view without the benefit, for example, of the choral elucidation of Fanny Assingham, leads to an unsettling and probably un-
intended ambiguity. In some of the crucial passages (for example,
pp. 155 and 161 in my text) the distinctions between the literal and
the metaphoric, ironic and straightforward meanings are so blurred
that alternate contradictory readings are possible. Dorothea Krook's
suggestion that the alternate meanings are to be accepted as a kind
of objective correlative of James's sense of the fusion in life of good
and evil seems to me not to be true to one's experience in reading
James;[20] that is, while acceptable as an intellectual proposition, I, at
least, do not find that I experience the alternatives as *all* possible and
thus as conveying a fused sense of paradox and complexity. The critical problem, thus, is not that of evaluating mannerist art as such
but that of distinguishing artistic lapses within the framework of the
general style. As I indicated in my discussion of art techniques and
parallels, my intention has not been to establish James as a complete mannerist but rather to suggest affinities with the mannerist
style and sensibility that help to explain some of the characteristics
of his mind and art.

My primary concern has been to show the diverse ways in which
James's cultivation of the art of seeing found expression in his practice and conception of the art of fiction. Beginning with its title,
The Golden Bowl, in spite of its special problems, may be viewed
as a summation of many of the visual art themes and techniques in
his fiction, As an echo of *Ecclesiastes*—"or ever the silver cord
be loosed, or the golden bowl be broken"—the title suggests the vulnerability of the Edwardian world of Eaton Square and the English
country house inhabited by Americans seemingly protected by their
armor of innocence. Inevitably, as the Preacher warns, the "days of
darkness" must come. The biblical reference should not, however, be
pressed too hard; it contributes to the parabolic dimension of the
novel without restricting meaning in the manner of simple allegory.
It also relates the contemporary world to the past, to a tradition of
Judeo-Christian wisdom. Unusually rich in connotation, the title
refers, however, also to the actual bowl in the novel. Functioning as
plot and moral revelation, the golden bowl typifies James's practice
throughout his fiction. Like the spoils of Poynton, it is passive yet
catalytic. Flawed, it is symbolic of a flawed world with which the
protagonists must come to terms. Besides the use of art objects and
art imagery—generalized and precise—to project themes and char-

acters, *The Golden Bowl* exemplifies James's fictional transmutation of the visual arts in other ways. In the novel's points of view, the analogy of the central, or recording, consciousness to the painter in relation to their fields of observation seems particularly apt. The elaboration of the nuances of thought and motive in combination with a taut balancing of scenes produces the characteristic Jamesian tension between classical form and picturesque indeterminateness. The endowment of perceptive, morally sensitive characters with the artist's open constructive imagination in contrast to the collector's perfectionist mentality and the identification of the associative aesthetic with the empathic imagination, while more complexly and ambiguously treated than in previous fiction, are the other aspects of *The Golden Bowl* that justify viewing it as the culmination in James's career of the conversion of his visual art experience into a literary form.

Notes

Notes—Chapter 1

1. Henry James, "A Small Boy and Others," in *Henry James: Autobiography,* ed. Frederick W. Dupee (New York, 1956), p. 13. Unless otherwise indicated, all James quotations with page references in this chapter are from this collected edition of the autobiographies. All citations from works by James will omit his name.

2. *The Art of the Novel: Critical Prefaces,* ed. Richard P. Blackmur (New York, 1934), pp. 153–54.

3. *Partial Portraits* (London and New York, 1888), p. 328.

4. James had also pored over Thackeray's Christmas books—*Doctor Birch and His Young Friends, Our Street,* and *Mrs. Perkins's Ball*—which, picture and text complementing each other, give the reader a vivid glimpse of English manners. James thought he could not exaggerate the influence of John Leech's illustrations of *Young Troublesome or Master Jacky's Holiday* and Richard Doyle's for the *Adventures of Brown, Jones, and Robinson* in forming the taste of the "fantastic little amateur" that he was. See *Partial Portraits,* pp. 331, 333.

5. Frank Weitenkampf, *The Illustrated Book* (Cambridge, Mass., 1938), p. 172.

6. Which specific set of Béranger "enriched by steel engravings" was owned by the James family is not known. The only sets (more than one volume) of his works illustrated with steel engravings and appearing before 1855 (the year the Jameses went abroad) were the original or reimpressions of the 1828 edition, which contained 103 engravings, according to Jules Brivois, *Bibliographie de l'oeuvre de P.-J. de Béranger* (Paris, 1876). My comments, therefore, are based on these illustrations.

7. The visual "experience of the present moment is never isolated. It is the most recent among an infinite number of sensory experiences that have occurred throughout the person's past life. Thus the new image gets into contact with the memory traces that have been perceived in the past. These traces of shapes interfere with each other on the basis of similarity, and the new image cannot escape this influence," according to Rudolph Arnheim, *Art and Visual Perception* (Berkeley and Los Angeles, 1954), p. 32.

8. Virgil Barker, *American Painting: History and Interpretation* (New York, 1950), p. 439.

9. *Ibid.,* p. 409.

10. Maurice E. Chernowitz, *Proust and Painting* (New York, 1945), p. 41.

11. Leon Edel, *Henry James: The Untried Years* (Philadelphia and New York, 1953), p. 118.

12. His attachment for Italy, James wrote in *A Small Boy,* started with this picture of a view of Florence from the convent of San Miniato, with a "contemplative monk seated on a terrace in the foreground" (p. 153).

13. The elder Henry James was the owner of a landscape by Charles Lefèvre exhibited in 1851 according to the *National Academy of Design Exhibition Record,*

1826–1860, ed. Mary B. Cowdrey (New York, 1943), I, 290. In 1837 Thomas Cole offered for sale a *View of Florence.* Perhaps it was this painting which the elder Henry James eventually purchased.

14. Richard Grant White, "Introduction," in *Companion to the Bryan Gallery of Christian Art: Containing a Critical Description of Pictures and Biographical Sketches of the Painter* (New York, 1853), pp. iv–v.

15. It has been banished to a dark corner of an aquarium in Melbourne, Australia. Eric George, *The Life and Death of Benjamin Robert Haydon, 1786–1846* (London, New York, and Toronto, 1948), p. v.

16. Sir Charles Holmes and C. H. Collins Baker, *The Making of the National Gallery* (London, 1924), p. 21.

17. *The Vernon Gallery of British Art*, ed. S. C. Hall (London, 1849–54), no pagination.

18. As this picture was exhibited at the Royal Academy in 1856, James must have seen it then, not in 1858 as stated in *A Small Boy.*

19. *The Novels and Tales of Henry James* (New York, 1907–9), XXIV, 234 (hereafter cited as NY).

20. "The Royal Academy, Exhibition the Eighty-Eighth: 1856," *Art Journal*, XVIII (June 1, 1856), 170.

21. John Ruskin, *Notes on Some of the Principal Pictures Exhibited in the Room of the Royal Academy and Society of Painters in Water Colours* (London, 1856), p. 29.

22. Royal Cortissoz, *John La Farge, A Memoir and a Study* (Boston and New York, 1911), p. 117.

23. *The Novels and Stories of Henry James, New and Complete Edition* (London,1921–23), XXVIII, 57 (hereafter cited as NS).

24. James's memory was at fault here. The only Atala painting in the Louvre in 1859 was Girodet's well-known *Atala in the Tomb*. Perhaps he confused Prudhon's *Slumber of Psyche* in the Wallace Collection with Gerard's *Cupid and Psyche*, which was in the Louvre collection at that time. My information comes from *Guide through the Galleries of the Imperial Museum of the Louvre* (Paris, 1859).

25. According to Thomas Sergeant Perry, Henry's main interest at Newport was literature, not art.

26. Martha A. S. Shannon, *Boston Days of William Morris Hunt* (Boston, 1923).

27. Frederick P. Vinton praised Hunt for being an extremely effective teacher in "William Morris Hunt," in *American Art and American Art Collection*, ed. Walter Montgomery (Boston, 1889), I, 81–109. "He taught me in five minutes the principle [of creating volume with chiaroscuro] of perhaps the greatest importance in painting" (p. 85).

28. *American Painting*, p. 619.

29. *John La Farge*, pp. 114–15.

30. "Introduction," in *The Art of the Novel*, p. xvii.

Notes—Chapter 2

1. *Notes on Some of the Principal Pictures . . .* , p. 11.

2. *England and the Italian Renaissance* (London, 1954), p. 151.

3. *Ibid.*, p. 61.

4. "An English Critic of French Painting," in *The Painter's Eye*, ed. John L. Sweeney (Cambridge, Mass., 1956), pp. 34–35. Including a perceptive introduction treating James's interest in the visual arts, this volume contains about half of James's art criticism, most of which had not previously appeared in book form.

5. *Ibid.*, p. 33. The pervasiveness of Ruskin's influence has been convincingly demonstrated by Roger B. Stein in *John Ruskin and Aesthetic Thought in America, 1840–1900* (Cambridge, Mass., 1967).

6. "Introduction," in *The Painter's Eye*, p. 17.

7. James to Norton, Aug. 9, 1871, and March 31, 1873, the Charles Eliot Norton Papers, by permission of the Harvard College Library, cited hereafter by CEN. Gautier's enthusiasm for Tintoretto in *Italia* probably helped interest James in this painter.

8. *Transatlantic Sketches* (Boston, 1875), p. 78.

9. *Ibid.*, p. 91.

10. *The Selected Letters of Henry James*, ed. Leon Edel (New York, 1955), p. 28.

11. *Portraits of Places* (Boston, 1884), p. 67.

12. *A Little Tour in France* (Boston and New York, 1885), p. 137.

13. E. V. Lucas, *Edwin Austin Abbey, Royal Academician: The Record of His Life and Work* (New York and London, 1921), I, 416.

14. *The Painter's Eye*, p. 33.

15. *Ibid.*, pp. 183–84. Between his first trip abroad as an adult in 1869 and his second in 1872, James's attitude toward art and the critical function seems to have undergone a change, as indicated in this passage which was not reprinted in *Transatlantic Sketches*: "I agree, on the whole, with X—, and with what he recently said about his own humor in these matters; that, having been on his first acquaintance with pictures, nothing, if not critical, and thought the lesson was incomplete and the opportunity slighted if he left a gallery without a headache, he had come, as he grew older, to regard them more as an entertainment and less as a solemnity, and to remind himself that, after all, it is the privilege of art to reconcile us to the human mind, and not to keep us in ill-humor with it" (*Independent*, XXVI, May 21, 1874, 1–2). About this same time he began to take a more relaxed attitude toward the duties of the literary critic, as noted by Cornelia Pulsifer Kelley, *The Early Development of Henry James*, University of Illinois Studies in Language and Literature, XV (May–Feb., 1930).

16. *Transatlantic Sketches*, p. 178.

17. *Portraits of Places*, pp. 68–69. In *Italian Hours* (Boston and New York, 1909), p. 182, "passion for representation" was changed to "the representational impulse."

18. *The Painter's Eye*, p. 43.

19. *Ibid.*, p. 45.

20. *Ibid.*, pp. 45–47.

21. *Ibid.*, pp. 140–43.

22. "Art: Boston," *Atlantic Monthly*, XXIX (March, 1872), 372.

23. *The Painter's Eye*, p. 92.

24. John Ruskin, *Modern Painters*, II (New York, 1871), 162.

25. C. R. Leslie, *Memoirs of the Life of John Constable, Esq., R.A.* (London, 1911), p. 243. Constable expressed a view of art which in its sane and single-minded concern with problems of painting itself makes Ruskin's categorical theorizing seem divorced from the realities of the creative process.

26. *Modern Painters*, II, 162–63.

27. *The Painter's Eye*, p. 228.

28. *Modern Painters*, II, 163. Both James and Ruskin used some of Coleridge's terms, making a similar distinction between "fancy" and "imagination," but neither seemed to have Coleridge's metaphysical conception of the imagination as "a repetition in the finite mind of the eternal act of creation in the infinite I AM," as set forth in the often-quoted passage from *Biographia Literaria*. Ruskin's conception of the imagination was admittedly "Coleridgian" but his experience of Tintoretto brought Ruskin to an awareness of the relationship of the imagination to the problems of life, according to Van Akin Burd, "Ruskin's Quest for a Theory of Imagination," MLQ, XVII (1956) 60–70.

29. *Portraits of Places*, p. 271.

30. *The American Scene* (New York, 1946), pp. 76–77.

31. *Transatlantic Sketches*, p. 398.

32. *A Little Tour in France*, p. 152. An exception to this attitude toward reconstruction is to be found in *Transatlantic Sketches* where he rather uneasily praised a completely reconstructed medieval manor-fortress as a "triumph of aesthetic culture" (p. 283).

33. *Ibid.*, pp. 196–97.

34. " 'Very Modern Rome'—An Unpublished Essay of Henry James," ed. Richard C. Harrier, *Harvard Library Bulletin*, VIII (Spring, 1954), 139. James, unlike Twain and Howells, managed through memory and imagination to reconcile a need for the past with the realist's devotion to the material present, as pointed out by Roger B. Salomon in "Realism as Disinheritance: Twain, Howells and James," *American Quarterly*, XVI (Winter, 1964), 531–44. The problem of the American's acceptance of the past is not, of course, peculiar to the realists. Hawthorne in *The Marble Faun*, to mention only one work, was overwhelmed by the very jumble in which James reveled.

35. *A Little Tour in France*, p. 184.

36. *Portraits of Places*, p. 70.

37. *Transatlantic Sketches*, p. 31.

38. *Modern Painters*, II, 166.

39. *The Painter's Eye*, pp. 184–85.

40. "Taine's Notes on England," *Nation*, XIV (Jan. 25, 1872), 59–60.

41. *The Painter's Eye*, p. 167.

42. "Gautier's Winter in Russia," *Nation*, XIX (Nov. 12, 1874), 321.

43. "Tableaux de siège," *Nation*, XIV (Jan. 25, 1872), 62.

44. "Gautier's Winter in Russia," p. 321.

45. "Tableaux de siège," p. 61.

46. Planche was one of the most extreme defenders of idealism, but even he after 1855 occasionally praised an artist having realistic tendencies, according to Thaddeus Ernest du Val, Jr., *The Subject of Realism in the "Revue des deux mondes" (1831–1865)* (Philadelphia, 1936), pp. 62–81. The *Revue* made concessions to realism, but its regular contributors were not converted to the new art.

47. Later in life James became noticeably more sympathetic to the ugly subject. For example, in the story "Glasses" (1896), the portrait painter finds the hero's ugly face more of a challenge than the perfection of the heroine's beauty.

48. *Partial Portraits*, p. 346.

49. *Ibid.*, pp. 346–47.

50. *Parisian Sketches: Letters to the "New York Tribune," 1875–1876*, ed. Leon Edel and Ilse Dusoir Lind (New York, 1957), p. 143.

51. *The Painter's Eye*, p. 97.

52. *Parisian Sketches*, p. 139.

53. *The Painter's Eye*, p. 63.

54. The breakdown of subject hierarchy brought about by the nineteenth-century revolution in art was a positive gain to art, but the common modern assumption that subject does not matter is certainly a superstition.

55. "Notes" [Paolo Veronese and Jean-François Millet], *Nation*, XX (June 17, 1875), 410.

Notes—Chapter 3

1. *Italian Painters of the Renaissance* (New York, 1957), pp. 23–24.

2. "*Italian Journeys* by W. D. Howells," *North American Review*, CVI (Jan., 1868), 337–38.

3. According to Wölfflin, the sixteenth-century, or "classic," painters tended to paint objects in outline to render volume, recording not only what the eye sees but what is known to the touch, while seventeenth-century baroque painters depreciated lines and began the process of surrendering to visual appearance which culminated in nineteenth-century impressionism. Wölfflin traces four other concomitant developments which distinguish the two styles: from recession in planes to diagonal recession, multiplicity to unity, absolute to relative clarity of subject, closed to open composition, in each instance the first term applying to classical Renaissance and the second to baroque art. He also shows how comparable changes were effected in architecture and sculpture. Later art historians refining on Wölfflin distinguish a third style, mannerism, which contains elements of both the classical Renaissance and baroque styles (Heinrich Wölfflin, *Principles of Art History*, trans. M. D. Hottinger, 7th ed., New York, [194–?]).

4. James had considerably more self-doubt about his taste in architecture than in painting or sculpture. For example, he wondered if he did not perhaps think too much of the Ca' Foscari: "These doubts and fears course rapidly through my mind—I am easily their victim when it is a question of architecture—as they are apt to do to-day, in Italy, almost anywhere, in the presence of the beautiful, of the desecrated or the neglected. We feel at such moments as if the eye of Mr. Ruskin were upon us; we grow nervous and lose our confidence. This makes me inevitably, in talking of Venice, seek a pusillanimous safety in the trivial and the obvious" ("The Grand Canal," in *Italian Hours*, p. 58).

5. *William Wetmore Story and His Friends* (New York, [1957]), I, 341.

6. *Ibid.*, I, 341.

7. *Transatlantic Sketches*, p. 302.

8. "'Very Modern Rome'—An Unpublished Essay of Henry James," 136. In a similar passage in *Transatlantic Sketches*, he makes an exception of the Roman Pantheon (p. 128).

9. *Transatlantic Sketches*, p. 125.

10. *Ibid.*, pp. 193–94.

11. *Italian Hours*, p. 58.

12. *A Little Tour in France*, pp. 163–64.
13. *Ibid.*, pp. 25–26.
14. "Lake George," *Nation*, XI (Aug. 25, 1870), 120.
15. *Principles of Art History*, p. 24.
16. *Portraits of Places*, p. 103.
17. *Principles of Art History*, p. 26. A sketch made by James in 1869 reproduced in *Henry James: The Untried Years* (facing p. 192) is of a picturesque subject—a half-timbered façade with a store window on the ground floor topped by rows of much smaller windows. James rather unsuccessfully tried to draw a foreshortened view and to suggest the play of light and shadow on the highly irregular surface. Of all possible aspects of a building, as Wölfflin points out, the front view is the least picturesque because "here the thing and its appearance fully coincide. But as soon as foreshortening comes in, the appearance separates from the thing, the picture-form becomes different from the object-form, and we speak of a picturesque movement-effect" (p. 25). Not only the attempted foreshortened view, but the lighting and irregular surface of the building James sketched have picturesque values.
18. *The Picturesque: Studies in a Point of View* (London and New York, 1927), p. 11.
19. Did James see picturesque effects because these paintings trained his eyes to see them, or was his response more or less independent, a result of an innate aesthetic sense? Undoubtedly, pictures influenced his perceptions of nature from the very first. But it must also be kept in mind that while paintings led him to see certain aspects of nature, he was so peculiarly sensitive to the ingredients of the picturesque—color, light, texture, and tone—that he could scarcely *not* appreciate picturesque effects. It was a condition of his vision.
20. *Portraits of Places*, p. 194.
21. *Ibid.*, p. 13.
22. *Transatlantic Sketches*, p. 272.
23. *A Little Tour in France*, p. 233.
24. *Essays in London and Elsewhere* (London, 1893), p. 14.
25. *Ibid.*, p. 13.
26. *Portraits of Places*, p. 80.
27. *Transatlantic Sketches*, p. 204.
28. *The Nude: A Study in Ideal Form* (New York, 1955), p. 51.
29. *Transatlantic Sketches*, p. 205.
30. *Transatlantic Sketches*, p. 131. The clause "the rarest . . . produced" was added in *Italian Hours* (p. 209). Significantly, as James records in his autobiography, when he was copying casts in William Morris Hunt's studio, he dreamed of being congratulated on his "sympathetic rendering of the sublime uplifted face of Michael Angelo's 'Captive' in the Louvre" (p. 284).
31. *Charity* is a massive statue of a seated woman holding two babies, one of whom is asleep, the other at her breast. An effect of serenity (as far as I can judge from photographs) is achieved through generalized modeling of her face and the folds of her garment. *Military Courage* resembles the visor-shadowed figure of *Contemplation* in the Medici Chapel. Dubois, it seems, in spite of his academicism, respected his medium and at least constructed figures having solidity.
32. [The Paris Salon of 1876] *Nation*, XXII (June 22, 1876), 397–98.
33. *A Little Tour in France*, pp. 107–8.
34. *The Selected Letters of Henry James*, p. 45.
35. *Parisian Sketches*, pp. 14–16.

36. *Ibid.*, p. 20.

37. F. O. Matthiessen, *The James Family* (New York, 1947), p. 255.

38. *Transatlantic Sketches*, p. 52.

39. *Ibid.*, p. 277.

40. *Ibid.*, p. 295.

41. *Principles of Art History*, p. 169. My comparison of these two paintings is based on Wölfflin's.

42. Henry to William James, as quoted in *Henry James: The Untried Years*, pp. 301–12. The comparison to Shakespeare was included in *Transatlantic Sketches*, p. 93. James similarly admired Balzac for his energy and the vastness of his literary canvas. In the light of James's own work, his desire to emulate these artists may suggest a gap between creative aspiration and achievement. James clearly did not realize a Balzacian breadth in the depiction of society. But the prodigious energy and epic scope are present in his works in "development," in the exhaustive working out of implications and relations.

43. James to Norton, Aug. 9, 1871, CEN. By "those good people at San Lorenzo," James must mean Michelangelo's sculpture in the Medici Chapel in the New Sacristy of the church of San Lorenzo.

44. *Transatlantic Sketches*, p. 90.

45. "The Grand Canal," in *Italian Hours*, p. 49.

46. *The Letters of Henry James*, ed. Percy Lubbock (New York, 1920), I, 378.

47. *Transatlantic Sketches*, p. 90.

48. *Ibid.*, p. 92.

49. *Ibid.*, p. 93.

50. Henry James to William James, Sept. 25, 1869, the James Family Papers, Houghton Library, Harvard University.

51. *Transatlantic Sketches*, pp. 92–93.

52. Walter Friedlaender, *David to Delacroix*, trans. Robert Goldwater (Cambridge, Mass., 1952). Friedlaender places Delacroix in the French baroque, or Rubenesque, tradition. Rubens himself was greatly influenced by Michelangelo, Titian, and Tintoretto.

53. *The Painter's Eye*, p. 184. La Farge's comments on Delacroix in *The Higher Life of Art* are of interest: "Delacroix felt the unexpressed rule that the human being never moves free in *space*, but always, being an animal, in relation to the space where he is, to the people around him, to innumerable influences of light, and air, wind, footing, and the possibility of touching others" (Royal Cortissoz, *John La Farge*, p. 149.)

54. *Transatlantic Sketches*, p. 295.

55. *Voices of Silence*, trans. Stuart Gilbert (New York, 1953), p. 444.

56. *Transatlantic Sketches*, p. 398. Sir Kenneth Clark has a qualifying opinion: "Rubens' nudes seem at first sight to have been tumbled out of a cornucopia of abundance; the more we study them the more we discover them to be under control" (*The Nude*, p. 142).

57. The semiapologetic tone of his references to Dutch and Flemish landscapists and genre painters indicates that while James relished them he considered them inferior to Italian painters in general. For example, he spoke of his fondness for David Teniers, "a singular genius, who combined the delicate with the groveling," as a "weakness" (*A Little Tour*, p. 165).

58. *Italian Painters*, p. 39.

59. *Voices of Silence*, p. 446.

60. "Pierre Loti," in *Essays in London and Elsewhere*, p. 183.

Notes—Chapter 4

1. For his analysis of the relationship of the Pre-Raphaelites, Pater, and Swinburne to the aesthetic movement of the 1880's, I am particularly indebted to Jerome Hamilton Buckley, *The Victorian Temper* (Cambridge, Mass., 1951).

2. *Letters*, I, 17.

3. *Selected Letters*, p. 27.

4. James explicitly made a point of the importance of individual observation in his reviews of Howells's *Italian Journeys* (chap. 3, note 2) and Taine's *Notes on England* (chap. 2, note 40), both reviews appearing before the publication of Pater's *Renaissance*.

5. *Letters*, I, 222.

6. *Partial Portraits*, p. 369.

7. *Partial Portraits*, pp. 370–71.

8. "The Decay of Lying," in *The Writings of Oscar Wilde* (London and New York, 1907), pp. 370–71.

9. I have treated this point in more detail in "The Artist and the Man in 'The Author of Beltraffio,'" *PMLA*, LXXXIII (March, 1968), 102–8. For a discussion of James's relation to Arnold see Alwyn Berland, "Henry James and the Aesthetic Tradition," *Journal of the History of Ideas*, 23 (July-Sept., 1962), 407–19.

10. The title itself has Pre-Raphaelite connotations. It is possible that James had in mind the Milanese painter Beltraffio, also spelled Boltraffio, a contemporary and follower of Leonardo da Vinci, who was popularized in England by Simeon Solomon. Solomon has been considered a link between the original English Pre-Raphaelites and the aesthetes of the 1880's.

11. *Selected Letters*, p. 147.

12. *The Victorian Temper*, p. 170.

13. Convincing evidence that James modeled Nash after Oscar Wilde is presented by Oscar Cargill in "Mr. James's Aesthetic Mr. Nash," *Nineteenth Century Fiction*, XII (Dec. 1957), 177–87.

14. Though James published stories in the *Yellow Book*—he said for money and as a favor to Harland—he did not send his brother William a copy with his story in it because he hated "too much the horrid aspect and company of the whole publication" (*Letters*, I, 217). His comments on Beardsley are to be found in *Letters*, II, 343.

15. *The Painter's Eye*, p. 143.

16. *Ibid.*, pp. 143–46.

17. *Ibid.*, pp. 164–65.

18. CEN, March 25, 1889.

19. *Letters*, I, 340.

20. *The Painter's Eye*, pp. 258–59. This last review was not taken into account by Donald M. Murray when he wrote, "Since Whistler, in his preoccupation with the strictly painterly qualities of form and color, had not produced a 'speaking' Irving, for instance, James could not consider it a picture at all" ("James and Whistler at the Grosvenor Gallery," *American Quarterly*, IV, Spring, 1952, 49–65).

While he correctly points out that James's traditionalism hampered his responsiveness to new movements in art, he fails to perceive that though James required a subject, he discriminated between a subject subdued to painterly purposes and one painted to tell a story and not fulfilling, in his words, its "plastic obligations."

21. *The Painter's Eye,* pp. 114–15.

22. *Ibid.,* p. 221.

23. *Ibid.,* pp. 217–18. A collation of the 1893 version of the Sargent essay reproduced in *The Painter's Eye* with the original 1887 text in *Harper's New Monthly Magazine* reveals that James made only minor stylistic revisions.

24. *Voices of Silence,* p. 117.

25. It is interesting that the very dangers James warned Sargent about in this essay proved in the long run, in Roger Fry's opinion, to have been his undoing. "That hand was a highly trained and obedient servant of his eye, and his eye took in at a glance those salient facts of appearance out of which the average man builds his world; and, as he never felt tempted to probe sensation deeper for those other relations which only emerge for a disinterested and prolonged contemplation, there was nothing to check his unbounded energy; nothing to prevent him from succeeding, as he did, every time" (*Transformations,* New York, 1956, p. 172).

26. *Portraits of Places,* p. 166.

27. *A Little Tour in France,* p. 102.

28. NY, XIII, 40.

29. "London," *Harper's Weekly,* XLI (Feb. 20, 1897), 183.

30. *The Notebooks of Henry James,* eds. F. O. Matthiessen and Kenneth B. Murdock (New York, 1947), p. 160 (hereafter cited as *Notebooks*).

31. Pp. 45–46.

32. *Henry James: Autobiography,* p. 287.

33. *Ibid.,* pp. 291–92.

34. *Ibid.,* p. 193.

35. *Edwin Austin Abbey,* I, 416–17. The quotation James selected is from Emerson's "On Art," in *Essays: First Series.* The rest of the passage is as follows: "The arts, as we know them, are but initial. Our best praise is given to what is aimed and promised, not to the actual result."

36. *The Painter's Eye,* p. 257.

37. *Roger Fry: A Biography* (New York, 1940), p. 180.

38. *Henry James: Autobiography,* pp. 568–69.

39. *Studies in the History of the Renaissance* (London and New York, 1888), p. 136. For a modern version of this view of the essential differences among the arts see Susanne K. Langer's *Philosophy in a New Key* or her *Problems of Art.*

40. *The Painter's Eye,* p. 35.

41. *Ibid.,* p. 88.

42. *Ibid.,* p. 35.

43. *Ibid.,* p. 118.

44. *Painting and Reality* (New York, 1957), p. 211.

45. *Aesthetics and History* (Garden City, 1948), p. 29.

46. "The Nude Renewed," *Griffin,* VI, (July, 1957).

47. "Matthew Arnold," in *Literary Reviews and Essays on American, English, and French Literature,* ed. Albert Mordell (New York, 1957), p. 344.

48. *The Painter's Eye,* p. 99.

49. *Ibid.,* pp. 214–15.

50. *Ibid.,* pp. 222–23. The first part of the last sentence also illustrates James's weakness as a critic: when he turned away from the picture to summarize his

reactions, he often resorted to generalizations applicable to almost any picture and adding little to an understanding of the one under consideration.

51. *Ibid.*, p. 151.

52. *Ibid.*, pp. 76–77.

53. "Letters of Henry James," ed. Richard C. Harrier, *Colby Library Quarterly*, 3d ser., no. 10 (May, 1953), p. 156.

54. "Henry James as Art Critic," *Listener*, LVI (Oct. 11, 1956), 572.

Notes—Chapter 5

1. *Henry James: Autobiography*, p. 294.

2. *Partial Portraits*, p. 378.

3. *Ibid.*

4. *Ibid.*, p. 379.

5. *Ibid.*, p. 404.

6. *Ibid.*, pp. 384–85.

7. *Ibid.*, pp. 385–86.

8. *Ibid.*, p. 390.

9. *Henry James and Robert Louis Stevenson*, ed. Janet Adam Smith (London, 1948), p. 239.

10. *English Hours* (Boston and New York, 1905), p. 294.

11. "William Dean Howells," in *The American Essays of Henry James*, ed. Leon Edel (New York, 1956), pp. 155–56.

12. "Alphonse Daudet," in *Literary Reviews and Essays on American, English, and French Literature*, p. 184.

13. "The Journal of the Brothers de Goncourt," in *Essays in London and Elsewhere* (London, 1893), p. 196.

14. *Ibid.*, p. 217.

15. *Ibid.*, p. 220.

16. *Picture and Text* (New York, 1893), p. 15.

17. "Preface to *The Golden Bowl*," in *The Art of the Novel*, pp. 332–33. Presumably James would have approved of Charles Demuth's water colors inspired by "The Turn of the Screw" and "The Beast in the Jungle." See John L. Sweeney, "The Demuth Pictures," *Kenyon Review*, V (Autumn, 1943), 522–32.

18. *Ibid.*, p. 333.

19. *The Art of the Novel*, p. 14.

20. *Ibid.*, p. 5. James's use of the architectural analogy to express his antithetical aims of "the organic and the scientific" is analyzed by J. A. Ward in *The Search for Form: Studies in the Structure of James's Fiction* (Chapel Hill, N.C., 1967).

21. *The Method of Henry James* (Philadelphia, 1954), p. 33.

22. *The Art of the Novel*, p. 278.

23. *Notes and Reviews by Henry James*, ed. Pierre de Chaignon la Rose (Cambridge, Mass., 1921), p. 24.

24. *Ibid.*, p. 25.

25. *The Art of the Novel*, p. 14

26. *Ibid.*, pp. 322–23.

27. *Ibid.*, p. 57.

28. *Ibid.*, p. 106.

29. *The Letters of Henry James,* II, 336; "The Lesson of Balzac," in *The Future of the Novel: Essays on the Art of Fiction,* ed. Leon Edel (New York, 1956), pp. 122–23.

30. "Our Hawthorne," *Partisan Review,* XXXI (Summer, 1964), 332.

31. *Image and Experience: Reflections on a Literary Revolution* (Lincoln, Neb., 1960), p. 78.

32. *The Art of the Novel,* p. 110.

33. *Roger Fry: A Biography,* p. 273.

34. *Aspects of the Novel* (New York, 1927), p. 228.

35. *Partial Portraits,* p. 378.

Notes—Chapter 6

1. The following works have been especially helpful in clarifying for me the problems of the comparative method in the study of literature and art: René Wellek, "The Parallelism between Literature and Art," *English Institute Annual,* 1941 (New York, 1942); G. Giovannini, "Method in the Study of Literature in Its Relation to the Other Fine Arts," *Journal of Aesthetics and Art Criticism,* VIII (March, 1950), 185–95; Susanne K. Langer, *Problems of Art: Ten Philosophical Lectures* (London, 1957); Jean H. Hagstrum, *The Sister Arts: The Tradition of Literary Pictorialism and English Poetry from Dryden to Gray* (Chicago, 1958).

2. The definition is my own, but I am indebted for this term to F. O. Matthiessen, "James and the Plastic Arts," *Kenyon Review,* V (Autumn, 1943), 533–50.

3. *Confidence* (Boston, 1880), p. 1.

4. *Ibid.,* p. 8.

5. *Principles of Art History,* p. 25.

6. *The American* (Boston, 1877), p. 1.

7. *Roderick Hudson* (Boston, 1876), pp. 112–13.

8. *The Portrait of a Lady* (Boston, 1882), p. 321.

9. "An Introductory Essay," in *The Sacred Fount* (New York, 1953), p. xx.

10. James used this phrase in describing his reactions to Paris in a letter of 1899 to his architect friend Edward P. Warren. See John Russell, "Henry James and the Leaning Tower," *New Statesman and Nation,* XXV (April 17, 1943), 254–55.

11. *The Painter's Eye,* p. 43.

12. *The Art of the Novel,* p. 8.

13. *Notebooks,* p. 409.

14. *Life in Letters of William Dean Howells,* ed. Mildred Howells (Garden City, 1928), I, 175.

15. *Travelling Companions* (New York, 1919), p. 20.

16. There is a discussion of James's use of Italian art for background and imagery in Robert L. Gale, "Henry James and Italy," *Nineteenth Century Fiction,*

XIV (Sept., 1959), 157–70. Gale does not analyze in detail the contextual significance of particular art images.

17. *The Painter's Eye*, p. 58.

18. *Ibid.*, p. 76

19. This identification was made by Miriam Allott, "The Bronzino Portrait in *The Wings of the Dove*," Modern Language Notes, LXVIII (Jan., 1953), 23–25.

20. Arthur McComb, *Agnolo Bronzino: His Life and Works* (Cambridge, Mass., 1928), p. 9.

21. *Letters*, I, 127.

22. His memory of the 1887 visit is recorded in the preface to *The Spoils of Poynton*. See *The Art of the Novel*, pp. 135–36.

23. This painting, now in the Boston Museum of Fine Arts, is by Walter A. Gay. Sargent's *Interior of a Palazzo in Venice* is of the grand *sala* of the Palazzo Barbaro. With its representation of figures (the Daniel Curtises, their son and his wife) in informal poses, this picture could be a frontispiece for one of James's depictions of modern life in a sumptuous old world setting.

24. *Portraits of Places*, pp. 29–30.

25. For an interesting interpretation of analogies between the Veronese's paintings and this scene, see Laurence B. Holland, "The Wings of the Dove," *Journal of English Literary History*, XXVI (Dec., 1959), 549–74.

26. That Susan "mixed this picture up with 'The Feast of Levi'" and that "the mistake" was hers, not James's, is suggested by Oscar Cargill in *The Novels of Henry James* (New York, 1961), p. 377. Certainly James knew both pictures—the less well-known *The Feast of Levi* he mentions seeing in *Transatlantic Sketches*, p. 76—but it was the general associations with Veronese that he drew on here. I believe the blurring is deliberate, not to show Susan in error; in this especially fluid and atmospheric scene, an allusion to a single painting would have created a static effect, reducing the symbolism to allegory.

27. *Italian Painters of the Renaissance*, pp. 47–48.

28. "The Relations between Poetry and Painting," in *The Necessary Angel* (New York, 1951), p. 169.

29. *David to Delacroix*, p. 113.

30. *The Painter's Eye*, p. 113.

31. *Ibid.*, p. 74.

32. *A Short History of Painting in America: The Story of 450 Years* (New York, 1963), p. 182.

33. *The Painter's Eye*, pp. 140 n., 141.

34. Edward E. Hale, "The Impressionism of Henry James," in *Faculty Papers of Union College*, II (Jan., 1931), 17. Hale points out that James had much in common with the impressionist sensibility, but he does not attempt to analyze specific impressionist characteristics of his work.

35. Arnold Hauser, *The Social History of Art*, trans. Stanley Goodman (New York, 1951), II, 873.

36. "The First Paragraph of *The Ambassadors*: An Explication (1960)," *Henry James*, ed. Tony Tanner, Modern Judgements series (London, 1968), p. 108.

37. *The Life of Forms in Art*, trans. Charles Beecher Hogan and George Kubler (New York, 1948), p. 15.

38. My discussion of mannerist art is based largely on Walter Friedlaender, *Mannerism and Anti-Mannerism in Italian Painting* (New York, 1957); Nikolaus Pevsner, "The Architecture of Mannerism," in *The Mint: A Miscellany of Literature, Art and Criticism*, ed. Geoffrey Grigson (London, 1946), pp. 116–38; and

I. L. Zupnik, "The 'Aesthetics' of the Early Mannerists," *Art Bulletin*, XXXV (Dec., 1953), 302–6.

39. *Mannerism and Anti-Mannerism*, p. 5.

40. *Ibid.*, p. 6.

41. "Architecture of Mannerism," p. 136.

42. *Tintoretto: The Paintings and Drawings* (New York, 1948), p. 44.

43. "Note sur Mallarmé et Poe," *La nouvelle revue française*, XXVII (Nov., 1926), 525.

44. *The Method of Henry James*, p. lxxxvii.

45. "The Vision of Grace: James's 'The Wings of the Dove,' " *Modern Fiction Studies*, III (Spring, 1957), 34.

46. *The Art of the Novel*, p. 84.

47. *Transatlantic Sketches*, pp. 91–92.

48. *Tintoretto*, p. 62.

49. *The Future of the Novel*, p. 156.

50. *Italian Hours*, pp. 49–50.

51. Giorgio Melchiori, *The Tightrope Walkers: Studies of Mannerism in Modern English Literature* (London, 1956), p. 23. Melchiori considers James a precursor of a twentieth-century mannerist style.

Notes—Chapter 7

1. *The American Novels and Stories of Henry James*, ed. F. O. Matthiessen (New York, 1951), pp. 1026–27. James probably rejected the idea of making Gray a painter because it would inevitably have involved placing him in a studio setting. Writing may be more readily indulged in, actually and as a secret ambition. Painting obviously involves paraphernalia.

2. *Partial Portraits*, p. 388.

3. *A Passionate Pilgrim and Other Tales* (Boston, 1875), p. 278.

4. Roger B. Stein considers "The Madonna of the Future" "a strong early statement of James's anti-idealistic view of the artist, though Theobald's failure is mitigated somewhat by our realization that the beauty of Italy is its past idealism, captured by the hands of Raphael, Michelangelo, Cellini, Mantegna, while the present is shabby and soiled" (*John Ruskin and Aesthetic Thought in America*, p. 213). "The story gains its symbolic dimension from the way in which the narrator scrutinizes, without quite committing himself to either one, two conflicting attitudes toward art and toward life," according to Robert Falk in *The Victorian Mode in American Fiction, 1865–1885* (East Lansing, Mich. 1965), p. 71. Later, however, he has qualified qualms about James's unequal distribution of "sympathy for the two 'artists' in their human roles" (p. 72). Though perceptive and sensitive to Jamesian complexities, both critics overemphasize the anti-idealism of the story.

5. *William Wetmore Story and His Friends*, I, 258.

6. Judging by the sculpture and by contemporary accounts of patrons, Margaret Farrand Thorp concludes that James was "scarcely exaggerating" in his portrayal of Leavenworth and his proposed commission. *The Literary Sculptors* (Durham, N.C., 1965), pp. 134, 156.

7. Leon Edel, *Henry James: The Untried Years*, p. 310.

8. *William Wetmore Story and His Friends*, I, 350.

9. *The Reminiscences of Augustus Saint-Gaudens*, ed. Homer Saint-Gaudens (New York, 1913), II, 65.

10. His antagonism is expressed, for example, in his report as United States Commissioner of Fine Arts, *Paris Universal Exhibition*, 1878.

11. *Parisian Sketches*, p. 15.

12. *Ibid.*, p. 20.

13. See chapter 3, p. 37.

14. *Parisian Sketches*, p. 20.

15. *The Painter's Eye*, p. 114.

16. James made significant revisions for the New York edition in his portrayal of Gloriani, aligning him with the great artist he was to become in *The Ambassadors*. See my note "Gloriani and the Tides of Taste," *Nineteenth-Century Fiction*, XVIII (June, 1963), 65–71.

17. *The Painter's Eye*, p. 56.

18. *Eight Uncollected Tales of Henry James*, ed. Edna Kenton (New Brunswick, N.J., 1950), p. 115.

19. James said of Hyppolite Flandrin, not a painter of "first force," that his singleness of aim "seems to remind us again that the main condition of success for an artist is not so much to have an extraordinary gift as to use without reservation that which he has." "[Mrs. Henrietta L. (Farrer) Lear's] A Christian Painter of the Nineteenth Century: Being the Life of Hyppolite Flandrin," *Nation*, XXI (Aug. 26, 1875), 138.

20. *The Art of the Novel*, p. 13.

21. *Ibid.*

22. I have availed myself here of the more elevated and moving phrasing of the New York edition (II, 524). In the 1875 version, Roderick's face "looked admirably handsome." The other revisions of this passage heighten Roderick's nobility, though it is implicit in the original. For example, in 1875 Singleton says "He was a beautiful fellow!"; in the New York edition, it is "He was the most beautiful of men!"

23. *Notebooks*, p. 103.

24. *The Art of the Novel*, p. 122.

25. *Painting and Reality*, p. 138.

26. Maurice Beebe suggests that many of James's characters who have the characteristics of the artist appear in other guises partially to avoid autobiographical identification. James does identify with his imaginative people, but clearly he does not consider imagination the prerogative of the artist alone. Beebe's chapter on James in *Ivory Towers and Sacred Founts: The Artist as Hero in Fiction from Goethe to Joyce* (New York, 1964) is highly stimulating but uneven. Other interesting discussions of the Jamesian "artist in life" are Quentin Anderson, *The American Henry James* (New Brunswick, N. J., 1957); and James Kraft, "'Madame de Mauves' and *Roderick Hudson*: The Development of James's International Style," *Texas Quarterly* (Autumn, 1968), pp. 143–60.

27. *The Europeans*, pp. 104–5.

28. *The Image of Europe in Henry James* (Dallas, 1958).

29. *The Art of the Novel*, p. 308.

30. *Ibid.*, p. 79.

31. *The Painter's Eye*, p. 196.

32. For my discussion in this chapter of the problems of the American artist,

I am indebted especially to Albert Ten Eyck Gardner, *Yankee Stonecutters: The First American School of Sculpture, 1800–1850* (New York, 1945); Oliver W. Larkin, *Art and Life in America* (New York, 1949); Otto Wittmann, Jr., "The Italian Experience (American Artists in Italy, 1830–1875)," *American Quarterly*, IV (1952), 3–15; Margaret Farrand Thorp, *The Literary Sculptors*.

33. *Book of the Artists, American Artist Life* (New York, 1867), p. 35.

34. *William Wetmore Story and His Friends*, I, 146.

35. Harriet Hosmer, *Letters and Memoirs*, ed. Cornelia Carr (New York, 1912), pp. 18–19.

36. *William Wetmore Story and His Friends*, I, 344.

37. *A Landscape Painter*, p. 54. That James was referring here to Manet's famous, at the time scandalous, painting is a theory of Giorgio Melchiori, "Il 'déjeuner sur l'herbe' di Henry James," *Studi Americani*, X (1964), 201–28.

38. In a note on Frank Duveneck's paintings James gave another reason why study in Europe was advisable: "We confess that, as things stand with us at present, almost any young artist of promise is likely to do better out of America than in it. We are fatally prone, in such cases, to use the superlative degree when the comparative is abundantly adequate, and to force second-rate power, even against its conscience, into attempting tasks of first-rate magnitude" *Nation*, XX, June 3, 1875, 376–77.

39. *The Wheel of Time* (New York, 1893), p. 134.

40. *The Painter's Eye*, p. 238.

41. *The Art of the Novel*, pp. 94–95.

42. *Ibid.*, p. 87.

43. *Ibid.*, p. 97.

44. *Ibid.*, pp. 96–97.

45. *Ibid.*, p. 83.

46. *Ibid.*, p. 95.

47. James at one period attended Whistler's *déjeuners*, but he associated mostly with rather conservative painters and sculptors. Although once considered radical, Sargent never experimented further with the impressionist technique after his Paris apprenticeship. The following is a list of James's artist friends and acquaintances: Edwin A. Abbey, Sir Lawrence Alma-Tadema, Hendrik C. Anderson, Frederick Barnard, Cecilia Beaux, Max Beerbohm, Eugene Benson, Jacques-Émile Blanche, Edward D. Boit, George H. Boughton, Sir Edward Burne-Jones, Philip Burne-Jones, Sarah Freeman Clarke, George Du Maurier, Frank Duveneck, John Elliott, Bay Emmet, Sir Luke Fildes, Kenneth Frazier, Daniel Chester French, Adolf von Hildebrand, Harriet Hosmer, William Holman Hunt, William Morris Hunt, Paul Joukowsky, John La Farge, Samuel Laurence, Lord Leighton, Sir John Everett Millais, Francis D. Millet, William Morris, Alfred Parsons, Joseph Pennell, Charles S. Reinhart, Dante Gabriel Rossetti, Sir William Rothenstein, Samuel Rowse, Augustus Saint-Gaudens, John Singer Sargent, Joseph Lindon Smith, Marcus Stone, Waldo Story, William Wetmore Story, Luther Terry, Paul Tilton, Frederick Walker, Edward P. Warren, James Abbott McNeill Whistler, and Thomas Woolner. I have excluded from the list amateurs, such as Lilla Perry, Lizzie Boott, and Ralph W. Curtis, as well as members of the James family. My list is not exhaustive as undoubtedly in the art and literary worlds of London and of the Anglo-American art colony in Rome he met and associated with other artists not mentioned in available sources.

48. Van Gogh, as quoted by Étienne Gilson in *Painting and Reality*, p. 215 n., thought that neither Balzac nor Zola understood much about painters. Similarly, in

Men and Memories (New York, 1931), II, 204, Sir William Rothenstein expressed the view that "no novelist, not even Henry James, has . . . done a convincing study of a painter or sculptor."

49. *Italian Hours*, p. 60.

Notes—Chapter 8

1. Especially stimulating critical studies on this subject are: F. O. Matthiessen, "James and the Plastic Arts," *Kenyon Review*, V (Autumn, 1943), 533–50; Adeline R. Tintner, "The Spoils of Henry James," *PMLA*, LXI (March, 1946), 239–51; G. H. Bantock, "Morals and Civilization in Henry James," *Cambridge Journal*, VII (Dec., 1953), 159–81; Edwin T. Bowden, *The Themes of Henry James: A System of Observation Through the Visual Arts* (New Haven, 1956); Barbara Melchiori, "The Taste of Henry James," *Studi Americani*, no. 3 (1957), 171–87; Frederick J. Hoffman, "Freedom and Conscious Form: Henry James and the American Self," *Virginia Quarterly Review*, XXXVII (Spring, 1961), 269–85.

2. "Henry James: The Poetics of Empiricism," in *Time, Place, and Idea, Essays on the Novel* (Carbondale and Edwardsville, Ill., 1968), pp. 8–9.

3. *The American*, p. 95.

4. *Travelling Companions*, p. 26.

5. NY, II, 158. Although this passage does not appear in the early edition of *The American*, it most aptly conveys the gist of the conversation between Valentin and Newman on pages 143–44 of the 1877 edition.

6. *The Comic Sense of Henry James: A Study of the Early Novels* (New York, 1960) pp. 95–144.

7. *The Europeans*, p. 244.

8. *The Portrait of a Lady*, pp. 175–76.

9. In the New York edition, James changed Watteau to Lancret. The painting as described in the novel resembles most closely Lancret's *Music Lesson* in the Louvre. It shows two women seated on the grass in front of a pedestal, the top of which is obscured by foliage; the guitar player in doublet, hose, and ruff stands to their left. As a minor and less serious painter of the school rather than its master, Lancret does seem more appropriate in the context than Watteau, which may be why James made the change.

10. NY, IV, 435. I quote from the New York edition here, as it is this version to which most critics refer in discussing the conclusion.

11. James's words from the dustjacket of *The Outcry* (London, 1911), as quoted in Leon Edel and Dan H. Laurence, *A Bibliography of Henry James* (London, 1957), p. 148.

12. *The Outcry* (London, 1911), p. 118. This is one of James's most topical works. Bender is barely a caricature of the American collectors of the time who periodically caused national crises in England, such as in 1905 when J. P. Morgan began to negotiate for the purchase of Velázquez's *Venus* from Rokeby Hall. It was saved for the nation by a fund to which Morgan himself contributed.

13. *The Art of the Novel*, p. 131. Nina Baym questions the trustworthiness of the Notebooks and the Prefaces as glosses to the text in a well-argued essay "Fleda

Vetch and the Plot of *The Spoils of Poynton,*" *PMLA*, 84 (Jan. 1969), 102–11. While an interpretation may rest upon authorial statements alone, the critic may certainly draw upon them providing, as with any other critical source, he uses them intelligently.

14. James separated the works in which the antithesis between the American and European outlook was central from those in which it was secondary. The subject of *The Wings of the Dove* and *The Golden Bowl* could have been, as he observes in the preface to "Lady Barbarina" (p. 199), "perfectly expressed had *all* the persons concerned been only American or only English or only Roman or whatever." Still, as he also notes, use is made in these works of the drama inherent in the international contrast. Thus, while *The Golden Bowl* is not about the differences between American and European manners and character, Adam and Maggie are inconceivable except as Americans.

15. "Introduction," *The Golden Bowl* (New York, 1952), p. ix.

16. These extreme views are held by Anderson (*The American Henry James*, p. 292) and Bowden (*The Themes of Henry James*, pp. 103–16). In Dorothea Krook's scheme he is "a figure of the Just God of Judaism and Christianity" (*The Ordeal of Consciousness in Henry James*, Cambridge, 1967, p. 286). While she is very perceptive on the aesthetic-moral aspects of the work, her allegorical interpretation is strained. For an inclusive summary and criticism of divergent opinions on *The Golden Bowl*, see Cargill, *The Novels of Henry James*, esp. pp. 401–11.

17. *The Art of the Novel*, p. 329.

18. *Ibid.*, p. 328.

19. *The Legend of the Master*, comp. Simon Nowell-Smith (London, 1947), p. 112.

20. *The Ordeal of Consciousness*, pp. 319–24.

Glossary

Glossary of Art Terms

Chiaroscuro   In the visual arts, patterns or contrasts of shade and light. In James, striking contrasts, e.g., Dorothea's tragedy (in *Middlemarch*) "abounds in fine shades, but it lacks, we think, the great dramatic chiaroscuro" (*The Future of the Novel*, p. 83).

Color   A frequently used metaphor in the ordinary sense of vividness or piquancy, e.g., Stendhal "is never pictorial . . . his style is perversely colorless" (*A Little Tour in France*, p. 163). Often used to express spirit or flavor, e.g., his father's books, James wrote, "could as little fail to flush with the strong colour, colour so remarkably given and not taken, projected and not reflected, colour of thought and faith and moral and expressional atmosphere, as they would leave us without that felt side-wind of their strong composition" (*Autobiography*, p. 334). James often used specific color and painting metaphors, e.g., George Eliot in *Silas Marner* "has come nearest the mildly rich tints of brown and gray, the mellow lights and the undreadful corner-shadows of the Dutch masters whom she emulates" (*Views and Reviews*, Boston, 1908, p. 9).

Perspective   Often used in James's discussions of the problem of foreshortening, e.g., in his analysis of "The Pupil," he used it to describe the indirect treatment of action through the center of consciousness so that "*all* the dimensions" (*The Art of the Novel*, p. 153) will be revealed. Also, used to express his ideal of author objectivity, the aesthetic distance between author and subject. H. G. Well's "autobiographic form" is objectionable because it sacrifices "a precious effect of *perspective*, indispensable . . . to beauty and authenticity" (*Letters*, 11, 334–35).

Photograph   His comments in the New York edition (1907–9) indicate his awareness by that time of the potentialities of photography as an art. However, in early reviews, *photograph* is used to designate literal reproduction of surface detail, *e.g.*, Trollope's manner has the "virtue of the photograph" because he is "true to common life" but fails to be "equally true to nature" (*Notes and Reviews*, pp. 70–74).

Picture (adjectivally, *pictorial, picturesque*)   The three most common uses are: the over-all composition; the part of the work which alternates with scene, presented through the center of consciousness; description. A character referred to as a "picture" or as a "figure" has been described but not dramatized or has been typed rather than individualized. Thus, James calls Hawthorne's Hepzibah Pyncheon "a masterly picture, . . . as her companions are pictures" (*Hawthorne*, Ithaca, N.Y., 1956, p. 100). *Picture* or *picturesque* is also used frequently, especially in the travel essays, to designate scenes in nature that "compose" into a picture, one that could be or has been painted. See chapter 3 for an extended discussion.

Portrait   Occasionally denotes a representation of type; more usually, the individualized characterization. James abjures the practice of using criticism to display private biases, engage in critical battles, or pass rancorous judgments. He advocates instead a kind of literary portraiture, a criticism which is empathic but disinterested, empirical rather than a priori, descriptive rather than prescriptive. The following passage on Robert Louis Stevenson states his position:

[Stevenson] gives us a new ground to wonder why the effort to fix a face and figure, to seize a literary character and transfer it to the canvas of the critic, should have fallen into such discredit among us, and have given way, to the mere multiplication of little private judgment-seats, where the scales and the judicial wig, both of them considerable awry, and not rendered more august by the company of a vicious-looking switch, have taken the place, as the symbols of office, of the kindly, disinterested palette and brush. It has become the fashion to be effective at the expense of the sitter, to make some little point, or inflict some little dig, with a heated party air, rather than to catch a talent in the fact, follow its line, and put a finger on its essence (*Partial Portraits*, pp. 137–38).

Likewise, the fiction writer should try to catch the likeness rather than exploit character for the sake of a thesis or moral judgment. Implied in the discussion of characters as *disponibles* in the New York edition preface to *The Portrait of a Lady* is the portrait painter's approach: the novelist begins with the vision of characters and then constructs relations and situations which will bring out the "sense of the creatures themselves" (*The Art of the Novel*,

p. 43). In another place, James contrasts Balzac's "love of each seized identity . . . the joy in their communicated and exhibited movement, in their standing on their feet and going of themselves and acting out their characters" with Thackeray's subservience of character to moral ends. Balzac's Valérie (*Les parents pauvres*) is a creation superior to Becky Sharp because "the English writer wants to make sure, first of all, of your moral judgment; the French is willing, while it waits a little, to risk, for the sake of his subject and its interest, your spiritual salvation" (*The Future of the Novel*, pp. 116–17). James's titles *The Portrait of a Lady*, *Portraits of Places*, and *Partial Portraits* are precise because his approach in these works is undidactic and empirical.

Sketch   In the visual arts, a drawing to be used as a basis for a more finished work or one of an unpretentious nature. The latter sense James had in mind in subtitling *The Europeans* "A Sketch" and in titling his first collecton of travel essays *Transatlantic Sketches*. James had literary precedents for *sketch* as a title: Irving's *Sketch Book by Geoffrey Crayon, Gent.*, Dickens's *Sketches by Boz*, Thackeray's subtitle to *Vanity Fair*, "Pen and Pencil Sketches of English Society." While making no claims to treat anything but the superficialities of life, Irving's and Dickens's works are nevertheless of a different literary genre. Similarly, no comparison in scope and dimension may be made between *The Europeans* and *Vanity Fair*. James's singular *sketch* to Thackeray's plural indicates the difference in intention. James used his subtitle to underscore his nouvelle's lightness of tone and simplicity of subject. The pictorial connotations of *Transatlantic Sketches*, given the contents, are apparent. Calling his essays in *A Little Tour in France* "notes," James in his 1900 preface said that they "were altogether governed by the pictorial spirit . . . if the written word may ever play the part of brush or pencil, they are sketches on 'drawing-paper' and nothing more. . . . There is no happy mean . . . between the sense and quest of the picture, and the surrender to it, and the sense and quest of the constitution, the inner springs of the subject—springs and connections social, economic, historic" (pp. iii–iv). Though James may hardly be said to have come to grips with complex underlying matter in it, *Portraits of Places* represents an effort to treat more than the picturesque surfaces of *Transatlantic Sketches*. *Portrait* as opposed to *sketch* denotes a real distinction.

Study   The preliminary sketches made for some part of a larger work or for the sake of acquiring skill. According to the *Oxford*

English Dictionary, a less usual sense is "a drawing, painting, or piece of sculpture designed to bring out the characteristics of the object represented, as they are revealed by especially careful observation." James "confesses" in his preface to *Daisy Miller* that he cannot remember the reasons why he added "A Study" to the title "unless they may have taken account simply of a certain flatness in my poor little heroine's literal denomination." Possibly, it may have been meant "as a deprecation, addressed to the reader, of any great critical hope of stirring scenes" (*The Art of the Novel,* pp. 268–69). It was apparently in the second sense that James originally used the term for he suppressed the qualifying epithet in the New York edition. His reason was that he came to realize that, while Daisy may have been based originally on observation, she was transmuted into a figure of "pure poetry."

Tone   James uses it in the sense of a harmony, or as analogous to a general effect of color with light and shade. He was pleased with the "sustained, preserved *tone* of '*The Tragic Muse*' . . . the inner harmony" (*The Art of the Novel,* p. 81). One of his favorite phrases is the "tone of time." For Ozenfant, "a little dirt can modify . . . much screaming color"; for James, the toning down and darkening of color by age can add "indescribable grace" to a work of art or of nature (*The Art of the Novel,* p. 10).

Values   In painting, the proportion of light or dark in a hue or a color, i.e., tones of a color, brilliance or darkness; also, the relation of parts or details in a picture with respect to darkness or lightness of color. In James's usage, *values* refers to a sense of proportion, a comprehension of subtle relations and meanings; e.g., to Taine's overestimation of Swift "we might add a hundred instances of the fatally defective perception of 'values' " ("[Taine's] English Literature" *Atlantic Monthly,* XXIX, April, 1872, 472).

Index

Index

Henry James
and the Visual Arts
was composed and printed by
Heritage Printers, Inc., Charlotte, N. C.
and was bound by
The Michie Company, Charlottesville, Virginia.
The paper is Warren's Olde Style
and the type is Baskerville.
Design is by Edward G. Foss.